SCHLESWIG IN IOWA

Best Wishes

Larry Grell

D1545910

SCHLESWIG IN IOWA

Larry Grill

Grill, Larry
        Schleswig in Iowa / by Larry Grill—1st ed.
        p. cm.
        Library of Congress Number: 99-90825
        ISBN #:   Hardcover   0-7388-0530-0
                            Softcover   0-7388-0531-9

        1. Schleswig (Iowa)—History   I. Title

    F629.S35G75 1999   977.7'45
                    QBI99-329

This book was printed in the United States of America.

To order additional copies of this book, contact:
Xlibris Corporation
1-888-7-XLIBRIS
www.Xlibris.com
Orders@Xlibris.com

CONTENTS

ACKNOWLEDGMENTS

Without a great deal of help this book could not have been completed. Much more needs to be said about the great value contributed to this effort than can be accomplished in this brief space, but the following people were invaluable to the completion of this work.

Elvera Hollander spent hours, days, and weeks editing and proofreading this material. Her efforts made the text much more readable and the details more accurate. Her efforts rounded out a research project into a presentable literary product, and the stamp of her impact is clearly visible on every page. She deserves much more credit than can be expressed in this short passage.

Leonard Hollander contributed a great deal of help. Over the years, he pointed out where many of the community's "skeletons" lie.

Dr. Joachim (Yogi) Reppmann, of Carlton College, Northfield, Minnesota, provided significant help by providing material for the text, establishing contacts as well as proofreading and editing.

Ann Smith, of the Mikkelsen Library, Augustana College, Sioux Falls, South Dakota, went out of her way to research materials for the book.

Keith Christie, of the Joslyn Art Museum, Omaha, Nebraska, spent a number of hours researching material on special projects.

Nancy Berta and the staff at the Schleswig Library were invaluable in helping find much of the bulk of the background information that was necessary for this project.

Ann Schneller in her *Crawford County History* pointed the way to many interesting facts and features.

A special thank you to all the people who shared facts, features, stories, and an understanding of how and why things occurred the way they did.

Finally, my father, Octavus Grill, who as a child was given the duty of entertaining his Grandmother, Lena Grill, who had moved into the home in the last years of her life, but it was she who enlightened him on the details of the development of Schleswig since the time of the first settlers and stirred a curiosity in him to pursue the interesting stories of the community. He was able to pass on both the stories and the curiosity.

I. INTRODUCTION

Schleswig in *Iowa*

The name Schleswig was originally given to a village that became a city in northern Germany. The meaning of the name is Village by the Schlei. A schlei is technically a sub-glacial outwash. When the glaciers that had come down across Northern Germany began to melt back, large amounts of water attempted to find a way back to the sea. The only way to do so was back under the glacier, and when the water found a way, it washed out a substantial channel. After the glaciers disappeared, the channel remained as a long, narrow bay which became known as the Schlei. Thus the name Schleswig can be translated as "Village by the Bay".

The name was used in Iowa because many of the founding fathers of our community came from the Schleswig area in Germany. It seems rather ironic because Schleswig, Iowa, is located on one of the highest and driest areas in the state, and how this came to be is the basis of this book.

In a hundred years of history, in a town of a thousand people, influenced by multiple forces, there are more interesting stories than one can possibly imagine. This book is not an attempt to tell them all. There is no way to even mention all the people who have influenced the events of the town.

This book is designed to give an overview of some of the highlights of what happened, and, as a result, it should be considered a very much condensed history. Hopefully, it will have included the truly influential events that helped to shape the profile of our town. The attempt is to develop how some of the things that did occur came about and a little of why they happened the way they did. The events portrayed are in approximate chronological order, but in some cases, this was altered to show more clearly the relationships and the pattern in which similar things developed. More emphasis was placed on being able to understand what happened rather than on the precise order in which things occurred. More detail on individuals, families and businesses can be obtained in the Schleswig Library's Family Histories Project, while many more pictorial scenes can be obtained on the video, *Schleswig, Iowa's 1st 100 Years,* written and produced by Elvera Hollander.

At any given time, the forces that influence the events of an area can be quite subtle. Even those people directly involved can be unaware of what is happening. Every effort has been made to unearth what forces were combining to achieve the results that are presented here. Intermixed with the explanation of events are anecdotes, antecedents, and points of interest to fill out the image of an active and vital community. A well-rounded picture of small-town-Iowa is the intention of this work.

In many aspects it is the story of any small town that developed in the northern Midwest where everyone faced many of the same problems and challenges. They were operating in the same environment and probably in a similar time frame. Each community had its own unique individuals, and they all contributed to their own unique solutions to the problems they confronted. So, while similar, each had its own individual imprint on history.

Good Reading

II. FOUNDATIONS

Small boys and dogs love to explore creeks and streams. Something is intriguing about these irregularities in the rolling curves of the landscape where there is always the prospect of discovering something new and different. Fields and cropland offer broad ranges of uniformity and consistency. All of the diversity of nature seems to be crowded into the creeks and streams. Flowing streams glisten in the sunlight. Wet rocks shine in multicolors. Fish flick through the waters. A multitude of sounds fill the air. The water tinkles over the streambed, birds sing in the trees, the wind rustles the leaves, a squirrel chatters, and rabbits rustle in the grasses and weeds. Side ditches and gullies offer a sense of mystery. Time just seems to disappear in these environs.

Every boy who grew up in the Schleswig area, and many of the girls as well, spent some time exploring the streams. As they grew up and needed an acceptable reason for such ventures, they became hunters. As adults farming the land, their first obligation was the stewardship of the soil, but when they would take a break, it was usually near a stream.

Streams and the land—water and soil—are the basis of all life in the area, especially of the people who live here. They are the sources of renewable wealth and fertility, but this evolution did not just happen easily or quickly. It took untold millions of years and scores of divergent processes to develop this resource upon which we have built our lives and our town.

Four and a half billion years ago all that existed here was a swirl of hot gases. All the elements we have now—iron, carbon, oxygen, nitrogen, etc—were here then, but they were so hot they were all in the form of gases. As this cloud of gases swirled in the sky, it cooled into heavy molecules and consolidated into a ball of liquid elements. The ball of liquid developed a hard crust with liquid in the center. The crust is several miles thick now, but lava will still come up through the surface occasionally in the form of lava flows and volcanos.

Our earth did not develop alone. At the time it was developing it was part of a system of dust disks and gas clouds that were congealing. The largest cloud became a ball of hot gases that did not cool because of the action of atomic fusion within the gases which kept the heat on. That cloud became our sun, and the companion clouds consolidated into a series of nine planets. Each of these objects took up space and reacted to each other in such a way that, while spinning themselves, they also revolved around the sun. The sun and planets are part of a group of a billion-star-and-planet system that make up our galaxy. This series of stars can be seen as the Milky Way in the night sky. It is swirling around a central object that has a gravitational field that is so strong not even light can resist it. Since no light can escape it nor is reflected off of it, the only thing we know about it is that it appears as a black hole in space. Black holes are created when large stars collapse into a very small object. As much as 50% to 60% of the matter and material in the universe may be tied up in black holes. Out beyond our galaxy are a billion other galaxies made up of billions of stars each, and each circles its own black hole or clusters of black holes that form a central cortex. Beyond that God only knows—so far. Man can only see as far as he can see light.

It took four and a half billion years for a stream to develop through a field, and it did not develop evenly nor smoothly. As the crust of the earth hardened, it would shrink, it would twist, and it would crack. Through the cracks lava would push upward and huge mountain ranges were formed along the cracks in the crust. Rocks that are formed by hot lava are igneous rocks. Our fields are made of various layers of soil over layers of various types of rock, and at the very bottom of the types of rock that can be identified is a large layer of igneous rock. This means that Iowa was a mountainous region a very long time ago, probably two billion years ago or more—in fact, so long ago this whole mountain range eroded away. There is some evidence that glaciers also occurred in these very early times that were so large they covered the entire earth and froze the surface of the oceans making the earth resemble a huge snowball.

Eventually the igneous rock eroded and formed sands and gravel which were washed into and settled in low areas. If they were put under enough pressure for long enough time, they would form sandstones. If they were broken down to finer particles, they would form the basis of soil. If they were then pressed for long periods of time, they would form slates and shales. Below our fields are layers of each of these types of rock. They form a concave basin under most of Iowa sloping to the Southwest. When life became prevalent on earth, sometime between 600 and 500 million years ago, Iowa went into a long period of time when it was under water below a shallow tropical sea where it stayed for hundreds of millions of years. During this time a slow build up of limestone covered everything. Today this limestone is being quarried at a number of sites around the state. A softer form of similar materials is gypsum which is formed when minerals-laden water is trapped in evaporation beds. Gypsum is found in a number of places in Iowa, one of the larger deposits being near Fort Dodge. This gypsum was used to carve out the Cardiff Giant, a hoax that was passed off as the remains of a prehistoric man in 1869.

The seas would drain down occasionally and plant life would proliferate. Huge ferns and early trees abounded. Layers of vegetation grew upon layers of vegetation a thick bed which was then covered and pressed. Coal was the result, and it is abundant in some parts of Iowa. However, in Crawford County there are only traces. It is a curiosity but not a significant factor.

At the end of the Cretaceous Period, some 65 million years ago, a unique phenomenon began. The crust of the earth not only cracked into sections or plates, but these plates began to shift, and entire continents began to move. Iowa was moved from the tropics to the temperate zones of the earth. This process, known as plate tectonics, changed the whole surface of the earth. The Rocky Mountains began to be formed, and the process is still going on today causing earthquakes in California and volcanos in Japan. Ridges in the middle of ocean floors and the Himalayas being pushed to the heavens have resulted from this action. This seemingly slow but vastly dramatic process is having a profound influence in shaping our world.

There are some interesting features about the bedrock below us. The oldest rock in Iowa is Sioux Quartzite, outcroppings of which are in Gitchie Manitou State Park in extreme northwest Iowa. The remains of Iowa's last volcano is also found in northwest Iowa near the town of Matlock. It was a violent eruption that took place about 1.7 billion years ago much like that of Mt.St. Helens. At Manson, Iowa, there is a twenty-mile wide circle where the bedrock is crushed and deformed into a crater-like depression. It is thought that a meteor landed there with terrific force some 50 or 60 million years ago.

One of the most unusual features in our makeup is related to the Mackenzie Fault. The fault starts at the southern tip of Lake Superior and runs down across Minnesota and across Iowa, taking a course through Mason City, Fort Dodge, Carroll, and Council Bluffs, and across southeastern Nebraska and out into Kansas. The fault is composed of two cracks through the crust of the earth roughly thirty miles apart. The Northern Boundary Fault came down between Breda and Carroll. The Thurman-Redfield Structural Zone ran somewhere west of Boone. The bedrock plates on each side of the fault spread apart, and the center zone sank, probably several miles. At that time Schleswig would have been on the rim of a huge rift valley just to the east of us. The whole area was subject to violent and frequent earthquakes. As the fault continued to spread, lava came up through the cracks and filled the valley to a depth of three to four miles. The lava cooled to form a layer of black basalt rock. The large plates of bedrock then stopped spreading and gradually reversed direction and came back together again.

In doing so they pushed the new block of rock in the rift valley high into the air, forming an enormous ridge called the Iowa Horst. This huge ridge isolated northwest Iowa form the rest of the State. All of this took place about a billion years ago. Over the next several million years the ridge eroded to the level of the surrounding land, giving our area a lot of this material. In Minnesota, the basalt rock from this formation has contributed iron and copper ore in northern Minnesota's iron range. Similar minerals have not been found in Iowa. There has been another source of value associated with this area, however. An energy source derived from bio-material and accumulated in the trough created by the rift—oil. In the late 1970's and early 1980's a number of oil wells were drilled in the Boyer, Iowa, area. They did find oil, and a good quality of oil, but not in commercial quantities. Amoco Oil Company drilled a major well near Halbur, Iowa, but sealed it without announcing the results of its effort. There had been an effort to accumulate mineral leases throughout the area, but they have largely been allowed to lapse.

A final unusual feature in Iowa's rock record is that there are areas that are missing. Huge layers of rock that reflect long periods of time, that are in the rock layers in most parts of the world, are just not here in Iowa. There are three such missing sections. One layer would have dated to the Pre Cambrian Era, sometime more than 550 million years ago. The second layer was from the Permian and Triassic Periods 230 million to 185 million years ago. (This is the same age as are the rocks that form the rim of the Grand Canyon.) The third gap in the record dates to the Tertiary Epoch, from 65 million years ago to three million years ago. Nebraska and South Dakota have substantial layers of Tertiary material, but Iowa has none. Why these gaps in the record exist is not certain. They may have eroded away entirely, or there may have been some reason why their development was limited. We can only guess at what was happening in Iowa during these times.

Our fields and streams don't show much of this record, largely because the latest geological stage covered up most of the older records. The climate changed, the average temperature dropping by about 6 to 8 degrees. The result was that in areas north of Iowa, in the Hudson Bay region, the snow that fell in the winter did not melt. Most of it stayed through the summers, and more accumulated during the next winter and the weight of the snow caused the crystals to reform into larger and more dense structures—glaciers. The thickness of the snow and ice grew to several thousand feet; in fact, it may have reached a depth of two miles or more. As it grew in thickness, it began to spread out. The outside edges were being pushed out from the center. Inch by inch it moved, year after year, until it covered a larger part of North America, and it would crush and scrape away anything that could be moved—trees, soil, even loose rocks would be crushed, ground up and shoved along with the ice.

During times when the temperatures were warmer, the ice would melt faster on the edges than it could move. In these times the glacier would retreat, and plants and animals would return to the plains. Then after thousands of years it would cool again, and the glaciers would creep forward. In the two and a half million years of the ice age, a number of major ice moves made their way across this area, and there is some evidence there may have been eight or more advances. When glaciers melted back, they dropped huge amounts of soil and debris. The Nebraskan Glacier, one of the earlier ones, left an average layer of 100 to 150 feet of sediments known as glacial till. A later glacier, the Kansan Glacier, left an average of 60 feet of till. In Crawford County the depth of the till ranges from 600 to 800 feet which is one of the thickest layers in the State. The last glacier retreated from this area about 10,000 years ago—a relatively short time ago in geological terms.

Iowa has proven to be the ideal place to study the effects of glaciers. Farther to the north, they have scraped everything off the bedrock leaving only circumstantial evidence of what may have happened at one time. Farther south only some glaciers would have arrived and may not have stayed long. In Iowa, the land was covered by most of the glaciers and covered with the debris from most of the retreats. Interestingly, much of what is known about glaciers in North America has come from studies in Iowa. Many features of glacial history are named after Iowa locations. The Aftonian Interglacial Period was named after Afton, Iowa, where the effects of it were being studied. The Yarmouth Interglacial Period was named when clear evidence of more than one glacier was discovered while digging a well near Yarmouth, Iowa. The best work on defining the Nebraskan Glacier was developed by efforts in Pottawattamie, Harrison, and Monona Counties. Iowa has developed such a reputation for glaciers that glacial activity anywhere in the world is compared to similar activity in Iowa. Iowa landscape has all of the unique features of glaciation—till left by glaciers, moraines where glacier advances stopped and dropped extra debris, kames, kettle lakes, erratic boulders and stones dropped almost anywhere, tear-shaped drumlin land forms, long, low paha hills, and many more. The Iowa Department of Natural Resources has developed the Glacial Landmarks Trail to identify some outstanding examples of these features in the Spirit Lake area and have published a brochure outlining the trail and explaining the sites.

Many other activities were taking place in the presence of glaciers besides the slow movement of ice sheets. The tremendous weight pressed down the crust of the earth which is still gradually rebounding in some areas. The massive amounts of water that are contained in the ice robbed the oceans of their liquid and caused sea levels to drop by as much as 300 feet. Much more coast land was exposed, sometimes with pronounced effects such as the emergence of a dry land path between Alaska and Siberia. The presence of such a cold block of ice caused a higher incidence of rainfall near the glacier since colder air can hold less water. The difference in temperatures in the area approaching a glacier results in a much windier climate. Strong winds, especially westerly winds, were particularly strong in this area. During the summers tremendous amounts of water melted from the front edges of the glacier, and the outwash created massive rivers only to become mere trickles in the cold of winters.

One of the more dynamic activities associated with glaciers is the development of loess. Loess is a fine, light-colored, wind-blown soil that has covered the surface of a large part of Iowa. When the glacial outwash slowed in winter, huge flooded river valleys would dry out, and the strong west winds would blow huge dust clouds over the surrounding land. In summer, the melt and outwash from the glaciers replenished the soil debris for the winter winds. In the Missouri River valley, the outwash was augmented by major erosion from the western states, and massive amounts of materials were available to be caught by the winds. The key factor in forming Loess soil is the wind rather than existence of the outwash. Loveland Loess, a significant feature in some parts of western Iowa, was formed when the nearest glacier was in Illinois. The Muddy Missouri was even muddier in these days, accumulating silt from western states as well as from the glaciers. As a result the thickest layer of loess lies along its north-south course. The loess is so thick it is recognized as its own land form. It is second only in size to the loess deposits just off the Gobi Desert in China. In Iowa, loess has covered most of the landscape in varying depths except where the last glacier scraped it away in a large V shaped area in the central part of the state. During the first weekend in June each year, the Loess Hills Prairie Seminars are held west of Castana in the heart of the hills. Experts in every area of study associated with the hills' environment share their knowledge with anyone interested, free of charge.

The last glacier, the Des Moines Lobe of the Wisconsin Glacier, came down from the north in a V shape. The tip of the V reached as far south as Des Moines. In this area loess-free soil is dark colored. Around the edges of a glacier is an area called a moraine, where the melting began to keep pace with the advance of the glacier. As a result, there would be excess melting along this line before the glacier began to retreat. The moraines would contain more material dropped from the melting ice, and the excess water would wash out much of the dirt and leave the heavier gravels—the result being major deposits of gravel. The closest such moraine to Schleswig is in the Wall Lake area. Significant amounts of gravel would wash out of these areas and form deposits along the water's path, such as the deposits along the Boyer River.

The land on which Schleswig was built is part of an area called the Southern Drift Plain. It is heavily glaciated land but missed the last two glaciers, and while loess wind deposits have covered much of the area, it is much thinner than land lying to our west. Our land had hundreds of thousands of years to erode. Hills and valleys were molded into shape, and drainage patterns were well established. This is much to the contrast of more recently glaciated lands to the east and north which must depend on extensive tiling to drain it. The base material of our land is the till dropped by the glaciers, which is a stable, durable material. While erosion shaped this land, it did not scar it nearly as sharply as in the loess hills to the west.

These are the base materials that underlie our community. But there has been a transformation that has taken place on the surface of the land. It has transformed the land into some of the most fertile soil in the world. The transition is a complex and involved process. The base material of ground-up rock, minerals, and materials dropped from the glaciers is allowed to weather to be mixed with the remains of living material–especially grasses and plants–to be eroded and leached by water, to be exposed to the sun's radiation, and to have these processes be repeated and varied over thousands of years. The result is that Schleswig has the most productive topsoil on earth. However, it is slipping away at an alarming rate. We are losing topsoil at one of the fastest rates in the world. It is estimated we lose on average 9.9 tons of topsoil per acre per year. When the pioneers first came to this country, the topsoil was as much as five to six feet deep. Today it is seldom as much as a foot deep.

There is a great deal of variation within the topsoil which has been divided into 450 series of soil types. Each has been named after the area where it was first identified. Each of these series has been broken down into a number of sub-characteristics called phases. The phases delineate the consistency of the soil and its slope and other more general features. There are also strata of soil at various depths called horizons. Schleswig soils are mainly variations of Marshall, Monona, and Judson soils.

The fields of home were formed by these processes, but what of the streams? To have streams water is needed. Water is necessary for the formation of soils. It is used to erode the landscapes. It fills our lakes and ponds. It provides for our streams and rivers. It has had a tremendous effect on our world and is essential for life. Where did it come from?

Water is made up of two hydrogen atoms and one oxygen atom combined into a very stable molecule. There were very likely representative samples of these gases included in the clouds of gases that congealed to form the earth. As the earth cooled, these gases could well have combined to form water vapor and condensed into liquid water. There is, however, a great deal of contrast between the other planets and moons in our solar system, where there is very little water, and the earth where two thirds of the surface is permanently flooded by oceans, where huge amounts of water are saturated in the soils, and massive ice caps cover the polar regions. A fair amount of water may have formed with the earth. There may be a large number of ice crystals in space and may be trapped by our atmosphere. We may also have had some close encounters with comets which are made up largely of ice crystals. We ended up, somehow, with a large supply of the water.

Water is an always-moving dynamic element. It runs down our streams and rivers to the oceans. It evaporates from the oceans, from plants, from the earth itself. The water vapor moves with air flows, and when it is encountered by colder conditions, it forms clouds and falls out as rain. It soaks into the porous layer of soils and fills the spaces between the grains of soil. When it comes to a soil horizon of more dense material, the water begins to move sideways in vein—which are the veins that supply most of our farm wells. The porous, upper layer of soil in this area is mainly formed from loess. Being windblown from the west, the loess is thicker on slopes that flow down to the east and north, and as a result, springs flowing into our streams are stronger on that side, and wells are more productive on these slopes. Some of the water will continue to seep downward until it comes to an impermeable layer of bedrock, where the water will build up to form a regional aquifer. Beneath Schleswig lies the Dakota Aquifer which is the water table under most of northwest Iowa. Schleswig's deep well extended down to this aquifer, but unfortunately, the quality of water in this aquifer is not considered good.

The site of Schleswig was picked because it was high on a ridge line. The site is unique because four small streams start at the boundaries of the town, each one going in a different direction. This also means the underground water veins flow away from Schleswig which has made it is difficult to find significant water supplies for our community. Another source of water is in the alluvial gravel deposits formed by glacial outwashes in our river valleys. Our closest one is in the Boyer River Valley, and Schleswig has developed an agreement with Denison and rural water networks to be part of a regional water system to derive our water through a twelve-mile water pipeline from these deposits.

The land is here, and so, too, is the water, but land and water would be very dull without life. However, our world is not dull! There is life, abundant life, all over the place. The diversity of life is all but unbelievable. There are trees, grasses, flowers, animals, birds, fish, insects, new life, old life, common life, rare life. Life has existed on earth for a vast amount of time. Evidence of life can be traced to, at least, the beginning of the Cambrian Period 550 million years ago, and there probably existed soft forms of life that left no trace for nearly as long before that.

Life is an interesting phenomenon. Life forms consist of fairly common elements–Carbon, calcium, oxygen, and a variety of trace elements. The chemicals that make up a man can be purchased for less than three dollars. The uniqueness of life is not in what it is, but in what it does, which makes a definition of life difficult. The elements that make up a life form are organized into a specific structure; they can transform energy from other elements through metabolism; and, they can reproduce themselves.

Life began on earth at a very early stage. When the conditions were right, some combinations of elements began to live off the energy of other elements but probably could not reproduce itself. When it "died", new life would have to be created. It appears that when the conditions are right, it is not so miraculous that life occurs; it is more likely to be difficult to prevent it from exploding all over the place. Within the structures of life, a double line of a formula developed that explained how it was organized. This formula can split and form a second organization duplicating the original. This DNA formula became the basis for reproduction. What is more miraculous than life itself is that it can adopt to new conditions as they change. Life can reproduce, mutate, and reproduce its mutations. Thus, as the earth changed, life changed to match it. One of the biggest challenges was when a poisonous gas developed on earth. Most forms of life died. Those that did not die were able to adapt to a way to use the poisonous gas to better metabolize the nutrients in its food. The poisonous gas was oxygen. The original atmosphere when life developed was rich in hydrogen and methane rather than in oxygen which is certainly strange, because today oxygen is so necessary for life.

The changing conditions on earth created many challenges to life. It reacted and changed and grew in complexity. Membranes to protect itself were developed, and shapes to take better advantage of its surroundings were created. Life developed into tubes to take in ocean waters to have better access to nutrients and developed digestive tracts. It developed the ability to flex and to move and to create appendages to help in movement. When conditions became particularly harsh, a characteristic developed whereby reproduction would not take place unless the environment could support at least two healthy adults. Thus God may have introduced sex as a method of birth control to limit reproduction to the level that could be sustained. Even with these considerations, life had its challenges. There were at least six times, and maybe as many as ten or more times, when catastrophes occurred when 75% or more of the life on earth perished. These earlier forms of life did leave evidence of their remains in the rock record. One of the most noted forms of life that did not survive was that of the dinosaurs. There is little evidence of dinosaurs around Schleswig, however. During the ages of the dinosaurs, Schleswig was under a shallow sea.

Life did survive. Its abundance and variety are astounding, and man has become its dominant form though he is a relatively recent player on the scene. Evidence of man goes back three to three and a half million years, a relatively brief time in the history of the earth. In that time there has been more than one type of man. The various species ranged from Australopithecus, to Homo Habilis to Neanderthal, but these earlier forms of man have become extinct. We, the survivors, from Australopithecus garhi to Homo Sapiens, are part of a long string of survivors.

The surviving forms of life have been grouped into divisions by biologists– kingdoms, phylums, classes, orders, families, genus, and species. The more closely related two forms of life are the more of these classifications they will share. Man shares the most characteristics with a group of animals called primates, a group including chimpanzees, gorillas, and monkeys. DNA testing reveals more similarities exist between man and chimpanzees than between chimpanzees and gorillas. Man is also part of a larger group containing all mammals and all warm blooded creatures including most animals and birds going back far enough to include a variety of dinosaurs. We share our internal skeletal structure with life forms that include fish. The theory that life may have started in primordial seas may be supported by the fact that the embryonic fluids in which a human baby is formed in its mother's womb are composed of the same salinity as existed in the primordial seas. We also have a digestive tract which we have in common with animals, birds, fish, and insects, worms and lesser forms of life. Then we arrive at our relationship with plant life. A major component in blood is Hemoglobin. It helps to provide oxygen and nutrients to the cells of our body. In plants the main component that helps transform sunlight into energy the plant can use is chlorophyl. Both hemoglobin and chlorophyl have very complex chemical formulas, but the only difference is one element. If it has an iron element, it is hemoglobin, but if it has a magnesium element, it is chlorophyl. Everything else in the formulas is the same. This probably holds a clue as to why so many of the medicines that are effective on man come from plants. Even the simplest form of life shares much with the most complex form. As a philosopher says, "We are all in this together."

Life in the Schleswig area developed in the same time frame but in its own unique fashion. For millions of years, Iowa was under a shallow tropical sea. Remains of prehistoric fish, trilobites, gastropods and other marine life which were the dominant forms of life are found in the limestone beds. When the water was sufficiently shallow, water plants also thrived. Crinoids, cephalopods, and brachiopods and many other such forms left a significant record. When land did surface, it produced prolific tree-sized ferns that were infested with huge insects. Layer after layer of vegetation was crushed down and pressed under heat until it became coal. When the continents split and began moving away from each other, Iowa was moved from the tropics to its current location in the temperate zone and permanently above sea level. This occurred about the time the dinosaurs disappeared. One theory of their demise is that it was caused by vertigo induced by plate tectonics.

It is becoming clearer that the dinosaurs did not become extinct. The larger varieties died, but it appears many of the smaller ones evolved into the birds of today. Thus something as familiar as the common chicken may have had an existence that predated man by hundreds of millions of years. This means it would have adapted to and survived all of the varieties of plagues and epidemics of the ages. Its resistance and endurance are recorded in its genes and musculature. Therein may lie the basis for the medicinal qualities of chicken soup.

Most of the recent life in the Schleswig area dated from the last glacial age. As the glaciers retreated, the surface became covered by tundra-like vegetation, and as the climate became warmer, it was replaced first by coniferous trees and then by deciduous trees. The weather became still warmer, the rivers slowed, and the rainfall declined to 30 inches a year or less, and the dominant vegetation became prairie grasses. It remained so for thousands of years. Big bluestem, Switch Grass and a wide variety of forbes and wild flowers, like the wild rose, spread their roots deep into the soil. Mammoths and giant sloths that lived during the late ice age gave way to Bison, elk, deer and a variety of smaller animals like badgers, raccoons, fox, wolves, gophers, mice, coyotes and much of the wildlife that is familiar today. The rivers were populated with fish. Lewis and Clark made numerous mention of mosquitos and insects in the river bottoms. Some of the life forms become very specific and interdependent. For example, on the tops of fast draining loess hills, yucca plants thrive, but they are totally dependent on the skipper moth for pollination, and the moth is dependent on the yucca for the incubation of its larvae. Neither could live without the other.

Major Stephen Watts Kearney on a journey through this country thirty years before there were any settlements said he could travel for more than a hundred miles without finding enough wood for a campfire. He also said he saw few buffalo, but herd after herd of elk were seen. The vast prairie dominance was caused by the dry climate and was aided by prairie fires which were frequent, some of which stretched from the Missouri to the Mississippi, and by the efforts of grazers such as elk nibbling off the woody shots that attempted to invade the grasses.

White settlers changed the nature of landscape faster than any other force. The first change was the disappearance of the wild life. The large animals were the first to go. Buffalo, which had never been abundant in Iowa, did not last long once the settlers came. The last buffalo in Crawford County was killed in Denison. It was found in the timber above town and chased into the city limits before it was brought down. It weighed nearly 1800 pounds and was killed in the year 1857. The last buffalo was killed in Ida County in 1862. Elk was highly prized for the quality of its meat. The last Elk in Crawford County was killed in 1855 and in Ida County in 1867. Some animals such as the black bear and the mountain lion had already disappeared from western Iowa. The grey wolf lasted into the 1860's. The passenger pigeon disappeared in the 1870's, the ruffled grouse in the 1880's, wild turkeys in the 1890's and the prairie chicken survived into the early twentieth century. Some of the smaller animals and migratory birds learned to live with man and survived to some extent. Their whole story is related in *A Country So Full Of Game* by James Dinsmore.

The prairie grasses also disappeared but not without a strong showing of resistence. The deep and tangled roots defied the settlers' attempts to convert the sod to farmland. The land near the rivers, where there were some groves, was settled first, and the grasslands were reserved for last. It wasn't until John Deere invented a steel plow that sod could be turned effectively. Even then it was plowed one year and left lay fallow. The following year it was cross plowed after which the settlers' attempted to cultivate it. Even then the grasses kept coming back to smother crops. With persistence the prairie was defeated and 98% of it has disappeared. Today it is only seen in preserves in some isolated rough areas and in some early cemeteries.

Our town is built on this land, and our economy depends on it. Our people use it for recreation, for sustenance, and as a foundation for all their activities. It is solid and enduring, but it is always changing. It has been revered, and it has been abused. It has an interesting story of its own, and the more one knows about it the more interesting it becomes. An excellent place to recognize its diversity is in the exhibits at the Battle Hill Museum in neighboring Battle Creek, Iowa (http://elwood.pionet.net/~bhmuseum/). Regardless of one's background, the land is fascinating just to observe.

Small boys and dogs love to explore creeks and streams. Something is intriguing about these irregularities in the rolling curves of the landscape where there is always the prospect of discovering something new and different. Fields and cropland offer broad ranges of uniformity and consistency. All of the diversity of nature seems to be crowded into the creeks and streams. Flowing streams glisten in the sunlight. Wet rocks shine in multicolors. Fish flick through the waters. A multitude of sounds fill the air. The water tinkles over the streambed, birds sing in the trees, the wind rustles the leaves, a squirrel chatters, and rabbits rustle in the grasses and weeds. Side ditches and gullies offer a sense of mystery. Time just seems to disappear in these environs.

III. NATIVE AMERICANS

There are footprints in the soil. By the streams, on the hills, in the valleys, there are footprints. People have passed by here. They had places to go, and they had things to do. They have been walking here for a very long time. Some of the footprints are old, and some of them are very fresh. Where we walk today, we are not walking on untrampled ground. There are footprints under the dust. They were made by people who enjoyed the freshness of the air at dawn, the warmth of noon, and the beauty of the sunset. We all liked it here.

The human race can trace its ancestry back some three and a half million years. The earliest traces of man come from the vicinity of a rift valley much like the one that once existed east of Schleswig. This rift valley is in east Africa, however. Some of the earliest traces are of manlike beings but are different from modern man. Some uncertainty exists in this evidence. Were these traces and fossils from early man or from relatives of man who did not survive in the evolutionary scene? Man did survive though and spread out from this center across the Middle East and into Asia and into Europe.

In Germany, in the Neandertal Valley, the remains of a man were found that were much different from those of modern man. This man was larger and appeared to be much stronger. Though this Neandertal man ceased to exist, it does appear to have lived in the same areas, at the same time, as modern man. He was thought to be dull and brutish, but some more recent discoveries have found flowers in grave sites and evidence of ceremony which would give Neandertals the image of having a more compassionate and caring nature. Since human remains are rather fragile, it is uncer-

tain when the last of the Neandertals left the earth. What is interesting is that in ancient German mythology, or Norse mythology,
or any mythology from Europe, there is one frequently reoccur-
ring theme. A race of giants existed that gave modern man a hard
time. Whether or not these tales of giants relate to a time when
Neandertal and modern man co-existed is a matter of speculation.
The only literary reference that can be ascribed to these giants is
the phrase, "Fee, Fi, Fo, Fum."

With the demise of the Neandertal man, the only humans on
earth were modern man, who propagated to all parts of the earth.
He even took to the waters and populated the distant islands of
the South Sea entering the Pacific Ocean as far as to the Hawaiian
Islands. When the glaciers tied up a large part of the water on
earth, and the sea levels were considerably lower, man found his
way over a newly-exposed land route to Alaska or around new ocean
rims to the new world. He seems to have spread quickly over most
of the Americas, and he may have arrived in Iowa in time to see
some of the last dust storms that formed the Loess Hills. Some
spear points were found in western Iowa that date to 10,000 to
12,000 years ago, and campsites have been discovered that are
over 8000 years old. The earliest remains of man in Iowa–a group
of four individuals–were found in the Loess Hills at Turin, Iowa,
deep in the loess by excavators in 1955. The remains have been
dated to nearly 5000 years ago.

The first men in America are referred to a Paleo-Indians, although the Kennewick Man and similar discoveries indicate there
may have been both Indian and Caucasian populations in America.
Only the Indian population survived. They were wanderers and
hunted the large animals that existed at the end of the glacial era–
the Mammoth, the Sloth, the Saber-tooth Cat, and the oversized
Bison Antiqutius (Occendentalis). Weapons–mainly spears and
clubs–were developed from stone. One unique leaf-shaped spear
point, known as the Clovis Point, has been found near Pearson,
Fort Dodge, Emmetsburg, and Sioux City and was likely used
throughout this whole area. These people were widely scattered

and lived lightly on the land leaving few traces of their existence. It has been suggested that these people were established over much of America before permanent artifacts were used. The use of a new artifact, such as the Clovis Point, appearing in widely diverse areas in a short period of time indicates it was traded through an existing population rather than having been spread by new exploration. There appear to have been at least three distinctive cultural patterns developed during this period, each more recent grouping seems to have been hunting a wider variety of animals. These humans lived here until about 8500 years ago.

When the climate thoroughly dried out and the land became a prairie, a new social organization appeared. More effort was needed to feed a family, and the stress lead to innovation. An atlatl was used to increase the efficiency of the spear. A wide range of animals and birds became part of the diet. Grains and seeds were collected and grown. Ground stone tools appeared. Grinding stones (manos) and slabs (metates) were used to process the grain. Several of these stones and slabs were found near stream beds south of Schleswig. These people were the first to notch their projectile points. Known as the Archaic Indians, they lived in small, widely-scattered groups, in a way of life that lasted six thousand years.

In the woodlands of the eastern United States a new way of life was developing, which became known appropriately enough as the Woodland Culture which lasted for 2000 years. These people lived a more settled life style. They hunted, but they depended more on crops and plants for sustenance. Living in more stable villages, they could develop more fragile possessions such as various forms of pottery which reduced the reliance on leather and cloth storage containers. Cloth had been developed although none of it has survived. The imprint of it was used to decorate the pottery, so we know it existed.

The population of the Woodland groups grew, and their culture became the dominant life style over much of the United States. One of their more impressive features was their burial rituals in which they developed the tradition of the use of burial mounds.

In the later stages of their development, effigy mounds were created. A large cluster of such burial mounds was reported by early settlers to be located five miles southwest of Denison in the Boyer River valley. Just southeast of Schleswig, such a burial mound was preserved on a farm until well into the twentieth century, until a financially distressed renter plowed it under to cultivate more land. Its exact location has been lost, although a stone-ground axe was found in the area.

After the time of Christ there were major developments in the Indian cultures in America. The Incas in Peru and the Mayas in Mexico developed cities and large-scale social organizations to support them. Massive buildings and temples were built and many cultural and scientific developments were made. The influences of change were not as dramatic locally, but changes were occurring. A Mississippian Culture was developing southeast of here centered around the Indian city of Cahokia. Cahokia was a city of 20,000 people located across the Mississippi River just east of St. Louis. It was the center of a huge trade organization that stretched from the Gulf of Mexico to the Great Lakes and to the Rocky Mountains. The Indians in Crawford County could obtain sea shells from Louisiana to grind into grit and harden their pottery, and they could get stone ground tools from central South Dakota and northern Minnesota. When Lewis and Clark made their expedition, they traveled as fast as they could to get to the west coast. When they arrived there, they discovered an Indian using an iron hatchet that they had traded to an Indian on the Missouri River just west of us. It had entered the trade routes and had crossed the continent faster than Lewis and Clarke could make it. It was an efficient system. However, Cahokia was not the only large city in the area. Blood Run was a city of 10,000 to 15,000 people in northwest Iowa on the Big Sioux River, and it is being developed as a historic site today.

Locally, a series of cultures developed that were associated with the Mississippian Culture such as the Great Oasis, the Mill Creek, and the Glenwood cultures. This life style was based on long term stable villages. Habitats were houses made of post and plaster walls and thatch roofs. The floors were recessed about 12 to 18 inches below ground level and storage pits were widely used. A wide variety of plants and animal foods were eaten. The M.A.D. archeological site, where the East Boyer River and the Boyer Rivers meet just west of Denison, has components of the Archaic Indian Culture, the Woodland Culture, and just above them the Glenwood Culture, all in the same small area. The Mississippian cultures disappeared from this area in 1200 to 1300 when severe climactic change called the Pacific Episode made life difficult as did pressure from a new people known as the Oneota.

The Oneota people lived on the fringes of the more occupied areas for many years. They were more nomadic and less well structured than many of the more settled peoples. The Oneota moved around frequently, occupying a site, moving on and later returning and re-occupying the site. Their society seems to be more patriarchally oriented since newly married couples would join the husband's family group. As a result, many of the traditions revolving around the home were more diversified and lacked strong traditions as was the case in the former cultures in which couples would join the girl's family group. Pottery making had no particular pattern. Homes were temporary and less stable. One recognizable feature of the Oneota was the use of red Catlinite or pipestone tablets on which images were drawn. It is thought the images were reminiscences of vision quests and were kept in medicine bundles for spiritual support. Hunting and foraging rather than growing crops was their lifestyle and they were more likely to raid their neighbors than become settled villagers. When bad crop years occurred, the Oneota were able to survive better than other cultures, and their raids put enough pressure on the settled cultures that most of those groups left the state. The Oneota held their way of life together long enough to meet the white man.

White settlement was concentrated on the east coast for many years, but its effects were felt far inland. Many tribes were displaced and forced to move into unfamiliar areas where some of them thrived and others declined. Many traditions were merged or dissolved. A Coalescent Tradition evolved in which the old traditions were transformed into more detailed tribal identities as they were first recorded in history. The Sioux, an unremarkable people from the east central United States, were forced out on the plains where they discovered a talent for horsemanship and become a dominant force over a wide area. The Cherokee, on the other hand, was one of the most highly developed tribes and was forced half way across the continent where they had difficulty surviving. The Oneota people came out of this process influencing a number of tribes, the most closely related being the Ioway tribe.

The Ioway tribe is directly descended from the Oneota, but they may not be the only descendants. The Ioway tribe at various times lived in almost all parts of the State of Iowa. The first contact that the Ioway had with white men took place when some of the tribe visited a French settlement at Green Bay, Wisconsin, in 1676. Records show that an explorer, Nicolas Perrot, visited the tribe in Iowa on the Upper Iowa River in 1685. However, they began losing their dominance in the 1700's. The Sac and Fox (Mesquaki) were affiliated with the Algonquian in the Northeast from where they were pushed west by pressure of white settlement into southeastern Iowa. The Sioux were also pushed out of the western Appalachian area and into the Michigan and Wisconsin area by white pressure and continued to be pushed south into southern Minnesota and northern Iowa by the Chippewa. Once the Sioux discovered the horse, they dominated the plains from here west. In western Iowa, the Ponca, Pawnee, and especially the Omaha moved in from the west and south causing the area of the Ioway tribe to be diminished rapidly.

In 1820, the Ioway tribe suffered a major defeat in a battle with the Sac and Fox tribes. In 1824, they conceded a large area of land in Iowa and Missouri to the United States Government, and in a series of treaties in 1830, 1832, and 1836 the tribe negotiated away all of its claims to land in Iowa. As a result they were moved to an area in northwest Missouri in 1836, and in 1838 they were moved again–this time to a reservation on the Kansas-Nebraska border just west of the Missouri River. After the Civil War many of the tribal members assimilated into the ways of the white society, however in the 1870's, the more traditional members of the tribe began moving to the Indian Territory in Oklahoma. Here they were given a separate reservation in 1883, but it was dissolved in 1890. Today the tribe has a small three square mile reservation where the Kansas-Nebraska border meets the Missouri River and a few scattered remnants in Oklahoma. The traditions, the culture, and the language of the Ioway tribe nearly became extinct as tribal membership was down to a few hundred but now there is an attempt to preserve these characteristics as the tribal membership is increasing (see http://www.ioway.org).

The Sac and Fox tribes had been relocated several times, and when they arrived in Iowa, they formed a confederation to work together to preserve their way of life as an organized group. They were able to defeat the Ioway and to hold the aggressive Sioux at bay, but the white community proved to be more difficult. U.S. Government policy was to keep the whites and Indians separate. Congress declared all land obtained in the Louisiana Purchase was not to be settled unless approved by the government. This meant Iowa was to be off limits to settlement, but that Illinois could be developed. The Sac and Fox maintained that they still had claim to hunting grounds in Illinois, but a difference of opinion rose as to how to approach this problem. Chief Keokuk of the Fox, who had established strong trading relations, was in favor of negotiating with the white man. He maintained they were too numerous to fight. The Sac War Chief Black Hawk disagreed. He had fought with Tecumseh on the side of the British in the War of 1812, and he was going to fight to hold his lands. In 1832, he led a group of tribesmen to occupy a former village site in Illinois. The white community considered this an invasion and called up the local militia. The Black Hawk War started and turned into a series of skirmishes as the militia drove the Indians up across Illinois, Wisconsin and back into Iowa. A number of tribes, who had pledged support left Black Hawk, stranded him and left him on his own. Black Hawk lost over half of his followers in the war that was named after him. One of the leaders of Illinois Militia was a young lieutenant from Springfield–Abraham Lincoln. For his efforts he received two land grants in Iowa. One of them is five miles south of Schleswig and the other is five miles north of Tama, Iowa. The Treaty that ended the Black Hawk War opened Iowa for settlement at least along a 50-mile wide strip near the Mississippi River.

The series of Indian treaties in Iowa resulted in a number of curious developments. A good part of Lee County was reserved for the support of the offspring of mixed parenthood, and, as a result, it became known as the Half-breed Tract. A frequently violated divide line was drawn between the lands held by the Sac and the Fox tribes and those held by the Sioux. The line was then widened to be a "Neutral Zone" that ran from the Mississippi River in northeast Iowa to the Des Moines River in Central Iowa, but it also failed. The Winabago Tribe was moved from Wisconsin into the strip to form a buffer between the tribes, but more resentment and instability resulted than there had been heretofore. Finally, in 1849, the army established Fort Atkinson in the strip and on the extreme west end of the neutral zone–Fort Dodge.

In each of the treaties, the Indians were asked to give up more land until by 1842 the Sac and Fox tribes sold all of their lands in Iowa. They were to give up possession of the land in a series of steps until by 1846 they were to be on a reservation in Kansas. They were not happy there, however, and soon longed to return to Iowa. They had kept some of the money they were paid for their land so they made overtures to Iowa officials to buy back some of their former lands. The Iowa legislature granted them this request; thus the Iowa legislature became the first governmental body to recognize an Indian as being legally able to exercise the rights of an individual under Common Law. The Fox or Mesquaki were able to purchase land, and as a result, owned their own reservation in Tama County.

The Sioux tribe occupied the northern part of Iowa from the

Mississippi to the Missouri, an area to which they were restricted by the Sac and Fox in the southeast and by the Omaha in the southwest. The Sioux tribe was an aggressive tribe and did not tolerate interference with their life style. They had signed away their rights to their lands in Iowa by 1851, but they were far from surrendering possession. Of all the tribes that Lewis and Clark encountered on their expedition, the Sioux were considered to be one of the most contentious. It may be easiest to demonstrate their nature by following the activities of one of their members— a man who did travel through this part of the country extensively.

On the northeast edge of Denison, Iowa, is a granite monument marking the location of Fort Purdy. Fort Purdy was not an army outpost on the frontier as its name may imply, but it was the strongly built home and grounds of John Purdy. Located high on a bluff overlooking the Boyer River Valley, it was easily defended and difficult to approach without being seen.

The Purdy place gained the title "Fort" during the Indian scare of 1856, though no battle was ever fought there; however, it did play a significant role in the events of the day. The Wahpeton-Santee Sioux War Chief Inkpaduta, also known as Scarlet Plume, and a band of disgruntled warriors crossed the Missouri River from Nebraska and were moving up the Little Sioux River Valley. They attacked the white settlers that had gathered at the community of Smithland, but the Indians were repulsed and left in an easterly-northeasterly direction.

Early day settlers were quite sensitive to threats of Indian unrest. Word of Inkpaduta's activities and the possibility of his coming in this direction spread quickly and prompted most settlers to leave their isolated homesteads and congregate in a more defensible site. The site selected was Fort Purdy. Settlers from Dunlap to Ida Grove congregated at the fort to wait out the threat. However, Inkpaduta, whose name translates to "Red On Top" or more familiarly, Scarlet Plume or Scarlet Point, and his band turned northward before they reached Denison. After they were sure the Indians had left the territory, the settlers returned to their homesteads. John Purdy was left the job of converting the "fort" back into a farm. The name "the Fort" was applied to his place for many years to come. Mr. Purdy did receive some benefit besides the fame attached to the name. He received some rent for storing the early county records in a safe place before a permanent court house was built.

To understand the significance of the events that lead to the establishment of the "Fort", it will be necessary to look back a few years. The opening of Iowa to white settlement had put new pressure on the Indian cultures in the state. The Indians were being steadily pushed out, and they resented it. They had been forced to sign treaties giving up title to their lands, and now they were being deprived of possession of it. While many Indians saw it was fruitless to resist the white man and looked for a way to coexist peacefully, there were also many who saw resistance as the only way to maintain dignity.

The first settlers in Crawford County were the Cornelius Dunham family who settled near Vail in 1849. In the next few years more families settled between the two branches of the Boyer River. In 1851, a group of Sioux decided they were far enough away from the army and could make a raid and teach these intruders a lesson. When many of the settlers were helping a new neighbor with a house-raising, the Indians struck the unprotected cabins and thoroughly looted them. At one cabin, they discovered a couple of young people who had been left home to tend to some chores. The young people were taken captive, and the Indians then headed for their regular camping grounds on the West Des Moines River. When the settlers found out what happened, they went after them in hot pursuit. Three of the settlers, Dunham, Reed and Butler, reported the incident to the army at Fort Dodge from where troops were sent to round up the most likely culprits. The Indians who were brought in protested their innocence, and said, if given a chance they could find out who the raiders were although they had probably already left the country. With the pressure of the army on them, the Indians did bring in the hostages and a major portion of the stolen goods. The rest, they said, had been lost or broken. The army was never able to identify for sure who the raiders were, but it was largely suspected that one of the instigators was Scarlet Plume, Chief Inkpaduta. Scarlet Plume headed a rowdy group that tested the tolerance of both the white and the Indian societies.

Harassment raids were problems, but a much more serious situation was developing at this time. From the earliest days of American history, there were always some men who could not survive in organized society. Border Ruffians, as they were called, lived just beyond the frontiers of civilization and survived off the land and often engaged in criminal activities. Early Iowa history has many stories of their colorful activities. It was the Ruffians who raided Colonel Davenport's prairie mansion and murdered him. The Ruffians started the town of Bellevue to base raids on the whole Mississippi River. There was a horse stealing operation headquartered outside Des Moines that stretched from Wisconsin to Missouri. At one time, the Ruffians totally controlled Benton County until the Vigilantes drove them out. One of the worst of these Ruffians was Henry Lott.

Henry Lott set up operations high on a bluff overlooking the valley where the Boone River joins the Des Moines River just north of the present day town of Stratford. His place became a refuge for every cutthroat, thief, and murderer in the area. His crew pilfered from whites and Indians alike. The Sioux Chief Sidominadota, Two Fingers, became disgusted seeing his braves go to trade with Lott and come back without their trade goods, without their horses, and with only a hangover in exchange. Then, when he heard that a large number of stolen Indian ponies had been seen in Lott's corral, he decided to take action. He and a group of warriors approached Lott's cabin and ordered him out of the country.

Sidominadota was distracted briefly when on a hunting trip he discovered a government survey crew camped on a sacred hill. Angered by the intrusion upon his hunting grounds and the desecration of the site, he attacked and scattered them near a small creek that was named for the battle.

When Sidominadota, flushed with his victory, returned to the Des Moines River country and found Lott still there, he organized a war party and attacked the cabin. Lott deserted his family and escaped by running down the frozen Des Moines River. Two of his sons attempted to follow suit. One made it; the other died of exposure in route. Mrs. Lott and the rest of the family were terrified but were unhurt by the Indians who did demolish the cabin and corrals and made off with all of his goods. The white community was not particularly upset by this raid.

Several years later, in 1853, Henry Lott turned up at Fort Dodge with plans to go about thirty miles north and set up a trading post for the Indians. He operated the post until some time in 1854, when Chief Sidominadota was camped nearby, and there were few other Indians around. Lott and his son approached the Chief saying they had heard there were elk farther up the Des Moines River and asked if he wanted to join them on a hunt. Sidominadota needed some meat and agreed to join the hunt. When they were away from camp, the Lotts ambushed the old Chief and killed him. They waited until dark and slipped back into camp and killed six more of the Chief's family in their sleep. The Indians were outraged, and there was a great deal of fear of a retaliatory raid. Major William Williams, who had purchased the site of Fort Dodge when the army left and laid out the town site, proposed a deal to the Indians. If the Indians would refrain from attacking the white settlement, he and a group of white men would run down Henry Lott and punish him for his crimes. The Indians agreed. Major Williams headed a posse that trailed Lott all the way to the Missouri River before they lost him. Later, they heard he did not stop until he reached California, where shortly after arriving, he was killed in a brawl.

By the time the posse returned to Fort Dodge, tensions had eased. Many of the Indians had gone back to their daily routines, but not all the Indians were ready to forget the incident. The most vocal was Inkpaduta. John Harlan in his five volume *History of Iowa* maintains Inkpaduta and Sidominadota were brothers, but Mackinlay Kantor, the prizewinning author from Webster City, stated they were not related at all. However, a society, where cousins are referred to in the same terms as brothers and sisters and aunts and uncles are referred to in similar terms as mothers and fathers, may not have the same definitions for relationships as do European societies. In any case, Inkpaduta felt a kinship with the old chief and was very irate over what had happened to him. Inkpaduta vented his anger and frustration over the death of Sidominadota and the general encroachment of the white settlers to whomever would listen. He began to attract a group of discontents and the disreputable elements of the surrounding tribes. He then decided to take a long circular trip to see if he could expand his following going to many of the local landmarks where he would expect tribes to be camped. He started north to the Blue Earth area in Minnesota and to the forested areas around the Minnesota River. He visited the buffalo drop cliffs near Luverne, the pipestone quarries with its oracles, and entered the Dakotas by the dells and the falls on the Big Sioux River. Everywhere he went, he attracted the disgruntled and belligerent into his following. He visited the Spirit Mound area in South Dakota and crossed to Nebraska near Devil's Nest and skirted the sand hills and returned to the Missouri River and Iowa where the Loess Hills are the highest and widest.

Here in the Loess Hills, they found a new white settlement starting which was called Smithland. They stopped here for a while to see what this place was like. It was late in the fall of 1856 and every sign pointed to a long hard winter, so the Indians began to collect food and supplies; they even "collected" some corn that belonged to one of the settlers. The settler became extremely upset and organized the homesteaders to drive the Indians away.

There was a battle of sorts. The Indians did not put up a sustained fight. They made a show of force, and there was a lot of shooting and hollering but then, surprisingly, the Indians withdrew. This was when the settlers to the east were gathering at Fort Purdy near Denison. Inkpaduta did not lead his band toward Denison, however, nor, for that matter, toward his old camping ground near Fort Dodge. Instead, he went up the Little Sioux through largely unsettled territory. His group did find a few settlers who had not heard his group was in the area. The Indians did harass them and caused a lot of property damage, but there was no bloodshed.

When they reached the major tribal landmark of the area, the Iowa great lakes, and found it, too, had been encroached upon by white men, that was just too much. All the haranguing by Inkpaduta and all the frustrations of the trail, especially at Smithland, burst forth in an explosion of tempers. One event fed into the next, and the result was every white settler in the area was killed or captured. In what would be later called the Spirit Lake Massacre, thirty-two people were killed and four women were taken captive.

The War Party moved north into Minnesota before pausing to reflect on what had just happened and to contemplate on what actions to take now. As soon as word of the massacre reached Fort Dodge, Major Williams put out a call for militia volunteers. As soon as they could be organized, he headed out with three companies comprising a hundred and ten men. It was a miserable trip. Snow drifts were often shoulder high, icy streams were waist deep–temperatures were zero and below–there were no tents and only a single blanket to wrap up in when sleeping on the frozen ground. Despite the conditions though, the militia made good time. As they approached the Estherville area, the scouts reported a large Indian camp in a nearby grove.

The militia organized for a fight and approached the grove. When they got there, they discovered a hurriedly deserted campsite. They were able to determine by the remains that it was not Inkpaduta's band but rather a group of Minnesota Sioux lead by Chief Sleepy Eye, who, when they saw the militia coming, headed back to the northeast to more peaceful hunting grounds.

The militia reached the massacre site and discovered there were four missing women and assumed they were captives. The trail of the Indians was found and was followed into Minnesota. Somewhere south of Springfield, they met a contingent of the regular army sent into this area from Fort Ridgley. The combined forces followed the Indians' trail for a short distance, but the regular army was more interested in protecting the villages to the east rather than following the Indians into the wilderness to the west. Major Williams, realizing the militia was not strong enough to follow Inkpaduta's band deep into Indian territory by itself, was forced to return to the massacre site. After burying the dead, they headed back to Fort Dodge. Two men were lost in a blizzard on the return trip.

Inkpaduta, having been routed from this victory camp by the appearance of the combined forces, moved his band to the west. He continued in that direction until he reached the Flandreau, South Dakota, area. On the way, his band killed two of the women captives; one because she was too fragile to keep up and the other because she was too insolent. Inkpaduta did eventually allow the two remaining captives, Mrs. Marble and the girl, Abbie Gardner, to be ransomed back through the efforts of a friendly tribe, who served as intermediaries.

These events are well documented to have occurred in this sequence. This is not, however, the way they were supposed to have happened. The Sioux had a much grander design in mind at the start of these activities. The plan was described by several Indians in later years and is borne out by inferences that can be drawn from the records of the events of the times. Inkpaduta was not supposed to have taken action on his own. He was to have gathered as large a force as he could and combined them with Sleepy Eye's band and with other Minnesota tribes lead by Chiefs like Chaska and Shakopee. The huge combined war party would then make a massive surprise raid down the Des Moines River Valley and clear all the white settlers out of their traditional hunting grounds.

This was why Inkpaduta did not put up more of a fight at Smithland and why there was no bloodshed on his way up the Little Sioux River. However, he had his followers so riled up and ready for battle by the time they reached Spirit Lake that when they found this landmark being infiltrated by settlers, he could no longer control them. The Spirit Lake Massacre was clearly a mistake from the Indians' point of view. In their heady exuberance they moved northward and missed contact with Sleepy Eye. The quick response by the militia from Fort Dodge surprised Sleepy Eye, who was not ready to take action on his own, and forced his band out of position by moving them to the northeast. The regular army, by moving in from Fort Ridgley much sooner than it would have moved had the massacre not occurred, probably disrupted the movements of other tribes who may have joined the action. By stopping south of Springfield, the army prevented Inkpaduta and Sleepy Eye from joining forces, and in fact, forced Inkpaduta to move to the west. Thus, a much greater tragedy was prevented from happening.

Had the tribes been able to form a combined war party and made a massive drive down the Des Moines River, they would have been able to clear out every settlement nearly as far as Boone before sufficient forces could have formed to stop them. If this had happened, the tribes would have likely turned west, and in a mopping up action, cleaned out the Raccoon and Boyer River Valleys and restored all their traditional hunting grounds. This is when Fort Purdy would have had its battle. It may well have been a battle it could not have won. Had things happened this way, the history of this area would have had to develop without such names as Jesse Denison, H.C. Laub, the McHenrys, the Doblers, the Masons, the Mooreheads, the Smiths or many others. Schleswig would also have had a very different beginning.

Before dismissing this possibility as a flight of fantasy, it should be pointed out that the Sioux did not drop this plan. They only postponed it. Only five years later, in 1862, many of the same Sioux Chiefs took advantage of a weakened army presence caused by the Civil War and made a massive surprise raid by a combined war party. This time they did not go down the Des Moines River but rather up the Minnesota River where the new settlers were at the time. There were hundreds of people killed before the hostilities were brought under control. One of the more interesting accounts of this is a novel by Frederick Manfred, from Doon, Iowa, in his book *Scarlet Plume*. It is the centerpiece of his Buckskin Man Series. His Scarlet Plume definitely is not Inkpaduta, but, some of his other characters do bear Inkpaduta's characteristics. A whole series of forts, manned by the Northern Border Brigade, was temporarily set up across northern Iowa to protect the settlers while these hostilities were taking place.

Inkpaduta was also involved in the battle of Whitestone Hill near Kulm, North Dakota, where General Sully and the Sixth Iowa Cavalry defeated the Sioux in the 1860's in retaliation for the Minnesota River raids. Inkpaduta and his band of Santees were there as well as groups from several other tribes. Inkpaduta surrounded an advance scouting party, but, rather than pursue his advantage, he decided to taunt and terrorize the surrounded troops through the night with the intention to finish them off the next morning. This gave General Sully the time necessary to bring up his main force and defeat the Sioux. There are statues, monuments, and a museum on the site. Inkpaduta was also thought to be involved in the looting and total destruction of Sioux Falls, South Dakota, in the early 1860's. For a while, almost every Indian atrocity in the upper Middle West was attributed to him.

In the 1870's, Inkpaduta was roaming the western hunting grounds with his band. Though he had become an elder leader, he still headed one of the most contentious groups of Indians on the plains. He was the leader of one of the groups that gathered for a powwow on the banks of a creek called the Greasy Grass. He was fishing one Sunday afternoon in July with his granddaughters in this stream which was also known as the Little Bighorn when Col. George Custer attacked. Inkpaduta was camped very near the place where Col. Custer concentrated his attack, and his warriors were likely some of the first to attempt to thwart the Cavalry. After the battle, Inkpaduta joined with Sitting Bull's Hunkpapa tribe and many others and fled to Canada for safety. It was a difficult and trying trip, but old Inkpaduta prevailed. However, while living in the north woods, the old fighter met his maker. He died of natural causes, defiant to the end.

Among the Sioux, Inkpaduta was considered a major War Chief, not because he was a particularly good strategist, but because he was willing to fight. Early in the powwow at the Little Big Horn, Inkpaduta was considered the most prominent Chief in attendance. Sitting Bull was a medicine man rather than a chief. Crazy Horse was a battle leader but was not considered a traditional chief. It was not until Gaul and some of the other more traditional chiefs arrived that Inkpaduta was reduced to an emeritus status because of his age and his generally contrary disposition.

Finally, the Indians were brought into the reservation system. Inkpaduta's Santee Sioux were located on a reservation in northeast Nebraska, about a hundred miles west of Schleswig. It was years, however, before Sitting Bull could return to the United States and join up with a former Iowa boy, Buffalo Bill Cody, to form a Wild West Show. Around here in Iowa, the stories about Inkpaduta and his band were told until about the turn of the last century, and then, except for the Spirit Lake massacre, they were generally forgotten.

Meyer's *History of Crawford County* has a picture of a building that was the last remaining structure in the Fort Purdy complex as of about 1911. Remnants of the fort were reported to have been found there through the 1950's. In the 1960's, the civil rights movement brought an awareness of minority problems. In the late sixties, the American Indian Movement brought attention specifically to Indian problems. While the Omahas were going to court to reclaim Iowa land, the Sioux took up arms and overran Wounded Knee, South Dakota. They took it from U. S. Bureau of Indian Affairs control in the early 1970's, and killed two of the FBI agents sent in to handle the situation. The incident was settled, but it did reawaken interest in Indian cultures in our society.

Near the town of Smithland, in 1987, a monument was set up to mark Inkpaduta's campsite of 1856. In 1990, the county conservation commissions in Woodbury, Cherokee, and Clay counties set up a canoe trail on the Little Sioux River from Smithland to Spencer and have called it the Inkpaduta Trail. It roughly follows the trail he took on his way to the Spirit Lake Massacre. In 1994, Hamilton county, the county where the Lott cabin was located, named a road after Inkpaduta in their 911 rural addressing program.

In Ida Grove, the Moorehead House and Stagecoach Station are also being restored. Local lore has it that Inkpaduta was well known in the area and had stopped there on occasion. In Okoboji, Iowa, the Gardner Cabin has been restored to 1856 condition and is open to the public, as is a replica of a fort and a village in Fort Dodge, Iowa. One of the more interesting related sites is a small cemetery on a high point just above the juncture of the Boone and Des Moines Rivers called Vegor's Cemetery. It has a monument to Mrs. Henry Lott, the first white woman to die in Webster County. Her grave and those of other pioneers are among a grouping of Indian mounds and commands a spectacular view of the rugged countryside surrounding the conjunction of the two river valleys.

In the last century, all of the forts in the upper Middle West including Fort Des Moines, Fort Dodge, Fort Ridgley and those farther west were controlled by Fort Snelling which is located at the very point above where the Minnesota River joins the Mississippi. Two small towns that started nearby grew up around it: Minneapolis and St. Paul. Today, the Fort is a living military history exhibit, circa. 1840. If in the area, it is well worth a stop. It is near the Minneapolis airport and the Mall of the Americas.

The old stone monument on the edge of Denison, commemorating a fort that never had a battle, still has quite a story behind it. When you see it, be reminded that one of the most influential men to affect the history of Crawford County was Chief Inkpaduta, Scarlet Plume–the Scourge of Fort Purdy.

The Omaha Indians with their rich and varied culture were the predominant tribe in the Schleswig area. Unfortunately, much of their heritage has been lost in the passage of time. Even the tales of their relationships with the white culture are becoming unfamiliar. The official record is rather brief and much detail is provided only by the oral traditions of historical folklore.

The Omaha were generally a peaceful tribe, but they were willing to stand their ground when necessary. One of the earlier stories about the Omaha involved a run-in they had with some early day Mormon farmers in 1853. The incident took place somewhere near the Boyer River. The story was told to anthropologist James Owen Dorsey and was recorded in the *Contributions to North American Ethnology*, Volume VI which was entitled "The Omaha Language," (1890) pp. 447–448. The episode which takes place on the Boyer River is included in a larger piece entitled "Acinapaji's War Party in 1853."

"We killed deer when we went on the autumnal hunt. We hunted all sorts of small leaping animals. When we approached any place to pitch the tents, we were in excellent spirits. Day after day we carried into camp different animals, such as deer, raccoons, badgers, skunks, and wild turkeys. We had ten lodges in our party. As we went, we camped for the night. And we camped again at night, being in excellent spirits.

At length we reached a place where some white farmers dwelt. They gave us food, which was very good. At length they assembled us. 'Come, ye Indians, we must talk together. Let us talk to each other at night.'

'Yes,' said we.

As they came for us when a part of the night had passed, we said, 'Let us go,' They came with us to a very large house. Behold, all of the whites had arrived. That place was beyond the Little Sioux River, at Boyer Creek, where the first white men were, across the country from this place. They talked with us. 'Oho! My friends, though I, for my part, talk with you, you will do just what I say,' said one.

'We will consider it. If it be good, we will do so,' said the Omahas.

'I am not willing for you to wander over this land,' said the white man.

White Buffalo in the Distance said, 'As you keep all your stock at home, you have no occasion to wander in search of them. You dwell nowhere else but at this place. But we have wild animals, which are beyond our dwelling place, though they are on our land.'

'Though you say so, the land is mine,' said the white man.

'The land is not yours. The President did not buy it. You have jumped on it, and I know it full well,' said White Buffalo in the Distance.

'If the President bought it, are you so intelligent that you would know about it?' said the white man, speaking in a sneering manner to the Omaha.

White Buffalo in the Distance hit the white man several times in the chest. 'Why do you consider me a fool? You are now dwelling a little beyond the bounds of the land belonging to the President. It is through me that you shall make yourself a person (i.e., you shall improve your condition at my expense). I wish to eat my animals that grow of their own accord, so I walk seeking them,' said White Buffalo in the Distance.

'Nevertheless, I am unwilling. If you go further, instead of obeying my words, we shall fight,' said the white man.

'I will go beyond. You may fight me. As the land is mine, I shall go,' said White Buffalo in the Distance.

'Yes, if you go tomorrow, I will go to you to see you. I shall collect the young white people all around, and go with them to see you,' said the white man.

Having removed the camp in the morning, we scattered to hunt for game. I went with three men. About forty white men arrived, and stood there to intercept us. They waved their hands at us, saying, 'Do not come any further,' As we still went on, they came with a rush, and tried to snatch our guns from us. When we refused to let them go, they shot at us: 'Ku! ku! ku!'

As we went back, we were driven towards the rest of our party. The leader of the white men said, 'Do not go. If you go, I will shoot at you.' We stood on an island; and the white men surrounded us.

'You have already shot at us,' said the Omaha.

The white men doubted their word, saying, 'It is not so about us.'

'You have already shot at us, so we will go at all hazards. I am following my trail in my own land. I am going to hunt. Why do you behave so? Make way for us. We will go to you,' said the White Buffalo in the Distance.

'If you speak saucily to me, I will shoot at you,' said the white man.

'Ho! If you wish to do that, do it,' said the Omahas. As they departed, the whites made way for them.

We went along a bluff, and then downhill, when we reached a creek. It was a good place for us to stay, so we remained there.

At length about two hundred white men came in sight. We were just thirty. We were in the hollow by the edge of the stream. Wanacejinga . . . arrived in sight. He looked at them. When he made a sudden signal, he was wounded in the arm. 'They have wounded me! There is cause for anger! They have wounded me severely,' he said.

'Oho! Come, let us attack them at any rate,' said the Omahas. We all stood, and gave the scalp yell. Having formed a line, we went to attack them. We scared off the white men. All of them were mounted, but only one Omaha, Agahamaci, was on a horse. He rode round and round, and gave us directions what to do, 'Miss in firing at the white men. Shoot elsewhere every time,' said he.

At length the Omahas intercepted the retreat of the whites. 'Come, stop pursuing. Let us cease. It is good not to injure even one of the white people, who are our own flesh and blood,' said Agahamaci. We returned to the women. Then we departed. We reached a place where we pitched the tents. There were a great many deer; they were exceedingly abundant.

Acinapaji, soon to be an Omaha War Chief.

While the relations between the Omaha and the white men were generally good, and there was a mutual respect between the Omaha and the Sac and Fox to the east, their relations with the Sioux to the north were anything but cordial. The Sioux were fond of making devastating and murderous raids on Omaha villages. Retaliation was the required response to preserve their hunting grounds, and the efforts of the Omaha were effective. The Sioux were careful not to be caught unaware in Omaha territory.

One incident that clearly demonstrated this point also involved one of the colorful characters in western Iowa–Charles Larpenteur. Charles Larpenteur's father was an envoy from Napoleon to the United States. After Napoleon fell, the Larpenteurs saw that discretion indicated it would be better to stay in the United States. Charles consequently went west to find his fortune in the 1820's. He saw the region develop from the earliest mountain rendevous to the final homesteading. He spent much of his life developing a career as a trader in the outposts on the upper Missouri. He preserved many of his memories in his autobiography, *Forty Years in the Fur Trade*. However, he maintained a home base just below where the Loess Hills meet the Missouri River Bottoms. His efforts to establish the new town he named Fontainebleau on the site were unsuccessful.

Larpenteur, while managing a fur trading post on the Missouri, had married an Assiniboine Sioux woman and brought her back to Iowa when he returned. While he was here, the Sioux raided the area, an action which agitated an Omaha war party who then turned up at Larpenteur's house looking for the Sioux. Larpenteur was afraid for his wife's safety. Since she and their daughter were out gathering berries and herbs he tried to misdirect the war party, but they discovered the women on their way back to the house. The Omaha recognized his wife as a Sioux and shot and killed her on the spot. They did spare his daughter because she had white blood as well as Sioux. Certain rules had to be maintained!

Locally, the best-known name associated with the Omaha tribe was Chief Yellow Smoke. From the earliest contact with white settlers until the last of the Indians were seen in this area, Chief Yellow Smoke was a household word. Everyone either knew him or had heard of him.

It is becoming fairly clear there were two and probably three Chiefs Yellow Smoke that had contact with white settlers–probably a son, father and grandfather. While this position in the tribe does not appear to be determined strictly by heredity, that does appear to have had a strong influence.

The position held by Yellow Smoke was an interesting one. In the Omaha Tribe, the leadership function was shared by a small group of Chiefs. Each had a specialty and an area of responsibility. Yellow Smoke was known as the Keeper of the Sacred Pole. There are a number of legends that date to antiquity concerning the origin of the Pole. The Pole is an eight-foot shaft with a scalp on one end, a medicine bag containing sacred items in the center, and a stake attached to the foot. It was meant to represent a man. To the Omaha, it was the essence of the perfect man. It represented the coming together of the forces of nature in a manifestation of its ultimate expression. To the tribe this is what it meant to be an Omaha.

When the tribe gathered for ceremonial purposes, the camp was formed in a circle with an opening to the east–a special arrangement with each clan having its location on the circle. The clans relating to the earth, such as the Buffalo clan, the Elk clan or the Turtle clan, formed the south side of the circle, and the clans relating to the sky, such as the Eagle clan, the Crow clan or the Thunder clan, on the north side, and the police society enforcing the traditional order. Within the circle were three tepees; one for the keeper of the Sacred White Buffalo Skin with the men in charge leading activities relating to the hunt; one for the keeper of the Two Sacred Peace Pipes with those in charge leading activities relating to war and peace with other tribes; the final one was for the keeper of the Sacred Pole. This responsibility was for maintaining the identity of the tribe. Yellow Smoke, as Keeper of the Sacred Pole, was responsible not only for the pole itself, but also for the ceremonies and traditions that went with it.

The earliest written record of Chief Yellow Smoke is a reference to an old Indian who was killed in a dispute in the Dunlap area in 1869. If this record is accurate, it probably refers to Yellow Smoke, the grandfather, since it corresponds with a number of folklore items. This Yellow Smoke was one of the first Indians with whom the early settlers in this area came in contact. He appears to have been a friendly and congenial person with a definite sporting bent. He enjoyed playing cards and gambling. He also discovered that his mere presence at the early country schools so terrified the students and teachers that they gave him all their lunches if he would just go away. He was glad to oblige since he now did not have to worry about groceries for several days. He also found he could enjoy the white man's whiskey and still beat him at his own games. This activity led to trouble, however.

After a successful evening of gambling, Yellow Smoke, the grandfather, was waylaid by some white men intent on stealing back their losings. He was stabbed in the process, and he, later, died of his wounds. Because of his prominence, the whole tribe came for the funeral ceremonies. Dunlap at this time was not a very large community and became apprehensive at the appearance of hundreds of Indians who came because a prominent tribal leader was killed there by white men. A delegation from the town met with the Indians and explained the border ruffians who had committed the murder had left as soon as the Indians started arriving. The town residents expressed their wish to reestablish friendly relations with the tribe. The Indians did identify the culprits, and when they were not found in the town, they did disperse after several days of ceremonies. It has been said a number of times,

Dunlap was lucky they were dealing with the Omaha tribe; had they been dealing with the Sioux, for instance, the Indians would have probably massacred the town first and checked the bodies later to see if they got the right men.

Chief Yellow Smoke, the father, held the position of keeper of the Sacred Pole during a time of crisis within the tribe. Since their culture was based on a nomadic life style, they could keep only a limited number of physical possessions, and they had to share the use of everything they had, including open access to the land. The main economic component of their life style was the Buffalo and almost everything they had was either from the Buffalo or used for the hunt of the animal. Their strong pride in being Omaha was their unifying force, and when the growing prominence of the white culture had the effect of destroying all the props which supported their society—the Buffalo was gone, travel was difficult, accumulating possessions did not seem satisfying. There was little left in which to take pride.

Chief Yellow Smoke maintained the traditions and ceremonies of the Sacred Pole as best he could. But when he became advanced in years, he began looking for someone to take over the responsibilities of his position. He could find no one. The young people had lost interest in tribal traditions and were unwilling to undertake the strenuous training involved. They could not see the relevance of the old ways. It was at this time Chief Iron Eye, also known as Joseph La Flesche, approached Yellow Smoke with an idea that some of the Chiefs had been discussing. The Bureau of Indian Affairs had made an arrangement with some of the leading museums in the country to send ethnologists to record the lifestyles of the major Indian tribes. This group of ethnologists received the respect of the Omaha Chiefs to the extent that they were considering turning over their sacred objects to the museums and describing the ceremonies and traditions, the songs and dances, so they could be preserved for future generations. It may not have been difficult to reveal the secrets of the Buffalo hunt; the Buffalo were gone. The last Buffalo hunt had occurred in the winter of 1875-

76. It may not have been difficult to reveal the secrets of warfare; tribal wars were not allowed by the white men. Even the most hostile of tribes had been subdued by this time. However, Yellow Smoke held the secrets and traditions that went to the very soul of tribal identity. To entrust these sacred objects and secrets to the very people who were responsible for their destruction would take a momentous act of faith. Yellow Smoke considered it for some time but in the end he consented. He could see no other way to preserve at least a portion of the tribal traditions even though he had sworn on his life to reveal much of it only to his successor.

Many of the sacred objects and legends had been transferred to the Whites by 1884, but because of the special nature of the Sacred Pole, arrangements for its transfer were not completed until 1888. In September of that year, Chief Yellow Smoke met with the White men in Chief Iron Eye's home. He made the transfers and in a somber and subdued manner revealed the secrets of the tribe that had been maintained for centuries. The supernatural implications of this act were reinforced when Chief Iron Eye came down with a high fever within hours of the meeting and within a few days lay dead in the very room where the secrets were revealed. Yellow Smoke also died within a very short time.

The name Yellow Smoke is a ceremonial name. It is derived from the part of the ceremonies of the Sacred Pole when the keeper added certain types of woods and herbs that produced a yellowish smoke which swirled up beside the pole and sometimes stained the tent. Yellow Smoke, the father's name in the Omaha language, was Shudenaci. The Bureau of Indian Affairs gave him the name Robert Morris.

Yellow Smoke, the son, had the most contact with white people. His travels through this area came at time when the frontier of white civilization came to Crawford County and passed on through. The land became settled, and he had much more opportunity to be in contact with the white people. Though he was probably not a Chief in the formal sense–too many of the traditions of the tribe had lapsed into disuse–but, because of his stature and personality, he attracted a number of fellow travelers, and he was probably referred to as Chief in deference to his family's past prominence. He was the subject of many of the stories that were passed down by pioneer families. He had a distinctive and interesting personality, and he was a gregarious and friendly person who enjoyed visiting with people along his travels. Once when he was visiting the Fred Jepsen farm, he became very curious about a livestock scale they were using and even had himself weighed. He often invited nearby farmers to his tepee for an evening of conversation over a leisurely pipe of tobacco. If the guests over-stayed their welcome, however, he would add some green twigs to the fire and stir it up. The tepee would soon be full of smoke and everyone would be forced out. This was his not-so-subtle way of saying the party was over.

There are enough stories about him and his followers to fill a book. Instances of hostility were rare. There are many accounts of help and cooperation. Many of the stories that survived involved two cultures investigating each other's peculiarities. Neither side appreciated the other's methods of preparing food, for instance, but, there was a great deal of respect for each other's insights into the uses of herbal medicines. Yellow Smoke traveled through this area well into the twentieth century. Even after fields and fences restricted his normal movements, he would be seen on the road as he traveled to attend the Mesquaki Pow-wows near Tama. He usually traveled seated in a chair mounted in the back of a wagon pulled by a team of horses driven by the women of the family.

Chief Yellow Smoke, the grandfather, is buried on a hilltop in the northeast corner of Harrison County. Chief Yellow Smoke, the father, apparently died in Nebraska and is presumably buried there. There is a small grove about a mile from the Vernon Voss Road, southeast of Schleswig, that for many years has been pointed out as the burial place of Chief Yellow Smoke, the son, who had been known to have said that he wanted to be buried on the old tribal hunting grounds, and that he wanted to be buried in a coffin in white man's style. This may be his grave site. It is near the route of a trail that was known to the early settlers as the Yellow Smoke Trail, which ran on the high ground roughly parallel to the present-day Vernon Voss Road.

Chief Iron Eye's son, Francis La Flesche, co-authored with Alice Fletcher a two-volume edition of *The Omaha Tribe*, which is considered the best work on the tribe. Iron Eye's daughter, Suzette La Flesche, better known as Bright Eyes, married Thomas Henry Tibbles, the journalist and editor for the *Omaha World-Herald*. These two did a great deal to publicize the plight of the Indians through lectures and articles. They played a major role along with General Crook, the old Indian fighter, and A.J. Poppleton, the railroad attorney, in the trial of Chief Standing Bear—a case which redefined the way Indians were recognized by the government. It paved the way for Indians like Yellow Smoke to be allocated particular plots of land in the reservation. This, in turn, helped the tribe win their law suit in the 1960's and 1970's to reclaim part of their reservation that became part of Iowa when the Missouri River changed course. The Nebraska Public Television Network has produced a very good video on the trial of Chief Standing Bear.

The Tibbles lived for a while in Bancroft, Nebraska, near Mrs Tibbles' people. While there they made the an acquaintance with one of the true greats of American literature, John Niehardt, who is best known for *Cycles of the West* and *Black Elk Speaks*. The Nebraska Historical Society has established a very interesting complex known as the Niehardt Center in Bancroft which is about an hour's drive west of Schleswig. It can be the subject of a very interesting afternoon excursion.

There are cycles that occur in history. Chief Yellow Smoke, the grandfather, liked the white man's games and liked to gamble. Now one of major sources of income and employment for the tribe is the WinneVegas Casino on reservation property near Sloan, Iowa, and the Omaha Casino near Onawa, Iowa.

When the Crawford County Conservation Board dedicated Yellow Smoke Park, a delegation from the Omaha tribe lead by Tribal Chairman Edward Cline attended. After the ceremonies,

Mr. Cline said the tribe was very aware of where the sacred objects of the tribe were in the museums, but they were reluctant to pursue a quest of obtaining their return. He said, by their very nature, the objects were sacred, and the tribe was apprehensive about the supernatural significance of their being mishandled. Too many of the ceremonies and traditions had been lost in time and the tribe did not want to be responsible for the consequences of their accidental misuse.

The tribe made a monetary donation to the development of the park at that time as well as providing a dance ceremony. The County presented the tribe with an engraved hunting knife in return. When the Crawford County Conservation Board celebrated its twenty-fifth anniversary, the Omaha again participated by sending a group of dancers to participate in the celebration.

However, more recently, the Omaha people changed their mind and began negotiating with the Peabody Museum at Harvard University. They decided it was time for the ancient artifacts to be returned to their people. In July of 1989, the most sacred of these objects, the Sacred Pole of the Omahas, was delivered to the tribe. In the delegation receiving this relic was the Tribal Chairman, Doran Morris, great, great grandson of the last Chief Yellow Smoke.

There were two major Indian battles in Iowa. The Black Hawk War which opened Iowa to white settlement, and the Spirit Lake Massacre which proved to be a last gesture as the Indians were forced out of the State. Crawford County is the only county in the Iowa that has a monument to both events. One is the Lincoln Land monument is located five miles south and a mile east of the town of Schleswig marking the land grant Lincoln received for services rendered in the Black Hawk war. The other is the Fort Purdy monument is located on the roadside at 1017 Old Ridge Road in far northeast Denison. The fort site, where the early settlers gathered to protect themselves from Inkpaduta and his band on their way to the Spirit Lake Massacre, is now the home of a local church. Additional memorials to our native American ancestors also exist in the county. The largest memorial to Indian affairs was reserved for a tribe with which the most peaceful relations were established. Yellow Smoke Park, the largest recreational area in the county, was named after the Chiefs Yellow Smoke. A major Indian interpretive center is also being proposed south of Charter Oak. We have done well in remembering our brothers.

There are footprints in the soil. By the streams, on the hills, in the valleys, there are footprints. People have passed by here. They had places to go, and they had things to do. They have been walking here for a very long time. Some of the footprints are old, and some of them are very fresh. Where we walk today, we are not walking on untrampled ground. There are footprints under the dust. They were made by people who enjoyed the freshness of the air at dawn, the warmth of noon, and the beauty of the sunset. We all liked it here.

IV. EXPLORATION

The wind is blowing through the tall grasses causing waves of green that spread from the horizon to here and from here to as far as the eye can see. The rains keep the grass growing and with the rain comes the rumbling of thunder. However, there is a different rumbling in the distance–and another wave coming–small, but growing–and growing. It is a wave of people! A different kind of people from those who had occupied the land–a light-skinned people. They are continuing to come. There is no stopping them. These people will take over the whole country– and it will never be the same. Strange things were done to the land. It was plowed, it was fenced, buildings were built on it and these people inhabited them. When they were finished they started all over again– and it will never be the same again.

The first of these people came to these shores in the North in small groups and looked around, staying a while, and leaving. For them it was an adventure. They came a viking. Long boats brought these Norsemen who were interested in exploring but not in settling. The Irish came in round boats covered with leather. Everyone who came left again. Getting here and returning were difficult, but when explorers came to the south of here, they did something different. They charted their course, and when they returned, they had a record to show of their travels. Others soon were following their path.

Now, with more frequent travel, their influence became more permanent. The Europeans brought their own ways–paying no attention to the long established life styles of the natives nor to their accomplishments. These new explorers were interested in the wealth they could send back to their native land. These new groups could not agree among themselves. Far to the south, the land was divided by the church between the Spanish and the Portugese. Spain and Portugal became wealthy from their imports, but at a terrible expense in lives, in values, in whole civilizations. The natives survived, however, and adopted the new ways and religions but changed them to fit their old ways as much as possible. In the North, the English and the French battled over control of the land. The English set up small, but highly developed settlements along a relatively small area of the coast. The French spread themselves out thinly over a large area of country.

The French arrived in our part of the country before the Spanish. DeSoto and his successors started up the Mississippi River, but they did not make it as far as Iowa. French explorers, Marquette and Joliet, came down the Mississippi from the Great Lakes and arrived in Iowa in 1673. French trappers and traders spread across the state during the 1700's where they checked out every creek and stream. One of them even left his name on the Boyer River. Meanwhile, the French and English settled their differences in the French and Indian War in 1763 by agreeing that everything east of the Mississippi River was to be English and everything west of the Mississippi was to be Spanish. The French lost the war and lost their possessions. The Spanish, however, never bothered to develop this area.

The English colonies revolted in 1776. They set up a new country somewhat to the east of this area. The only contact that Iowa had with the Revolutionary War was that some of the lead from Julian Dubuque's mines made it there in the form of bullets. Several years later Napoleon attempted to conquer all of Europe, and in the process, he took over Spain, and in 1800, he relieved them of the title to Louisiana which included this area. He was blocked from getting to it by the British in the Carribean, so he sold it to the United States in 1803. The territory became known as the Louisiana Purchase.

President Thomas Jefferson bought this land which included the area from here west. Not knowing of what it consisted, he sent his secretary, Meriwether Lewis, and General George Rogers Clark's brother, William Clark, to head an expedition to find out. They left St. Louis in May of 1804 with tons of supplies in a keel boat, a somewhat smaller pirogue, and canoes which had to be propelled upstream against the fast-moving Missouri River. Some six hundred miles later, they came to Iowa around the end of July 1804. A number of first time experiences were encountered as they worked their way up the Iowa coast. They met the first Indians—a group of Otes and Missouris to whom they gave gifts, demonstrated a close rank drill, and explained their relation to the United States. The chiefs were presented with Presidential Peace Metals, and in return, the Indians gave them watermelons.

A number of animals in this area were not known to science at the time including coyotes, terns, and bull snakes. A number of other things that were known but had not been encountered until they got to Iowa included Buffalo, badgers, and pelicans. One island was so full of pelicans, which were molting winter feathers, that there was a blanket of feathers on the water seventy yards wide and three miles long. The numbers of deer and elk were so large they were almost unimaginable. At one sitting, the group was able to land 490 catfish and 300 of other species of fish. The mosquitoes were so thick they could not fire a gun accurately.

It was in Iowa that Lewis and Clark lost the only man to die on the expedition. Sergeant Charles Floyd died of acute appendicitis and was buried on a loess bluff near Sioux City where today an obelisk stands in his memory. The expedition returned through this area on the return trip in early September of 1806. Since they were in a hurry to get home by the time they passed here, they were making sixty to eighty miles a day. The only thing that slowed them was that Lewis had been accidentally wounded by one of his men, and travel for him was uncomfortable.

Lewis and Clark opened the trail west. It didn't take long to find use for the trail. Within months mountain men were heading out to explore the great unknown territory that lay out there. Some of them, like John Colter and George Drouillard, were former members of the expedition, but they were soon joined by many others. Numerous men were recruited by the newly-formed fur companies which were thriving since the demand for beaver pelts in Europe was huge. French trappers had been moderately successful, but now there was big money to be made, and big organizations were formed to exploit it. Many of the organizers were Frenchmen who had worked earlier as trappers—men like Auguste Chouteau, Pierre Chouteau, and Charles Gratiot who had been some of the original organizers of the City of St. Louis. An aggressive young Spaniard just starting to make a name for himself at this time was Manual Lisa. He set a pattern for later fur trade activities by going up stream and setting up a series of forts. Thus he was trading directly with the Indians and trappers before they could reach his competition in St. Louis. Several of his forts were along the Iowa portions of the Missouri River, one of them being Fort Lisa, located somewhat south of the mouth of the Boyer River. It became the most important trading post on the river in the decade after 1811.

During the first thirty years of the 1800's there was more activity in western Iowa than there was in eastern Iowa. Through a series of treaties with Indians, Iowa was declared off limits to white settlement. Both the military and the Indians enforced the provisions of the treaties in eastern Iowa. The exception was Julian Dubuque's lead mines. He had obtained Spanish permission to work his mines and was already set up before the territory became a possession of the United States. He had generally good relations with the Indians, although it was said the ones he hired he did work very hard.

Just how far west Iowa extended was not defined at the time, but it was considered to have included a large section of the fur trapping territory. The lucrative fur trade, and curiosity of the explorers following Lewis and Clark, demanded that the Missouri River be opened as a natural travel route.

The military took some interest in the area, too. They established Fort Atkinson just north of present-day Omaha near Fort Calhoun which was only a few miles from one of Manual Lisa's trading posts. One of the officers assigned here was Captain Stephen Watts Kearney. In 1820, he was assigned the duty to take a small expedition across Iowa and southern Minnesota to Camp Coldwater near present day Minneapolis. The purpose of his mission was to make observations of the land he covered and to determine if a feasible road could be built through the area.

His party left Fort Atkinson at 7:00 A.M. on July 2, 1820. Two hours later he passed Manual Lisa's trading post and continued on to the Boyer River. He proceeded up the south side of the river and crossed the Boyer near the present day Dow City. They camped near the river on July 5. The following is an excerpt from Kearney's journal for July 6, 1820.

> "Last night we found quite cool, & three blankets, for a covering were by no means uncomfortable. The mosquitoes, however, were very troublesome & tho' I am benefitted by Lieut. Talcot's mosquito net, we had not sufficiently secured it to prevent the entrance of theses annoying little insects.
>
> Crossed the creek, which we called Morgan's Creek, & were engaged till 11:00 A.M. in continually de & ascending high hills, with no indication of timber, or of a single tree, when we halted on a ravine with a little water for our dinner, having previously crossed two others, of similar character—at 1:00 P.M., recommenced our march, & after proceeding a few miles, saw from the summit of a high hill some timber, to the West, at however, a very great distance; from this point the hills commence running in a different direction, viz N. & S & we find the traveling somewhat easier, as we are enabled to take advantage of the ridges—halted at sunset near a small drain of water, but without wood, having made 22 miles & over a country, tho' without timber, yet pretty well watered by small drains—
>
> The dull monotony of traveling over the Prairies is occasionally interrupted by the feats of Horsemanship dis-

played by our squaw, & the affection & gallantry shewn toward her & her papoose (an infant of but four months old) by the Indian Guide.

Four of our party went in pursuit of a gang of elk which we observed, a mile from our camp, but returned unsuccessful, about 9:00 P.M.

On the night of July 6, 1820, the Stephen Watts Kearney Expedition camped on the site of Schleswig, Iowa. The journal, as contained in the *Annals of Iowa*, Vol. X, (1912), continued for July 7, as follows:

> "*In consequence of having no timber, & being desirous of procuring some, started at 4:00 A.M. & continued our course North for 10 miles, when we halted on a ravine for breakfast. The country is gradually assuming a more level appearance & many elk are seen, to the right & left of us, but at too great a distance to pursue—we have headed the Head waters of the Soldier River, which is laid down on the maps incorrectly: inasmuch as it is made to appear a very considerable stream, & having its source near the Racoon branch, of the Des Moines: proceeded on our route: saw many gangs of buck elks, & some of our party fired at them, but at too great distance to kill any: shot a badger, which was given to the Guide, who has been all day very sick, in consequence of living on salt provisions, which he is unaccustomed to—halted at 6:00 P.M. on a ravine, with no timber, the want of which we began to feel— made today 21 miles.*"

They continued without finding enough wood for a campfire until they reached the Little Sioux River at the present site of the town of Peterson, Iowa. It was in this area that they saw their first buffalo which they chased for two miles and shot five times before they were able to bring it down. Some time before reaching the

Little Sioux, Captain Kearney left his command and traveled on a side trip to visit the grave of a local Indian Chief–Shaton de Tou (Red Hawk) of the Sisseton Sioux whom Kearney had met when he was fighting against him in the War of 1812.

The Shawnee Chief, Tecumseh, and his brother, The Prophet, formed a vast Indian Confederation in which they wanted to form a combined force of all western Indians who had a grievance against the American settlers. A large number of followers joined the confederacy and instigated a number of smaller uprisings. When the War of 1812 began, they sided with the British. General William Henry Harrison defeated the combined forces near Detroit where Tecumseh, who had been given the rank of General and commanded one flank of the British line, was killed in the battle. The Indian ranks dissolved after the battle. The two most influential Indian leaders from Iowa who had joined the Confederacy were Red Hawk of Sioux and Black Hawk of Sauk. It had been during this fight that Capt. Kearney and Red Hawk had met.

Kearney described Red Hawk's grave as a circular mound 12 feet in diameter and six feet high with a 12-foot pole erected in the center located on a high hill overlooking a vast amount of country. He estimated the time of death as shortly after he returned from the war. The exact location of the grave is no longer known.

Traffic on the Missouri River was being propelled more and more by the fur trade. The fur trade had been dominated for over a hundred years by the Hudson's Bay Company which was headquartered far up in Canada. For many years its only competition was the Northwest Company, a French company that operated mainly in the Pacific Coast area. There were a few more modest regional companies such as the Chouteau brothers and Manuel Lisa in St. Louis. One of the goals of the Lewis and Clark expedition had been to claim as much of the rich fur territory as possible for the United States and to evaluate the potential of this extremely rich trade. John Jacob Astor's American Fur Company marked the United States' major entry into the industry. He set up a transcontinental operation that could export directly from the west coast to the Orient, but the War of 1812 curtailed his operations east of the Rocky Mountains. However, he worked the western area extensively. William Ashley and Col. Andrew Henry developed a rival Rocky Mountain Fur Company. They each developed strings of forts and trading posts up the Missouri across Iowa, the Dakotas, and Montana all the way into the heart of the Rocky Mountains. Where it was impractical to build permanent facilities, temporary rendevous were organized where several weeks of trading, partying, and revelry occurred in the high mountain meadows. Tremendous fortunes were made in this trade. When John Jacob Astor died his estate was estimated at $20,000,000.00 in 1827 dollars. Many of the areas close to the trade centers, such as the Boyer River Valley, were cleaned out of its furs early.

Chief Black Hawk had a strong influence on the development of Iowa. He had been part of the Indian Confederacy and joined forces with the British in the War of 1812 during which his major contribution was to destroy the original Fort Madison and force the Americans out of Iowa. Then in the early 1830's, he engaged in the activities that are referred as the Black Hawk War. He was deserted by many of his supporters and chased across Illinois and Wisconsin. By the time he returned to Iowa, his forces were decimated and he was captured.

Black Hawk's major influence was not in his military efforts but in the political fallout that resulted from his activities. The treaty that ended the war opened up Iowa for white settlement for the first time and settlers swarmed in. The government offered the militia land grants in lieu of payment for their services in battle. The Lincoln land grant near Schleswig was one of these. Many of the first grants of title to land in Iowa were similar land grants.

Governmentally, Iowa was first technically administered by Meriwether Lewis when he was appointed Governor of all the Louisiana Territory. However, it was William Clark who had been appointed Superintendent of Indian Affairs who had more actual influence.

When Louisiana was admitted as a State, Iowa was attached to Missouri Territory, and William Clark was appointed Governor. When Missouri was admitted as a state, we attached to Michigan Territory. The Missouri Compromise under which Missouri was admitted as a State provided that no territory farther north could be a slave owning territory. Thus Iowa's status as a free territory was mandated. This was very agreeable to most Iowans since support for slavery was not strong here. Iowa was also attached to Wisconsin Territory for a time. For all practical terms, there was no effective administration in Iowa from 1821 until it became Iowa Territory in 1838, and some interesting situations developed because of this lack of jurisdiction. Patrick O'Connor killed his mining partner, George O'Keaf. Fearing the outcome of a local trial, he appealed to the Governor of Missouri, who claimed not to have jurisdiction, and he appealed to the Governor of Michigan, who also claimed no jurisdiction. The local minor's jury found him guilty and sentenced him to death. He countered that since there was no jurisdiction for an appeal, there was no constitutional authority to try him. He had a good point; but, they hanged him anyway.

The Smith brothers were rough and rowdy friends of O'Connor and were not happy the way he had been treated. Consequently, they cornered Woodbury Massey, the foreman of the jury and shot him. The Massey family responded by killing Bill Smith. The younger Smith brother was known as a ruthless killer, and he swore to avenge his brother's death by killing the remaining Massey. When Smith appeared, Massey was working in a remote area, unarmed. Fearing she would not be able to get a warning to him in time, Louisa Massey went to meet the ruffian, but rather than appeal to him, when she got close enough, she pulled out a gun and shot him dead! In doing so she saved her man, and her action captured the imagination of the public. She become Iowa's famous lady gunfighter, and Louisa County was even named after her.

This lack of official authority created a rowdy start to Iowa's history. Every outlaw and ne'er-do-well that was forced out of the

more civilized areas farther east set up operations here. One gang
of outlaws became so powerful they took over the entire town of
Bellevue. From there they controlled the outlaw activity along the
Mississippi River over the full length of the State until 1840, when
a pitched battle between the outlaws and a posse of concerned
citizens finally drove the outlaws out of the State. Some of the
ruffians associated with this gang later returned and murdered
Col. Davenport in his Rock Island home. Benton County also
became completely controlled by outlaws, and one gang of horse
thieves just west of Des Moines operated from Wisconsin to Missouri. Henry Lott had his notorious operation at the mouth of the
Boone River.

The State did not have the resources to combat these nefarious
activities, so the people took things in their own hands and organized vigilance committees. Members were known as Vigilantes,
or, more popularly, as Regulators. In some areas, such as where the
Wapsipinicon River ran near Scott, Cedar, and Clinton Counties,
they took on fanciful names like the Wapsi Rangers, a group boast-
ing of more than a hundred members at its peak. These groups
were most effective against large and easily identifiable opposition,
being less effective on small scale and less serious activities. Unfortunately, there was no one else capable of providing for the common defense at this time, and the trend moved westward across
Iowa.

Another problem in these early days was the title to land.
White settlers were prohibited from entering Iowa until after the
Black Hawk War when the land was to be surveyed by government
surveyors and then auctioned off. However, the process was slow—
much too slow—for many of the settlers, who would move in, find
a good site, and set up a farming operation. But a problem resulted when the land was auctioned. Huge tracks of land would be
sold to Eastern speculators for as little as $1.25 and acre. When
the speculators would begin to partition and develop the land,
they would have the local authorities evict the squatters. The developed farms could then be sold for a large profit. Claims Clubs

were established by the settlers to protect their interest and evictions would be prevented physically. A lot of political pressure on how to find a better solution was put on the authorities. In some cases, preemption laws were enacted in which a squatter, if he could show that he had substantially improved a property, could preempt the auction by paying a minimum amount and getting title before the auction. These laws were hit or miss until Congress passed a national preemption law in 1841, but it still remained difficult for the government to keep their survey teams ahead of the settlers in time to head off conflict. The surveyors used a system established in the Northwest Ordinance of 1787 all across the State. Sections of a mile square were organized into townships of 36 sections with one section set aside for the support of schools.

Along the Missouri River, the traffic was becoming heavier and heavier. The fur trade was hitting its peak, and there was a constant flow of furs and trade goods. Miners were beginning to take some interest in the mountains, and other groups were finding the river an easy access route to the vast new areas of the West. Father DeSmit and other missionaries were traveling to the new territories. James Catlin was looking for new views to paint as was Swiss painter, Karl Bodner. Many other adventurers with diverse interests from the East, and from many other parts of the world, were traveling through during these years. Prince Maximilian of Germany, John Jacob Audubon, and John C. Fremont were some of the more illustrious visitors. Most of the travelers were going down the Ohio and Mississippi Rivers to St. Louis and back up the Missouri to Independence before starting west, but there was always a trickle of travelers crossing Iowa as a short cut to the Oregon trail.

By this time, settlers were pouring into eastern Iowa. Within six years after Iowa was opened for settlement, there were enough people to apply for status as a separate territory. The Territory of Iowa was established by an act of Congress and signed by President Martin Van Buren to go into effect on July 4, 1838. The boundaries of the Territory included everything north of the State of Missouri between the Mississippi and Missouri Rivers all the way to the Canadian border. The first governor was Robert Lucas, the former governor of Ohio. He was a man with the experience necessary to get Iowa off to a good start. Problems did arise, however. A war was nearly started with Missouri. Missourians claimed a border much farther north than was originally established, and a Sheriff from Missouri attempted to collect taxes in Iowa but was repelled. Some timber men also came north to harvest some "bee trees" in Iowa, thus giving the affair the name the Honey War. The Missourians formed a *posse comitatus* of several hundred men to enforce their position. Governor Lucas sent Iowa troops down to "clean out" the place, but fortunately the groups managed to avoid finding each other and Congress later set the official boundary between Iowa and Missouri.

The event that really opened up western Iowa was the Mormon migration. The Mormons discovered that the freedom of religion sometimes meant the freedom to persecute a religious difference rather than freedom from persecution. They moved from New York to Ohio to Missouri and back to Illinois without finding a comfortable place in which to practice their religion. In 1846, they decided to find an unsettled territory in the West where they would not have to worry about persecution by non-believers. Mass migrations across southern Iowa were to go completely cross the state. Present day Highway 34 roughly shows the trek of the first group; the second was slightly to the north; and today's Interstate 80 roughly marks the trek of the third group. The first expedition camped the first winter near Council Bluffs which at the time was named Kanesville. A debate among the faithful took place as to whether it would be better to stay together and form a single homogeneous community, or whether it would be better to separate and live among the general population as did other denominations. In the Spring, the bulk of the people joined Brigham Young on his trek to find a community of their own, eventually settling in Salt Lake City, Utah. There was a significant minority, however, who stayed and spread over the loess hills area joining or starting new settlements. One such group settled on the north branch of the Boyer River naming their community Mason's Grove. Later when they attempted to get a post office, the postal authorities required a new name which they chose to be Deloit.

By the middle of the 1840's Iowa had grown to the size that it was considering statehood. A national political trend was very beneficial for this prospect. In order to maintain the balance of power in Congress, whenever a slave state was admitted to the union, a free state also had to be admitted. Texas, to be a slave state, was pushing hard for membership in the Union. A new free state was needed. There was some question as to whether Iowa was ready for statehood, but it was needed. Some of the earlier leaders tried to take advantage of this and pushed for as large a State as possible. They proposed a boundary starting at Sioux City and running northeast to Mankato, Minnesota, and following the Minnesota River to the Mississippi. If this boundary had been accepted, the Mall of America would almost have been in Iowa today. Congress, however, rejected this idea, and, as a result, statehood for Iowa was delayed for a while. The dispute was resolved in favor of the present boundary, and President Polk signed the statehood bill on December 28, 1846.

In 1848, gold was discovered in California. While the West was of general interest to most people and of considerable interest to specific groups such as fur trappers, Mormons, and hopeful new landowners, it now became the consuming interest of the whole nation. Everyone wanted to go west or to have contacts with people who did go west. A mass movement was underway, and Iowa was right on the path.

Crawford County was established by the Iowa Legislature as part of the County Organization Act of 1851. It was named after William Harris Crawford who had run for President, in 1824, against John Quincy Adams. There were too few people in the county to formally organize it, however, and it was attached to Shelby County for administration. Prior to that time it had been considered part of Benton County and later of Pottawatamie county.

The settlers, when they came to Crawford County, found wide stretches of open prairie where the only trees were along some of the rivers and some of the major streams. The prairie sod was so thick and tangled that the groves became the desired locations.

The first settler in Crawford County was Cornelius Dunham. He came from Vermont and in several stages moved west settling near the East Boyer River in 1849. He brought a large family and was joined by the Prentice, Reed, Butler, and Blake families. This community became known as Dunham's Grove, and when the railroad came, the town of Vail, Iowa, was established nearby.

In 1851, Jesse Mason settled at Mason's Grove (present day Deloit) on the north Boyer. Soon after, he was joined by the Skinner and Johnson families, and the following year Thomas Dobson came and set up a mill on the river which became the center of commercial activity in the county for a number of years.

A wagon train of ox-drawn covered wagons arrived and settled in the Coon Grove area south of where the two branches of the Boyer River join. Included were New Englanders, Scots, and Pennsylvania Deutsche. The Friend, Bassett, and Baer families were in this group. They had a very difficult first winter but became established the following summer.

Finally, the county was organized when there were enough people to provide a petition requesting it. Temporary officers were selected in April of 1855, and later that year, permanent officers were elected. Judge John R. Bassett of Coon Grove was the principal driving force of the county. The first county road was proposed to run from Dunham's Grove (Vail) to Mason's Grove (Deloit). By the end of 1856 the population of the county was 235. A preliminary survey of the county was begun by Surveyor Anderson and was completed by Morris McHenry.

Jesse Denison arrived in 1855 as an agent of the Providence Western Land Company, a Rhode Island company, which had purchased a large number of land grants issued to soldiers by the Federal government for services in the military. Issuing land grants had been a common form of payment since the founding of the country. Mr. Denison would see that the deeds acquired on the east coast from former soldiers, who had no intention to move west, were properly recorded at the Federal land office for this area which was in Kanesville (Council Bluffs). He would then do what he could to increase the value of the land and resell it at a profit. One of the early observations that Mr. Denison made was that the current talk about a railroad across Iowa proposed routes which would make the East Boyer valley a likely route for the railroad to Nebraska. Consequently, he acquired as much land along the route as he could. Realizing that Mason's Grove was too far off the route of the railroad to benefit from it, he proposed a new town on the confluence of the two branches of the Boyer River. It could take advantage of a new railroad and become a regional center of commerce, since it was nearly equidistant from Fort Dodge, Council Bluffs and Des Moines. The new town was to be named Denison. To get it off to a good start, he offered a block of city lots to the county for a court house square and offered to build a court house if Denison was named the county seat. The County Commissioners accepted this proposal. Until this time the county records had been kept in the homes of the county officials or at Fort Purdy.

John Purdy had been storing many of the county records at his "Fort" where they had been held from the time his place was used as a refuse in the Indian scare of 1856 until the new courthouse was ready. Jesse Denison recruited Henry C. Laub from Mason's Grove to build the court house. It was to be built from locally produced brick and was completed in 1859. Mr. Laub was an exceptional organizer and a major force in developing the new town of Denison. A mercantile empire, centered in Denison, that extended over six counties was the result of his efforts.

The hot topic of conversation at the time was politics. The new Republican Party had nominated a virtual neighbor, Abraham Lincoln from Illinois, for the presidency. All of the old arguments about slavery and freedom were dragged up and rehashed. New questions about whether the Federal Government should back westward expansion by backing the railroads were brought up.

Should the government put in high tariffs to protect our new industrial base or promote free trade to encourage our raw agriculture products? There were many things to talk about.

The economic issues carried long-term weight, but slavery was
the hot emotional issue at the time. Iowa had always been a free
state having led the nation when in 1839 the Iowa Supreme Court,
in the *Case of Ralph*, said that when a slave came to Iowa with the
consent of his master, he was not a "fugitive slave" and could not
be forced to return. As the debate heated, more direct action was
taken. The Underground Railroad which provided passage for fugitive slaves to Canada became very active in Iowa. One of the
major stops on these routes was just south of our area at Lewis,
Iowa, where the Hitchcock family was quite active. The militant
John Brown had several training camps in southern Iowa to train
his raiders in combat before they engaged in action in the Kansas
disputes. The actions were becoming more violent, and they were
coming closer.

Lincoln was elected President in 1860, and the South seceded
from the Union. It was a move not provided for in the Constitution, but it would take the Civil War to stop the South. The odds
were long against the South from the start. They did not have a
manufacturing base, so all their equipment would have to be imported, and they did not have a navy to keep their ports open.
Their agriculturally based economy was thinly populated. The
heavily populated cities were in the north so it was not surprising
the North won the war. What was surprising is that it took five
years to get the job done. The South had spirit and good generals
whereas it took Lincoln three years just to find the military leadership needed to accomplish his goals.

In Crawford County the effects of the War were slow in coming. Jesse Denison had been elected to the state legislature and
was instrumental in getting an allocation from Governor Kirkwood
of 40 Enfield rifles in 1861 for civil defense purposes in case any
activity arose here. Later in 1861 there was a call for volunteers for
the army. As a result the county officials organized a sign-up pro-

cedure and collected money for a bonus for the two men who did sign up. In 1863, President Lincoln made a call for additional volunteers. This time the county voted a bonus of $300.00 per person and a monthly subsidy to the family. Seven men signed up, but two were rejected after a physical examination. In 1865 another call came and Crawford County's quota came to six men. This time the men had to be selected, and four of the six paid someone else to take their place. War stories had been making it back to Crawford County.

While the war was going on, the railroads were not being forgotten. The national talk was about a transcontinental railroad which would tie the gold fields of California with the manufacturing plants in the East and everything in between. Iowa was on the direct route and the rails were already past the Mississippi River. The Mississippi and Missouri Railroad (Rock Island Line) was organized in Davenport in 1853, and Antoine Le Claire turned the first spade full of dirt for its construction. Later that year, General Grenville Dodge completed a survey to Council Bluffs. The first railroad bridge across the Mississippi River was opened in 1856, and in the same year, the government granted the railroads title to every other section in the townships on either side of a line of track they laid. If those sections had already been claimed, an available section was substituted. By 1859, the rails had reached Ottumwa, and by 1861 they had reached Cedar Falls.

Progress on the rails was slow and was interrupted by the war. In 1864, Congress appropriated $100,000,000 in addition to the land grants to stir up interest in the project, but there were no takers. Anyone interested thought it would cost even more than the $100,000,000 and it would take some time to be able to recoup the investment. A plan was then proposed in 1866 to allow the railroads to issue their own bonds which would be guaranteed by the Government. Thus, more money could be raised, and it would cost the government less. A company called the "Credit Mobilier" was organized to administer it which gave the railroad companies the incentive they needed. The rush to lay rails was on!

Four railroads were racing to become the first rail line across Iowa. The most likely to win was the Mississippi and Missouri (later named the Rock Island Line) since they already had a good start. Also in the running were the Burlington and Missouri (later named the Burlington Northern) and the Illinois Central. However, there were many setbacks in their progress. The money panic of 1857 closed down the credit market and the money supply. Then the Civil War took national priority for a time. When things did get going in earnest with government support, it was the least likely company that actually won. It began as the Iowa Central Air Line Railroad Co. But in 1856 the officers absconded with the funds, and the company went into bankruptcy. The workers had to be paid in groceries and dry goods, and, as a result, the first end of rail was known as the Calico Road. A new company, the Cedar Rapids, Iowa and Nebraska was set up to take over the construction, and it was to lay the tracks from near Clinton to Cedar Rapids before it ran out of money. Finally, the Cedar Rapids and Missouri Railroad was organized and John Insley Blair was put in charge. He drove the company, and drove it hard, to complete its objective. Under Mr. Blair's leadership, his company made it across the state a full two years ahead of any of the other lines. This line later became the Chicago and Northwestern Railroad, a major link in the first transcontinental railroad.

This was the railroad that came through Ames, Carroll and down the East Boyer River valley, heading for Denison. Jesse Denison's vision had been correct. It was powered by John Blair's force of will and manned by a work gang of immigrants far away from home and by war veterans from disrupted homes. They were a rowdy crew that worked hard and played harder. Denison became the base camp for the last hundred miles of construction. The men camped or lived in temporary flop houses down by the tracks, an area which became known as the Navy Yard District, probably because of its proximity to the river. With them came the saloons, gambling houses, and every other device known to separate the men from their wages. The workers and their followers totally overwhelmed the civil authorities. Here was a town of several hundred people who suddenly had a work crew and followers numbering in the thousands. Denison was the wildest, widest open town in the nation for a while. It took years for it to settle down—if it ever did entirely.

However, there were other kinds people coming into the county, too. Most of the newcomers were looking for farmland, and the countryside was soon developed. Much of the Big Bluestem Prairie Grass was being plowed under and another type of grass–corn– was being planted to replace it. On a warm summer night, one could "hear it grow" and during the day, one could see the tassels wave in the breeze.

The wind is blowing through the tall grasses causing waves of green that spread from the horizon to here and from here to as far as the eye can see. The rains keep the grass growing and with the rain comes the rumbling of thunder. However, there is a different rumbling in the distance–and another wave coming–small, but growing–and growing. It is a wave of people! A different kind of people from those who had occupied the land–a light-skinned people. They are continuing to come. There is no stopping them. These people will take over the whole country– and it will never be the same. Strange things were done to the land. It was plowed, it was fenced, buildings were built on it and these people inhabited them. When they were finished they started all over again– and it will never be the same again.

V. SETTLING IN

1870–1899

There is smoke on the horizon—over there. There has never been smoke on the horizon over there before. There must be someone new over there. Doesn't look like a bad place to build a home—over there. I wonder what kind of people they are. We have been getting a lot of different kinds of people here recently, and the ones who worked stayed and succeeded. The rest moved on. A lot of developments have been occurring around here creating a lot of improvements, but there is a ways to go. As long as we all work together, things will come together. Neighbors will have to work together to make neighborhoods. Communities will grow, and life will be better for everyone. If we keep at it, this place may amount to something yet!

The first settlers were from New England. They were Americans looking for new land—cheap land—of which there was plenty. Quite a stream of emigrants came but not huge numbers. Of these numbers who were moving into this area, many were Mormons. They found their promised land right here in Crawford County, leaving a strong imprint on the development of the county. Thomas Dodson became their first minister.

A second wave of English-speaking Americans came this way who were not interested in farming the land, however. Their interests lay in making their fortune by providing services and support to the settlers. They were the surveyors, the land agents, the lawyers, the bankers, the politicians, the county officials, the representatives, the educators, the physicians, the merchants—the ones who hoped to be the leaders of the community. English was the official language of the government, and those who could speak it fluently and understood the basic procedures had an inside track to becoming the prominent citizens of the era. Many came with that idea in mind.

The first commercial enterprises in the county were the mills built on the Boyer River. The Dobson mill at Mason's grove had an eight-foot drop at the head of its run. Most mills powered both a saw head to cut lumber and a burr to grind grain. The Rev. Jesse Denison became the prominent land agent as the representative of the Providence Western Land Company. Morris McHenry became the official surveyor, the first school teacher, the county treasurer, a land agent, a merchant, a banker, and a deed abstractor. He brought in his brother, William A. Mc Henry, who became the most prominent banker in the region and an importer of purebred livestock. Henry Laub became the predominant merchant. At its peak, his empire numbered 32 mercantile stores and numerous other businesses. John Bassett became the county Judge. J.S. Miricle was the first attorney. Sam Kennedy was the Sheriff. As the community grew, it was becoming structured.

From the time Cornelius Dunham came into a virgin prairie as the first settler, it took only a little over fifteen years for the railroad to come through Denison. Once the railroad arrived, the pace of settlement became even faster. The Chicago Northwestern Railroad Company, the Providence Western Land Company, and the American Emigrant Company all set up huge advertizing campaigns to bring people into the county. Ads were placed all along the east coast and in many northern European countries. As a result, the people came in waves often via New Orleans, St. Louis, and Davenport moving west along the railroad tracks.

Peoples arrived from numerous European countries including a group of immigrants from Bohemia, now the Czech Republic, who settled in Milford Township where they added their energetic behavior and colorful life style to the fabric of local society. They, like many groups to come, maintained their culture and customs for years. However, the only thing of real permanence that survived the years was the cemetery they established.

A large and active settlement of Swedish people called Swede Bend was located in Webster County on the Des Moines River near the present day town of Stratford. In 1867, they became so numerous they began to look for a location to start a new settlement. Consequently, they sent a delegation to investigate the Missouri River bottoms for a likely spot. The delegation did not like what they saw. The land was too swampy and subject to floods. On the way back to Swede Bend, they stopped in Denison. Jesse Denison learned of their purpose and approached them suggesting they look at some land he had available to the north of Deloit. They did look at it and liked what they saw.

As a result, a group of Swedes came and settled in Stockholm Township. They proved to be a magnet for many more of their fellow countrymen, and when there were sufficient numbers, they established their own Post Office, naming their location Kiron. It was the first Post Office in the county that was not on the Boyer River. The name Kiron was selected by Andrew Norelius but there is some disagreement as to where he derived his inspiration. Harold Dilts in *From Ackley to Zwingle, A Collection of the Origins of Iowa Place Names*, says he named it after Kirin, a major city in northern China near Manchuria. Arthur Allen in *Northwest Iowa, Its History and Traditions* says it was named after Kidron, a brook mentioned in the Old Testament of the Bible. Either place was a long distance from Sweden, but then, so was Kiron, Iowa. Some of the first settlers in this area were the Olsens, the Noreliuses, and the Engbergs.

The Swedes proved to be industrious people and good organizers. Through hard work and cooperation they broke up the prairie and developed substantial farms. Around their Post Office they built a town also calling it Kiron. Soon a solid array of support businesses were established there and several churches were built in the surrounding countryside.

Swede Bend was bypassed by the railroads, and the commercial traffic on the Des Moines River dried up. Swede Bend slowly deteriorated until today there is only a historical marker two miles west and two miles south of Stratford, Iowa, indicating where it had been. The Church where they worshiped was moved to a church camp on Twin Lakes, north of Rockwell City. Community services are held there each Sunday during the summer season.

By far the largest group of immigrants to come was the Germans, who settled in Goodrich township and spread up through Otter Creek Township and across Morgan Township and into other areas of the county. When the railroads and land companies began advertizing for settlers, they did not have to go far to find interested Germans. Scott and Clinton Counties in eastern Iowa had been filling up with Germans for the last twenty years. A revolution had occurred in Germany and throughout Europe in 1848, and the young republican radicals, who formed the first democratic parliament and proved to be the more educated and able leaders, had lost. Many of them became political refugees in America to escape punishment, following the trade routes from northern Germany to New Orleans and then up the Mississippi River. Many of the early revolutionaries liked the land and climate around Davenport, Iowa, where large numbers of them settled. They wrote many letters to friends back in Germany and many articles for German newspapers in which they encouraged many more Germans to immigrate. Many of them who came to Iowa were from the Schleswig-Holstein area in northern Germany.

Many of the German immigrants who came to Scott and Clinton Counties in the 1850's and 1860's were of modest means. Working and saving their money to buy their own land was their goal. But they were frustrated by the fact that the land values were growing just a little faster than their ability to save. When the advertisements offering western land appeared in the late 1860's and 1870's, there was a great deal of interest. Here was good land that was affordable to be bought, and the new railroad made it easily accessible. On this frontier of civilization, there was opportunity.

People bought their land and came out to develop it. The prairie did not surrender easily, however. It had to be plowed and left to lay fallow through the first winter. The following year it was cross plowed, and the beginning of a crop could be attempted. However, it was several years before it could be called a productive field. During the first year the best that could be hoped for was enough garden vegetables to survive the winter. Lack of time did not permit developing livestock herds, and, as a result, meat was at a premium. This was prairie land, so there were no trees and, as a result, no lumber. The first homes were likely to be dugouts in the side of a hill extended with thick sod walls. Such a home could be warm against the winter cold, but it would offer no protection from mice, insects, nor snakes, and spring rains caused problems. Most pioneer housewives demanded something better and soon! The sod house era in Crawford County history was rather brief and little remains of it.

As soon as possible grain, or labor, or whatever was available, was bartered at the mill in Mason's Grove for enough lumber to build some kind of house. This early home was usually replaced with a more substantial version when the settlers became more prosperous. Some of the early settlers in the area were C.F. Dahms, the Putizier Brothers, Claus Mundt, Fred Kastner, the Lehfeldt Brothers, Jurgen Grill, and J. Sievers.

In the 1880's and beyond there were large numbers of Germans and Danes who came over directly from the old Country. Not only were there more Germans in Crawford County than any other group, but also there were more Germans in Iowa than any other group. At least one out of every three people had a Germanic background.

Let us look a little closer at the Germans. The first German in America was Tyrker, foster father of Leif Ericson, and a member of his crew when he made his voyage to the new world in the year 1001. Tyrker discovered wild grapes near the settlement, thus giving Ericson the inspiration for the name of the new land—Vinland.

Germans were in nearly every settlement from Jamestown on through the development of the colonies. They were valued for their industry and expertise. At one time the colony of Pennsylvania held an election on which language, English or German, should be the official school language. German came in a very close second—losing by only one vote. But let's go back a bit farther and pick up a bit of German history.

There were Germans in Germany long before anyone bothered to record what they were doing there. The best way to trace them is through their language patterns. The Germanic Languages include all the languages from Scandinavia through most of northern and central Europe, and, in some aspects, as far as the Middle East. This vast area may give a clue as to the origin of the Germanic peoples and may also be clues to the early activities of the Germans in their myths and legends which have been handed down for generations. It is difficult, though, to determine how much is fact, and how much is fable.

The first recording of German activities occurred when they came into contact with the Romans. Tacitus was one of the first historians to write extensively about the Germans who were organized in groups or tribes and would live in one area until the crops started declining; then they moved to a new area to break new ground. It was known as the time of the "Wandering Nations." The trained Roman legions had little trouble handling individual tribes, but the number of tribes seemed to be endless. In 9 A.D., a German, who had been trained to fight in the legions, named Hermann, organized a number of tribes and defeated the Roman, Varus, in the Teutoberg Forest, north of Cologne. The Romans built the Limes, a wall along their northern border for protection. It was second in size only to the great wall of China. In times of peace, the Romans were very interested in trading with the Germans. They especially prized the grain used in "Schwarzbrot"– their dark bread–and smoked Westphalian hams.

A number of leaders arose among the German peoples who organized many, if not all of the people temporarily, but none of these leaders were able to establish a permanent operating central government. As a consequence, the German peoples were soon back to their many-splintered groups–a trend which continued for 1800 years. Charlemagne was the first conqueror to unite all the German people when he concluded a thirty-year fight with the northern Saxons under the leadership of Wittekind. Charlemagne was crowned Emperor of the Roman Empire by Pope Leo III in 800 A.D. which started what was known as the Holy Roman Empire–a concept that influenced policies for hundreds of years. Every aggressor wanted the blessing of the Church, so he could count on the support of the clergy in the conquered territory. On the other hand, the Church wanted to increase its power and wealth by influencing secular affairs. Feudalism resulted. A conqueror would award large tracts of land to his supporters, and in return the supporters would provide taxes and armies. The nobleman would then "lease" the land to the peasants in return for a share of the crop and military service, resulting in the establishment of isolated kingdoms which disrupted transportation and communications. Learning and culture declined, and the era became known as the Dark Ages.

The German people during this time settled into villages and cities and developed many skills and crafts for which they later became famous. Governmental influence was not necessary for a number of these accomplishments. The Teutonic Order of Knights took it upon itself to conquer the tribes of Prussia and controlled that area for centuries. The Hanseatic League of Merchants operated its own fleet of ships on a larger scale than many countries. The center of the Hanseatic League was in Lubeck on the Baltic Sea to the south of Schleswig-Holstein. The Low German, or Platt Deutsche, they spoke became the business language of the world from 12th through the 16th centuries. Low German is a regional language developed by the Angles and Saxons before they invaded and dominated the British Isles, and, as a result, it has elements of both the German and what was to become the English language. Low German went into decline when Martin Luther translated the Bible into High German, and that became the predominant language of the country, but Low German survived in northern Germany. (On December 1, 1998, Low German was officially recognized as a minority language by the European Council.)

The Renaissance marked a rebirth of learning, literature, and the arts in the 14th, 15th and 16th centuries. Many great advancements took place. However, the Church attempted to resist change and to entrench its secular advantages. The Reformation then resulted in the splintering of the Church into scores of Protestant sects. Many of the German princes endorsed the Protestant movement as a way to escape Church domination, and the result was the Thirty-Years War–1618-1648–that devastated central Europe. Thousands of people were killed either in battle or by starvation in the desolation caused by the roving armies. In the end, no side was able to gain a full victory.

A final consolidation of Germany was accomplished through the efforts of Otto von Bismark in the late 1800's. He consolidated the country under the Hohenzollerns, the Prussian ruling family, and guided Germany through a number of wars and negotiations and brought it to the position of a major world power. One of the many wars was against Denmark, and the two duchies–Schleswig and Holstein–became Prussian provinces through his efforts.

The Germans brought with them not only a sense of history but a whole way of life and a set of ideas when they came to America. The German imagination is wonderfully complex and colorful. From before recorded time, the German pantheon of Gods, including Thor, Woden, Frieda, and Tyr, is fascinating. There was the huge ash tree that reached from Earth to Heaven where one would "knock on wood" to alert the Gods to an incoming prayer. A celestial Valhalla existed where the spirits of fallen warriors would gather to celebrate past glories. The beautiful Valkyries would flutter over a battle ground and determine the fate of individuals. Many elements of German Lore have survived in our culture today. Santa Claus, the Yule Log, and the Christmas Tree have all become major parts of our heritage. The children's stories, the fairy tales, are the most enduring. The German fairy tales are the most wonderful and imaginative in the world. They involved mystical and magical qualities, magnificent castles and nobility, friendly and talkative animals, strange and weird happenings. In them is usually a moral or an eternal truth to help explain our contemporary world to a child. Some examples of these stories include Hansel and Gretel, the Pied Piper of Hamelin, Snow White and the Seven Dwarfs, Rumpelstiltskin, and Cinderella. The tales are so numerous that they have been collected and printed in volumes of stories–the Mother Goose Stories, Grimm's Fairy Tales, and the Stories of Hans Christian Anderson–to name a few. Without the German fairy tales, Disneyland and Saturday morning TV would be rather skimpy fare. In addition to the stories, there are rhymes and songs that have been passed from generation to generation–little songs about rabbits and hunters to wake up by, and rhymes about the sandman or about gremlins to go to sleep by. The variety of songs and dances and rituals is almost unending.

Symbols and taboos also abound, and superstition reigned. One performed certain things in certain events to ensure good luck, like waving your left hand and reciting a short rhyme when you unexpectedly come upon a white horse. Broken mirrors, black cats, and walking under ladders portended bad luck–such things vary widely from one part of Germany to another and are very numerous.

Folk medicine offers another area of interesting ideas. A large variety of cures and preventions to almost any human condition such as poultices of various concoctions have proven effective over the years. Magic spells and incantations had curative effects as well. A washcloth soaked in a special concoction and held over a wart for a certain period of time and then buried in the moonlight while reciting special phrases repeatedly would cause the wart to disappear. These special procedures could only be learned from a member of the opposite sex, at a prescribed rate over an extended period of time.

The settlers, when they arrived, came with a fully developed and colorful culture. They had many, many interesting ideas when they landed and thought up many more after they got here. Many of the old ideas were changed to fit the new conditions, but there were some ideas though that were not even attempted here. In Europe, the main agricultural building was the hausbarn. It was a large building with the family home on one end, and grain storage and livestock pens on the other end–all of it under one roof. It was a universal design used over a large area in the Old Country. Not one hausbarn was built in Crawford County, in Iowa, or in America. Manning, Iowa, is reconstructing one now that was disassembled in Germany and sent over here. It may be the only hausbarn in thousands of miles. It will be part of their German Immigrant Heritage Museum Complex.

If there was one topic of conversation in Crawford County that kept pace with the talk of railroad construction, it was the availability and price of land. In this area the availability of land was keyed to the repurchase of military service land grants. The primary players were the Providence Western Land Company and Silas Dow's operation in Dow City. Soon a number of additional operations, not all of them reputable, were begun. When Jurgen Grill came west to find farmland in the fall of 1873, he was shown a very handsome piece of land in Section 15 of Otter Creek Township. He agreed to buy it, made a payment on it and returned to Scott County. He spent the winter finishing up any business he had there, obtained the supplies he needed and prepared his family for a move to the frontier. The next spring he arrived to claim his land. There was someone else already working the land! The land agents had sold the good land a number of times and then switched the section numbers on the deeds. Jurgen discovered he had bought some rougher land in Section 14 of Otter Creek Township. Not knowing what else to do, he and his family stayed and developed it. Fortunately, he was working with his brother, Clause Grill, who stayed and worked in Scott County helping support the homestead here. Once the farm was functional, Clause came out to help work it and later the farm was split and Clause started his own operation. The land agents, by their fast dealing, did get a little better price out of some lesser land. The settlers, like Jurgen Grill, although disadvantaged at first, did stay and develop the land, and when he died, the estate Mr. Grill left included more than 400 acres of land at a time when 40 acres would support a family. There is little doubt who, in the long run, came out with the better end of the deal. As Arthur Allen in *Northwest Iowa, Its History and Traditions*, quoted William Familton, a land agent at that time, "*When I sold prairie lands to those German farmers at from $5.00 to $7.50 per acre, I used to drive home ashamed of myself for having played them for suckers. Now, they are rich, and I—well, I wish I could buy that land back at $7.50 per acre.*

A very different kind of land developer came on the scene in the mid 1870's. The Close Brothers arrived. They were a pair of energetic, cultured, and well-financed young men from England who had ties with the aristocracy and high financial circles of Europe. Denison society was taken by storm. The town had never seen the likes of the Close brothers before. They were self-assured, talented, and gregarious. William organized a Sunday School, and Frederic lead a local choir. All the young ladies in the area were swept off their feet. The business practices of the new arrivals were rather unusual, too. Well financed by their European backers, the brothers would buy up large tracks of land. Instead of just subdividing the land and reselling it, as the previous developers had done, the Close Brothers would hire a crew, fence the land, build a house and a barn and dig a well on the property. When they sold it, it was an operating farm, and, as a result, brought a much better price.

The Close Brothers operated largely in Soldier and Charter Oak Townships although they worked wherever they could find open land. Their operation worked so well that individual farmers would pattern their buildings and operation after that used by the brothers. When the open land in this area had been developed, the brothers moved to the Kingsley and Le Mars area. They eventu-

ally developed a large part of northwest Iowa where they founded
the prestigious and gentile Prairie Club, which was also known as
the British Club of Le Mars. They were definitely a major force in
Iowa history.

Agriculture in one form or another was involved in more than
95% of all business activity and was open to anyone. The technology was not overly difficult, but it did require a great deal of labor.
Those who did not pay attention to the technology or to the markets for their products did not do well in their efforts. Those who
were unwilling to put in the work required did not succeed at all.
Those who did, could make a living from their crops, and they did
build substantial wealth from accumulating land. Nevertheless,
problems did exist. Nature provided a number of plagues ranging
from inclement weather to insect infestations. One of the most
devastating occurrences was that of a prairie fire. Prairie fires were
a natural phenomena that rejuvenated the grass prairies, but when
the prairies were broken up into individual farms, the fires became
problems. Before settlements there were stories of prairie fires that
swept from the Missouri to the Mississippi Rivers. Even a small
fire could be devastating to a farmer and the year 1874 was a
particularly bad year for fires in our county. The whole neighborhood would turn out to help fight such a potential disaster. The
fires were dangerous, too. In 1879, Mrs. John Struck was caught
in a fire and received deep and painful burns over most of her
body.

Man-made problems also prevailed. The most serious financial problem that could arise was a money panic. Money supply,
being tied to the value of gold, could not expand to meet the
needs of an expanding economy, and when the economy turned
down, there was no money to be had. Such panics came about
every ten to fifteen years. At one time, in the 1870's, in such a
panic, a significant number of farmers in Crawford County went
broke, and thousands of acres of land went up for auction and
brought less than ten cents an acre. The farmers who could survive
such a crisis were able to do well in the long run.

On the political scene in Iowa, the Republican Party became the dominant force after the Civil War. There were two factions—one lead by Senator and Secretary of the Interior James Harlan and the other by General Grenville Dodge. The predominant issues were the total and unquestioned good of the railroads, and the need for more immigrants to provide the muscle to develop the state. A political scandal of major proportions was developing. The Republican politicians who set up the Credit Mobilier to finance railroad construction became the controlling body of the organization, and for every dollar that went to help build railroads, a dollar went into their pockets. The public was outraged. The Iowa politicians were very quiet about any contacts they may have had in the mess, but as more and more word of scandal was revealed, it became clear that President Grant's administration was corrupt from one end to the other. Almost every Republican politician and interest group had its fingers in the public coffers.

As the landscape began to fill with developed farming operations, a need for support services developed. The Germans in Otter Creek township either had to take a day's trip to Denison for supplies or to take a slightly shorter trip to the Swedish community of Kiron. To fill this need, Albrecht Boock set up a store on his farm in Section 31 of Otter Creek Township. It worked out so well he soon added more facilities including a large dance hall. When he applied for a Post Office, it was assigned the name of Morgan, Iowa, which became the center of the German community.

As the town grew, Mr. Boock brought in additional help. He set up Detlef Wieck as a blacksmith toward the south end of the property and brought in Paul Voss to help with the tavern and dance hall. A large number of events, from regular dances to insurance and other business meetings, were held there. In good weather, nine pin games which were taken quite seriously were set up in the pasture. As the community became more organized, they reestablished the old German tradition of the Kinderfest. In late spring, after the crops had been planted, everyone gathered for a day-long festival. Most of the daytime activities were directed toward children's activities which consisted of a crock-mashing contest by blindfolded participants, a sharpshooter's contest with rotating windmill blades as a target, and many other special contests. In the afternoon, there was a dance for the children and in the evening there was a dinner followed by an adult dance. The children were laid down to sleep in the family wagons. The adult dance would sometimes last until nearly dawn. Many times the music was punctuated with fisticuffs. These were very spirited times.

During the rest of the year the farmers would come to Morgan on a Saturday or on a rainy day to pick up supplies. Farmers would come on a team and wagon while the younger folks would ride horseback. Sometimes people would walk in during the evening– sometimes from a number of miles around. The finest of home-cooked meals could be had for 25 cents and the evening gatherings were a source of the news of the day, and occasionally even a piece of gossip. The social events of the area centered on this developing community, and it took on the appearance of a thriving town as more businesses and services were offered. A second center was attempted some twelve miles to the west by the name of Como, but it did not have the cohesive appeal of Morgan, and it faded away. Everyone was aware that he was doing something new here. He was breaking new ground; he had new neighbors; and he had new problems. It was a new country! Everyone had an optimistic view of what could be accomplished, and most people were willing to work together to get the job done.

Many of the skills that the settlers had learned elsewhere had to be modified to fit their current needs. They learned the proper rate of seeding oats was to have twelve grains of seed in the area of a horse's hoof. The proper time to plant corn was when the leaf of an oak tree was the size of a Squirrel's ear. They learned that a hundred days after a heavy fog it would rain. When they were working in the field and a cloud bank came over indicating a new weather front, they knew they had until it got to about fifteen degrees from the far horizon before it would start to rain. They knew if they left a plow in the ground at night, it would not scour in the morning. They learned what would work here.

One of the necessities of every community proved to be the setting up of a cemetery. The need for a cemetery in the German community arose in 1872 with the death of Nick Thompson. Two acres of virgin prairie in Section 25 of Morgan Township was unofficially designated as a cemetery, and on Easter Sunday, April 14, 1872, Nick Thompson was buried in a grave dug by Henry Hollmann and Carsten Holdorf. The wooden marker has long since disappeared. On June 26, 1878, all of Section 25 was sold to Hans and Catherine Nissen. When the cemetery situation was explained, the Nissens agreed to sell the land to the newly formed Morgan Cemetery Association. In a show of respect, the new cemetery was named the Nissen Cemetery. In the new official cemetery the first lot was sold to Johan Bendixen. The first person buried under the new association rules was Herman Mundt.

Public transportation in the early days was largely provided by the stagecoach, the main stage routes being in an east-west direction. One major route ran from Fort Dodge to Sioux City with the Moorehead House near Ida Grove as a major stop where a coach from either direction would stop each day. Denison was a hub for traffic, one line coming in from Fort Dodge, another form Lyons, Iowa, near Clinton by way of Des Moines, and a third going to Council Bluffs. In later years a route was directed to Onawa.

Another major route was provided by the Iowa legislature in 1856, and it was established in the following years. It extended from Keokuk through Des Moines to Sioux City. It came through Adel, Panora, Roselle, crossed Crawford County near Arcadia and Boyer, and crossed southern Ida County to a point near Battle Creek. Here it joined the road from Fort Dodge and Ida Grove. The combined road went down the Maple River Valley for a short distance then turned west and near Smithland turned north and followed the edge of the Loess Hills to Sioux City. In the pre-railroad days this became a heavily-traveled stagecoach and freight route. Very little remains to mark this trail. Bob Rickers of Vail,

Iowa, has been able to locate a number of scars left by this trail including one where the route could be traced across a field by a line where the soybeans matured slightly sooner than the rest of the field.

The stagecoach routes were displaced when the railroads arrived, which was in 1867 in Denison, and 1877 in Ida Grove. A number of short runs did continue to operate on north-south routes, however. In 1874, A.O. West, the proprietor of the Ida House in Ida Grove, started a stage route from Ida Grove to Denison. It was scheduled to make three runs a week, and although its route is uncertain, it probably would have favored the "ridge road" on the high ground. The same year, E.H. "Grandpa" Barnes set up a freight line along the same path. How long the stage lines were used is uncertain. There is some evidence that the stagecoach to Holstein was operating into the middle of the 1880's, which is long after the arrival of the railroads.

A stagecoach waystation appears to have been established on the east edge of Section 24 of Morgan Township. It would have been approximately half way between Ida Grove and Denison. It would have provided a rest for the passengers as a fresh team of horses was hitched to the coach. There was a barn with extra horse stalls and a place for a farrier to work as well as a house on the property. The station grounds were split off into a three-acre estate when Claus Mundt sold the larger farm of which it was a part in 1882. Heinrich Sucksdorf bought the acreage in 1894 and attached it to his farm across the road in Section 19 of Otter Creek Township.

Dr. Giles Moorehead wrote of his memories of the stagecoach days in *Historical Collections of Ida County* as follows:

> "*The coaches were luxuriant, having glass doors, fine upholstering and long elliptical springs that made riding in them very comfortable. They carried six passengers inside and as many as could crowd onto the top. The drivers were expert horsemen and took great pride in their beautiful teams. . . . When a coach*

approached to within half a mile the driver blew a horn and
hearing this the hostler and stable man hurried to the dismount-
ing platform. The coach rolled in at an easy trot, the brakes
creaked, the driver threw his lines to the hostler, the stable man
attended the lead team, the express messenger who sat beside the
driver opened the door and assisted passengers out. He then
delivered the mail and all went for dinner. When they came out
a 'fresh four' had been hitched to the coach, the hostler with lines
in hand stood at attention, passengers were loaded in, the driver
took his seat, the lines were handed him by the hostler and with
a word to the horses they were off at a brisk trot."

One memorable weather event that occurred during this time happened on Easter Sunday in 1878. Those who witnessed the events said shortly after the noon meal the air became very calm and heavy. There was a high, overcast sky and the light took on a yellowish hue. A deep and steady rumbling was heard whereupon one farmer ran to a hill behind his house and saw a massive tornado coming at some distance. He ran back to the house and to get a yardstick which he held steady on the top of a fence post, then he sighted along it to the tornado. His theory was that if the tornado stayed on the track of the yardstick, it was coming straight for him, and they would have to take shelter immediately. Fortunately, the tornado veered off the yardstick track indicating the tornado would miss them. The tornado started in Hanover Township and just missed Morgan and Kiron and went as far as Pocahontas before it dispersed. At the John Zage farm four miles south of Schleswig, the house and all the buildings were destroyed. The wind ripped a board off of a granary and impaled seven-year-old Fred Zage killing him. Most of the buildings were also destroyed at the John Marquardt farm. Here the tornado picked up a white pony and lifted it high in the sky, and then dropped it to its death. Mrs. Marquardt was also caught by the wind but escaped without injury. Several miles farther east, the storm came close enough to a farm place to twist a corn crib but spared the rest of the buildings. It is still considered on of the worst tornados on record in Iowa.

One of the more important and most lasting organizations in the area was founded in 1879–the German Mutual Insurance Company. The full name was actually the Mutual Fire, Lightning, Tornado and Wind Storm Insurance Association of German Farmers of Crawford and Ida Counties–but that was a mouthful. The risks involved in farming on the prairie were enormous, and any way to reduce them was welcomed with enthusiasm. The first officers of this organization were C.J. Holling, President; Herm Heilckesen, Secretary; Hans Brodersen, Assistant; and Carl Hensen, Treasurer. Each officer maintained the records that pertained to that office, and once a year they had a membership meeting, which in the early years, was held in Morgan, since they had no office. It was an organization that all of the members thought was essential to the operation of their farms and to the survival of their community.

Iowa politics was dominated by a single force in these years—Senator William Boyd Allison. He built an organization so tight no one could get into Iowa politics unless he went through the "Allison Machine," or, as it was called, the "Iowa Regency." From this tight organization, he was able to pull many Iowans to positions of prominence on the national level. He was able to use his organization to elect Senators Jonathan Dolliver and William Kenyon, Speaker of the House David Henderson from Dubuque, as well as numerous congressmen, that he was able to get appointed to many influential committees. He was able to influence many presidential appointments such as that of Tama Jim Wilson to be Secretary of Agriculture, George Evans Roberts as director of the Mint, and Maurice O'Connor as Solicitor for the Treasury.

Anyone interested in a political career had only one opportunity in Iowa and that was through the Allison Regency. A case in point is that of a small town banker from Denison, Iowa–Leslie M. Shaw. He began by making speeches against William Jennings Bryan. Bryan, a Nebraska Democrat, was promoting the use of

Silver coinage to increase the money supply to help out the farmers and small businessmen in times of the money panics. Shaw gave numerous speeches promoting the big business line of keeping money tightly tied to gold. His efforts and loyalty did not go unnoticed, for he was offered the nomination for the Governorship of the State. With the party backing, he easily won. While in office, he actively supported and promoted the party line, and, as a reward, Senator Allison recommended him for the position as Secretary of the Treasury. President Theodore Roosevelt accepted the recommendation and made the appointment. Governor Shaw's former law partner, James Perry Conner, was appointed to a judgeship, and when Jonathan P. Dolliver was elevated from Congressman to Senator, Conner was picked to fill his Congressional seat. When Secretary Shaw retired and proposed to have a marble and granite courthouse built in Denison as a monument to his career, he was able to bring in President Teddy Roosevelt to speak on his behalf to a tight money constituency. He got his courthouse. If you were loyal to the Regency, there were few limits to what you could accomplish.

Senator Allison did not promote a strong ideology, however. He was interested in maintaining his position in office and the power it brought him in a variety of areas. To increase the effect of his actions, he became increasingly reluctant to state a position in advance of taking action. It became a game between the press and the Senator. The reporters tried every trick to get the Senator to reveal his sentiments, and he succeeded in remaining non-committal. The positions he took were sure to be politically, socially, and economically correct for his day. He promoted the interests of power and wealth. He favored the railroads, the new Republican Party in Iowa, the Civil War, the Radical Reconstruction of the South, and the concentration of wealth in the "Robber Barons" of the major industrial groups. They were positions that served him well.

At the Republican Presidential Convention of 1888, the leading contenders were James G. Blaine and William Boyd Allison of

Iowa. After a number of ballots, it became clear that Blaine could not receive the necessary votes. He withdrew and threw his support to Benjamin Harrison, but Allison put together a coalition that could lead to victory. At the last minute, Senator Depew of New York broke up the coalition, because Republican Governor Larribee of Iowa had put through the first truly effective Railroad reform law in the nation. Senator Allison, the acknowledged leader of the Republican party in Iowa, was tainted in that his railroad support was questioned. After numerous more ballots were taken, Harrison was able to get the nomination by the narrowest of margins. It was said by political commentators of the time, never had anyone come so close to becoming President of the United States and not make it.

By the turn of the century, Senator Allison had consolidated his power to the extent he was known not only as "Mr. Iowa" but also as "Mr. Republican, U.S.A." There were four U.S. Senators who could block any piece of legislation in Congress or could see that it was approved. They were Senator Nelson Aldrich of Rhode Island, Senator Orville Platt of Connecticut, Senator John Coit Spooner of Wisconsin and Senator William Boyd Allison of Iowa. Senator Allison's personal power and the many Iowans he had projected into Federal office on all levels meant that if anyone wanted to achieve anything on the national level, they would have to see the people from Iowa first. Senator Allison held this power until his death in 1908. He died as he began campaigning for his sixth term in the Senate. For 47 years Congress had felt his influence. The politicians had an easy time in these years. Most people did not have the time nor the inclination to get involved, and the winning of the Civil War put the new Republican Party in a dominant position. It was mainly those who wanted to take advantage of the political process who became involved.

The same could be said of the religious community in the early years. Jesse Denison was a Presbyterian minister; Henry Laub was an active Methodist; and the Close Brothers were heavily involved in the Episcopal Church. However, the homesteaders were not nearly so concerned with the organized church. They led a much more isolated life where the wonders of God were around them all day. They could pause any time to spend a few minutes appreciating the splendor and beauty of God's work, but they also spent many hours struggling to build a farm that was at the mercy of nature. The farmer had to work largely on his own. When he needed help or wanted to socialize, he had to depend on the scattering of neighbors around him. He did not have the privilege of seeking out kindred spirits. He certainly did not want to promote any divisive elements that would limit his access to these essential contacts.

The early settler looked at organized religion as such a divisive force. Splitting hairs over interpretations of religious doctrine seemed counter productive. The circuit riding ministers had a tough sell and many had a hard time making any progress. Just the same, there were some success stories. The Reverend Mr. Black of the Methodist Church succeeded well enough that by 1884 there was a Church conference in Deloit that attracted 1500 people. (The Reverend Mr. Black was immortalized in a song of the same name by Billy Edd Wheeler and Jed Peters which was popularized by the Kingston Trio with renditions by Faron Young, Johnny Cash, and others. He was also mentioned in the song "Mule Train" by Frankie Laine.) The Deloit Mormons were able to invite the brother of Joseph Smith, the founder of the religion, to speak to their congregation.

Although they met with resistence, the circuit riders were persistent. They did, however, have one inside track in that they could provide services and validation in times of transition. They could provide established and accepted processes for funerals, weddings, baptisms and comfort in times of crisis and stress. Gradually churches were established, and they did disrupt the social patterns of the pioneer communities. Fortunately, by the time this disruption occurred, the countryside was well enough developed and populated that the support networks in the neighborhoods, while changing, were still viable.

An Insurance meeting at the town of Morgan in the early 1880's. The scene is near the Dance Hall with the other buildings hidden by the trees. Albrecht Boock, in a vest but no top coat, is standing behind the table. Paul Voss is the bartender in the white shirt by the keg.

The town of Hohenzollern in the late 1890's. The man in a vest and no top coat here is Jurgen Schroeder.

Churches were established both in the countryside and in the new towns that were developing. The first church in the German area was the Hanover Township Lutheran Church which was established in 1873, and another was organized in Grant Township in 1880. Many ceremonies were conducted in the homes, however. Well into the twentieth century most funerals, weddings, and baptisms were held in the home rather than in the Church. It was well into the 1930's and 1940's before more contemporary church-centered service patterns were established.

Not everything, however, was going smoothly in the German community. Horses were becoming an increasingly valuable asset, and they began to disappear with some regularity. The dimensions of the problem grew to the extent that an organized effort had to be made to stop the thievery. One farmer took the train to Nebraska to visit some relatives. While there, a neighbor showed a new team he just purchased. The Iowa farmer was amazed because he had an identical team back home. When he got home, he found that not only had his horses been stolen, but they had almost beaten him to Nebraska! In another incident, young Herman Reimers heard a noise outside one night and went to his bedroom window just as his father, John Reimers, burst out the front door of the house with a rifle in his hands. At the same moment his pony burst out of the barn with a rider on his back and headed down the pasture. His father emptied his rifle at the fleeing horse and rider, but the moonlight did not give enough light for a clear target. Temper and tensions grew as the problem continued. One incident that demonstrated this occurred in the town of Morgan. A number of farmers were discussing the problem over a few of beers, and the mood became ugly. The men decided that one happy-go-lucky young farm hand by the name of Brink was a likely suspect. Unfortunately, the young man picked that time to show up. They cornered him and demanded he confess and reveal the rest of the culprits. As it turned out, he was innocent, but before cooler heads could prevail, they had him up on the back of a wagon with a rope around his neck. One farmer was prodding him toward the end gate with a pitchfork and saying, "Heist him up! Heist him up, boys. If he won't talk, heist him up!" Fortunately, he was rescued in time.

It was shrewd old Fredericka Kastner who came up with an idea. The Kastners were some of the very first settlers in the area. Her idea was to hire one of the cowboys who drifted through now and then and have him infiltrate the gang and find out who was involved. Since no one had a better idea, the farmers in the neighborhood agreed to pool some money and see if they could find someone to tackle the job. After some time, they did find a man who would give it a try. They gave him the cover of being a hired hand for the Kastners. If he found out anything, he would pass it on to the Kastners, and they would get word to the authorities.

After some time in hanging around the dives of the county and letting it be known that he would do most anything for money, our man began making acquaintances with kindred spirits. In a short time, he began to uncover who was involved in the thefts, but it was much more difficult to discover who the ringleaders were. It actually took months but finally the whole story unfolded.

There were two ringleaders. One was a farmer from Morgan Township and one was from Goodrich Township. The thieves were a group of toughs from Denison who would not come into farm country until the man from Morgan Township had set up a theft. Then they would take the horses to the farm in Goodrich Township and remain there until it was safe to move them. In due time, they would take the horses east through Mason's Grove and down to the railroad near Dunham's Grove and ship them by rail to wherever the horse market was "hot" at the time, often in Chicago.

The toughs were convicted, but there was not enough evidence to convict the ringleaders, but community pressure drove the farmer in Morgan Township back to eastern Iowa. The man in Goodrich did not move out and denied his involvement until his dying day.

There are a few interesting sidelines to this story. The man in

Goodrich Township was also the man with the pitchfork in the incident at the town of Morgan. Years later, a newspaper account of one of the first burials at the Morgan Cemetery, said that one of the men who had been identified as a ringleader was a pallbearer, but the name of the deceased was not known. This led some to speculate that maybe old John Reimers had been a better shot than he thought.

The worst blizzard in the German Settlement was the Black Blizzard on Friday, January 12, 1888. It was a huge storm that covered the Dakotas, Nebraska, Kansas, and western Iowa. The weather before the storm was unusually mild and the day was overcast and very quiet. About 4:30 in the afternoon the wind rose and the storm struck with unexpected violence. Winds up to sixty miles an hour and heavy dense snow moved in quickly. The temperature dropped rapidly, and it became very dark from the heavy snow and the wind which whipped dust in the air. The storm lasted all night. In the morning the sun came out, and it was clear, but it was bitterly cold and stayed that way for the rest of the month. The snow drifts were fifteen to twenty feet high across the landscape.

On that day, Mr. and Mrs. Jurgen Jepsen and their family were helping his brother, John Jepsen, with some butchering. As the storm began, the Jurgen Jepsens decided to leave for home despite an invitation to stay the night. The two farms were not far apart. Jurgen Jepsen lived at 2274 Ave. H and John Jepsen lived at 1650 Hwy 59–both farms were in the same section. When the full brunt of the storm hit, the Jurgen Jepsens were crossing a field toward home. Unable to see in the howling dark storm, they lost their direction, and to add to their distress the double-tree on the wagon broke, and the frightened horses ran away. Mr. Jepsen overturned the wagon box and put Mrs. Jepsen and his three sons under it for shelter. He then went after the horses. When he did not return, Mrs. Jepsen went out to find him. She became disoriented in the storm and wandered until she collapsed and died in the cold. When her frozen body was discovered, she was only fifty feet from the wagon box. Jurgen Jepsen spent the night walking the fields. The next morning he was found near a neighbor's farm. He survived but never fully recovered from the ordeal. The Jepsen children all survived. The youngest, Ted, only a year old, had a frozen hand which somewhat crippled him, but he later became a prominent carpenter in the area despite his handicap.

By 1890, not only had all the land been settled but also a number of the settlers were becoming prosperous–they had worked hard for that prosperity. However, not all of them had started from scratch. Some of the immigrants had financial backing and had brought investment capital with them. Others had extended families in this country that were helping to support them until they could get started. Others were very talented in the skill of making money and advancing their net worth. The settlers were a diverse group, who had a wide variety of skills which they used to great accomplishment. Many of them were doing well, but there were also a number of them who were marginal at best. A social structure was becoming evident, and some farmers were clearly doing better than others. However, they all met and socialized at one common site: the town of Morgan.

Some growing dissatisfaction with this arrangement was becoming apparent. Some of the more successful families thought they should have a better place to meet. There was a strong competitive bent in German communities. Most of them originated in northern Germany, the part of the country that had a long tradition of being aggressive and competitive, much to the contrast of the southern part of Germany which was more laid back and easy going. It was the successful northern German immigrants who wanted to be a little more conspicuous in presenting their status.

The man to provide them with the opportunity to do so was Jurgen Schroeder. Mr. Schroeder decided to start a competing center by building a new commercial operation on his farm just four miles from Morgan. He began with a small grocery store next to his house to test the market. It succeeded so well that he built a larger one and added a saloon. Soon additional services and a dance hall were added. To add to its more exclusive nature, the new town was named after the royal family of Germany–Hohenzollern. The name was suggested by Doctor Richard Fuester who operated a medical practice from his farm several miles north of the new town.

Hohenzollern was located approximately at 2075 D Ave. The Schroeder's house and stores were in a line diagonal to the road all facing east with a wind break planted behind them. There were two streets—one past the store fronts and leading to a large barn that served as a livery stable, and one that ran from a blacksmith shop and dance hall, which had been built farther to the east, to a produce station which had been located near a stream to the southwest. The two streets crossed each other

In these days before refrigeration it was difficult to keep food from spoiling. Two approaches to remedy this problem were used in Hohenzollern—one was to let creek water trickle around the containers as was done with the cream at the produce station, and the other was to dig a dry well and lower the products into it. Such a dry well was located high on the hill behind the buildings. Since the well was closer to the saloon, it was the place where the beer was kept. The problem with the well was that it was difficult to get the product in and out of the well. When time was of the essence, one of the techniques used was to lower a small boy into the well and have him attach the desired container to a rope, and both he and the beer would be hoisted out of the recesses. Chris Gierstorf often told of his times of service at the end of the rope.

The town of Morgan maintained its businesses at this time, too. Unfortunately, its growth was somewhat curtailed by the new competition. At its peak Morgan had a General Store, a large dance hall and saloon, a blacksmith shop and a number of smaller activities and buildings. Most of the businesses were in the low ground around the original site of the Albrecht Boock farm, and there were also a half a dozen houses on the hillside to the south. The basement depressions of these houses was evident well into the 1950's and 1960's. The town was located at approximately 2285 F Ave. about a mile east of the Morgan Cemetery. The community was also referred to by the nickname the "Ten-Mile House" since it was just ten miles from the county seat, Denison. Many of the farmers were loyal in their support of the older community, but many others split their business between the two towns.

Not all of the commercial and social activity was centered in the towns, however. Both towns sent out "peddler wagons" on sales routes to the various farms as well as "pickup routes" to collect produce. A number of service people, such as tinkers and knife sharpeners, harness repair, rope splicers, etc., plied their businesses from door to door, Jacob Stuber, being one of the best known for his talents in these areas. There were a variety of businesses that became established in the countryside, too. The Bliesman Store offered merchandise to an area about six miles north of Morgan; Peter Langholz had a blacksmith shop five miles to the northeast; Pete Suhr was a well-digger; and the Bielenberg Hall in Section 27 of Grant Township provided an alternative social setting. House parties and barn dances throughout the community offered a lively social life.

For a barn dance, the hayloft of a barn was cleaned out to provide a dance floor. Seating was supplied by attaching wooden planks to the walls. Often special stairs were installed for the occasion–sometimes borrowed from the cellar in the house–since workday access to a hayloft was usually a ladder which would have been awkward for a social occasion. Hay chaff was used to keep the floor slick for dancing which was performed to the music of a band playing from a platform supported by some remaining hay. A hearty lunch would be prepared in the house, and an ample supply of beer was usually on hand. As the evening progressed, the music was complimented by many rousing choruses of old German folk songs, performed with gusto.

The distances to the activities were not too great. As it was described by Lillian Jakso and Emma Struck, *"girls walked to Hohenzollern, single boys rode horseback and families had their surreys. After the dance boys 'walked' their best girl home in the moonlight, sauntering over the soft, dusty country road. Their horses trailed on behind. No one minded the dry dust. It was the mud that created a real problem."*

The schools were also centers of entertainment and business meetings. As was designated by the original survey of the county, an acre in every other section was reserved for use by a local school. The schools were constructed, and many gatherings held there were centered around activities in which the students were involved such as holiday presentations which were for their families. The schools were also used for other civic activities such as voting centers and meeting halls for special occasions. The arrangement of a school house two miles in every direction also made them handy as landmarks. One could always keep track of the distances he traveled by the schools he passed. They were handy references when giving directions. When schools were closed for the summer, school yards were used as parks for picnics.

Problems of another sort were surfacing during this time. The immigrants who first come to this country grew up in a tight, closed society in which rules of conduct were well thought out and enforced. The next generation that was growing up on our frontier did not have the pressure from society to conform. They did not see the need for all the rules of the old country, and the diversity of the new society made it difficult to decide which rules were important. This diversity was apparent as when young Louie Grill went to school six miles northeast of Morgan. When he rose in the morning, he spoke German in the household; when he arrived at the classroom he had to speak English; when he went to to the playground, he had to learn Swedish since many of his playmates came from the Swedish community. When he and his brothers would go to a social event, such as a dance, it would seldom end without a fight. It was not uncommon for someone to claim to be the toughest man in a bar and to challenge anyone to disprove it. Challenges seldom went unaccepted. It was a rough and tumble time when even the country, itself, was trying to discover its identity as a world power. New values had to be worked out, and it took a lot of trial and error to find them. It was the reestablishment of order by the authorities that finally settled the country down which made it a hard time in which to grow up, but it was also an interesting time.

The main topic of conversation still was usually the railroads that were the instruments of change of almost every feature of life in the United States. Something new and different was always being done by them. The Milwaukee and Rock Island built tracks through Manning and Manila crossing the Northwestern tracks just on the east side of Dow City and on up to Sioux City. The crossing resulted in the town of Arion being established despite resistance by Dow City. There was also talk of rails being laid north of Denison up the Boyer River Valley. At one time or another survey crews had checked out almost every farm in the country, but nothing resulted from their efforts.

Occasionally, though, other topics would come up for discussion. When a peddler was found murdered half way to Denison one day, it caught a lot of attention for a while. They thought his name was Jackson. He had been stabbed, although some thought an ax had been used to kill him. Many stories went around, and a lot of apprehension was caused, but when no farther incidents occurred, nerves began to settle down even though the authorities made no progress in solving the case. Some people thought it had happened as part of a robbery attempt; others thought a dispute with one of the settlers had gotten out of hand. It was a crime that was never solved.

Railroad talk really heated up in the late 1890 when it became clear there would be a real contest between the Chicago Northwestern and the Illinois Central as to which line would be able to lay tracks up the North Boyer Valley. As it turned, out both lines constructed tracks that lay parallel to the river. The Chicago Northwestern went through Deloit and Boyer. The Illinois Central founded the towns of Ells and Brogan.

A new company was formed proposing a railroad to be called the Boyer Valley Line. It proposed to construct a rail line from Boyer to Mondamin and across the Missouri River to Nebraska. The final survey crews were out in 1898 and construction was underway in 1899. The route stayed on the ridge lines, and, as a result, there were many fewer streams to cross and bridges to build. Difficulty in finding water for the steam engines was encountered, but it was much more economical to lay the tracks by staying on the ridge. The ridge lines were far from being straight, and consequently the tracks curved around in all directions. The line picked up the nickname the "Punkin Vine Line," and in some circles it was called the "High Line."

The work on the tracks was very labor intensive. The grades for the tracks were made with mule-drawn slip scrapers with either one or two men providing the leverage to get the blade of the scoop into the ground and to dump it when it arrived at the proper location. It was tough going! Two miles a day could be made if they really pushed it, and the foremen were pushing. If an animal should die on the job, it was unhitched, buried in the grade, and the work kept right on. The only thing that slowed construction was bad weather. Even the railroad bosses could not control the weather.

A siding every eight or nine miles was built to allow freight to be picked up or dropped off. When the rails arrived at Kiron, a siding was not put down until the workers were over a mile beyond the town. The townspeople were not happy about it, but there was nothing they could do; they had move to the new site if they wanted to take advantage of access to the railroad. Some buildings they moved to the new site, but most of the businesses were built up new. The new site was also named Kiron and "Old Kiron" faded and disappeared.

When the rails arrived in the German settlements, everyone was glad to see them come, but they did not go through either the towns of Morgan or Hohenzollern. It took a course between them, missing them both. A siding was laid down about a mile and half east of Hohenzollern and about two and a half miles north of Morgan which spelled the end for both towns.

The siding was located on the Heinrich Sucksdorf's farm. The rail crews camped at the Jacob Jensen and Ed and Wilhelm Reimer's farms, camping out in tents except in inclement weather when they moved into farm buildings. They were a rough, hard–working bunch. Usually they were too tired from the work to cause much trouble, although there was one story that one crew member had been stabbed with a knife while working here. It is not known if he survived, or, for that matter, if he was severely injured. At the next siding down the tracks, a new town, Ricketts, was started.

The coming of the railroad changed the whole countryside into a settled and productive agricultural community. Tremendous changes were yet to be made, but things were well on their way. There is still smoke on the horizon, but it was a new kind of smoke. It was the black coal smoke puffing out of a steam engine as it came down the railroad track.

There is smoke on the horizon–over there. There has never been smoke on the horizon over there before. There must be someone new over there. Doesn't look like a bad place build a home–over there. I wonder what kind of people they are. We have been getting a lot of different kinds of people here recently, and the ones who worked stayed and succeeded. The rest moved on. A lot of developments have been occurring around here creating a lot of improvements, but there is a ways to go. As long as we all work together, things will come together. Neighbors will have to work together to make neighborhoods. Communities will grow, and life will be better for everyone. If we keep at it, this place may amount to something yet!

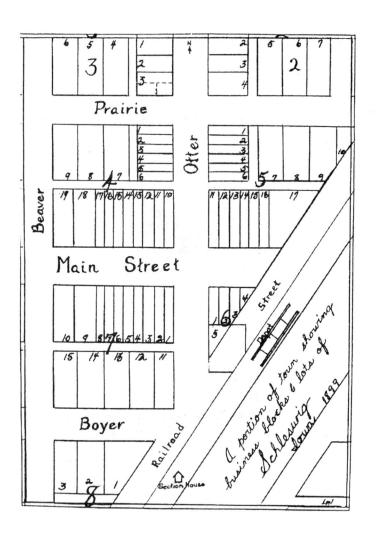

A portion of town showing business blocks & lots of Schleswig, Iowa 1899

VI. THE NEW TOWN

1899-1914

A new century is starting. There is promise in the air. New ideas, fresh approaches, and interesting inventions are coming faster and faster. No one would have thought it would have turned out this way. Many of the old things will be left behind. Some things that were so well established slipped away while other things that did not seem so important grew large. It might be good to see what is coming, but that is not so important. There are so many interesting things that are happening right now. Who would have thought things would have developed in such strange ways and still worked out? The trick is to keep the good things coming.

Heinrich Suckstorf's farm became the center of attention. Once the railroad, which became part of the Chicago Northwestern system, decided where to locate the siding, the Western Lot Company bought the farm for which they gave Heinrich and Catherine Suckstorf seventy dollars an acre in March of 1899. It was a very good price for the day. Ironically the railroad had selected a site for its siding just across the road from the old stagecoach station—which the Suckstorfs retained for a home. The farm was subdivided, and a plan for a new town was laid out. A number of suggestions about what to call the new town were offered. Some suggested it be named after Heinrich, but he said no. He would rather have it named after the province in Germany from where many of the settlers had come—Schleswig-Holstein. The Holstein part of the name was already in use by a community twenty-five miles to the north, leaving the Schleswig part of the name. That was agreeable to the vast majority of those concerned. Schleswig, Iowa, came into being.

The railroad siding was located in Section 19 of Otter Creek Township. The railroad tracks were laid at about a 55'-degree angle across the corner of the section and the town plat that was developed at the time covered the land located only west of the tracks. A depot was to be located halfway along the siding, and Main Street (now Cedar Street) was laid out running west from the depot over a low rise. A block west was a cross street, Otter Street (Second Street). The land along these streets was divided into commercial lots. A block on either side was set up for residential lots, and, in May an auction was held to sell the lots. The commercial lots sold for as high as $600.00 and the residential lots sold for as much as $90.00 apiece. A break was taken at noon for a picnic dinner alongside the new tracks. It was quite a sight—the railroad men in suits, ties, and top hats; the farmers were in overalls, and their wives in full skirts and bonnets and the businessmen keeping a close eye on everything that was going on—and on each other. Work horses and wagons and surreys with fancy high-stepping teams all lined the picnic area by the siding. The construction area had been laid out across the fields with not a tree in sight except a few that were starting at the former Suckstorf farm site. Lines of stakes and strings ran here and there, and it took a bit of imagination to see what was meant to be here. Imagination was not in short supply, however, and the whole scene was spirited and happy.

The big question of the day was whether the commercial district of the new town would be along Main Street or along Otter Street. There would be easier access to the depot on the east-west running Main Street, but there were more commercial lots on the north-south running Otter Street. A great deal of interest arose about where the two main players in this question would locate. Jurgen Schroeder, the organizer of the town of Hohenzollern, bought several lots on Otter Street, a block north of Main Street. Albrecht Boock and his three sons, Herman, Emil, and Ernest, who were the organizers of the town of Morgan, bought lots on Otter Street, a block south of Main Street. This set the scene for Otter Street to be the main commercial street, but there was plenty of opportunity for those who bought on Main Street as well. Some of the other purchasers of interest were Baxter and Reed, the banking interest from Ida Grove, Dr. Schneller from Ute, who wanted to establish a Drug Store, and a variety of local interests.

Once the auction was over, the pace of activity skyrocketed. Everyone wanted to get in on the action immediately. The tracks were laid to Schleswig, but the railroad was far from being complete, since the construction crews were still working on a thirty-foot cut through a hillside just west of town. However, once that was completed, the grade went quickly down to the next siding where the new town of Ricketts was established.

Jurgen Schroeder decided the best way to get set up and operating quickly in the new town would be to move his existing buildings to the new site and start operating. He contracted with the Hollenbeck Brothers from Omaha to move six buildings at a cost of $1100.00 which would take six weeks to accomplish. The Boock family decided not to move their buildings from Morgan. Their buildings were considerably older, and the distance was farther, so they decided to build new in the new town of Schleswig, and with some luck they might be open before Schroeder. The railroad was not operational yet, so the lumber had to be hauled in wagons from Denison. The lumber was purchased from a fellow German with local connections–Herman Grill ran the Independent Lumber Yard in Denison. When the first wagon load arrived, a young carpenter, Albert Schultz, jumped off the wagon and grabbed two boards and nailed them together. From that day until he died at the age of 90, he claimed the honor of driving the first nail in the town of Schleswig.

The Boock Brothers set up a farm implement and supply store at 221 Second Street where they also operated a produce station and a service and repair shop. They sold John Deere, Rock Island, International and Pioneer implements, as well as, hardware, plumbing supplies and buggies. All became bustling businesses from the day they opened their doors. Jurgen Schroeder moved his buildings into the north end of Otter (Second) Street. The lumbering teams of horses slowly turning a horse-powered wench, which had to be continually reset, moved entire buildings supported by beams sixteen inches square and 60 feet long. Certainly, it must have been quite a sight to see. He located three buildings on the north end of the 100 block, and in them he established a General Merchandise, a Hardware Store, A Saloon with food, and the Post Office. A dance hall, which was located at 113 Birch Street; a livery barn which was located along the alley behind the commercial buildings—the portion of the barn that still remains was covered with metal siding and roofing—and a blacksmith shop were the other buildings which he had moved into the new town. However, his blacksmith wanted to start out on his own, so Mr. Schroeder converted his building into a personal residence for himself located at 103 Birch Street. It took all of the six weeks to get all of the buildings moved to their new locations.

The first tragedy in the community occurred at this time. Jurgen Schroeder's wife, Johanna, was unable to take the stress and excitement of the move and died. Jurgen had four children from his first wife, Wilhelmina—Matilda, Willie, Maggie, and Herman who were pretty well grown at this time. Willie had become his father's right-hand man, driving the supply wagon to Denison and the route wagon around to the farmsteads. With his second wife, Johanna, Jurgen had four more children;—Olga, Eddie, Frieda, and Walter who were all small at the time. He later married a third time to Tina Frahm, and they had one son, Raymond. It was quite a trying time for the Schroeder family.

While this activity was occurring at the ends of Otter Street, the rest of the town was also active. Jurgen Krohnke constructed a large tie barn and livery stable across the street east of the Boock Brothers at 204 Second Street. C. W. Christiansen built a grocery store on Second Street. Baxter and Reed built a brick bank on the intersection of Main and Otter Streets. Dr. Schneller built a frame building for a drug store at 121 Cedar St. Broder Petersen built a hotel and tavern at 201 Cedar St. Henry Krohnke built a butcher shop at 107 Second St. Neils Koch set up a blacksmith shop between Jurgen Schroeder's store and his dance hall at 115 Birch St. Detlef Wieck, who had been the blacksmith at Morgan, set up shop at 215 Birch Street. Three lumber yards set up operations– Noble and Dessel at 219 Birch St., Steward Lumber at 34 Second St., and Green Bay Lumber at 31 Second St. Dr. Fuester set up a doctor's office, and a rooming house was built near the depot. Construction of one kind or another was taking place everywhere in the new town.

By the end of the year, there were also two grain elevators along the railroad tracks, the Trans-Mississippi Elevator Co. and the Snider, Nye and Company Elevator of Fremont, Nebraska. Albert von Doren operated Schroeder's Hardware store, and Claus Gottburg set up a furniture store. A jewelry store, a second drug store, a real estate office, a café, several barber shops, a millinery shop, and a contractor also located in the new town. Max Hueschen started a newspaper, and both Leopold and Knutsen set up harness shops. The name Schleswig, Iowa, was not official until the Post Office accepted it in place of Hohenzollern, which took place on January 1, 1900, and Jurgen Schroeder was retained as Postmaster.

Schleswig, unlike many other beginning towns, did not start slowly and quietly. It erupted, loudly and busily, out of the sod of the rich prairie ground. There was the tumultuous excitement of having the leading technology of the time, the railroad, coming here. It was followed by the spectacles of a whole town being picked up and moved to a new site, another whole town being shut down overnight and being built up again on a new site, and all kinds of new activity everywhere. Within eighteen months, the new town had a full-range commercial district and more than three hundred residents.

It was said that many German farmers built a large and solid barn first while living in rather modest housing until the farm made enough money for a "good" house. So it was with the town of Schleswig. The business district was built up first. Then housing followed. The residential area was in the northwest part of town where a number of new houses were constructed. The demand outran the ability of the carpenters, however, and a number of houses were moved in from the countryside to fill the need. One of the first houses constructed was for Theodore Rohwer at 23 First Street. Heinrich Suckstorf, who sold the land that formed the town site, built a home just across the road in the next section at 417 Hwy 59.

From the time the trains began running on a regular schedule on July 24, 1899, Schleswig was the most active depot on the Punkin Vine Line. Large amounts of produce, grain, and livestock were shipped to and from Schleswig, where the demand for goods for the new town and the growing countryside was phenomenal. Travelers and salesmen found rail travel fast and economical, it being easy to ride to Boyer and switch cars to Denison in the morning and reverse the trip in the afternoon. The railroads soon had special excursion trains to go to and back from the resort area at Lake View on Sundays. "The modern age" had come to farm country.

In January of 1900, an election was held to determine if the town should be incorporated. The issue passed overwhelmingly by a vote of 32 to 2. The paperwork was completed and accepted in February of 1900. The first Mayor was Herman Boock. Other officers were S. W. Myers, Clerk, and Theodore Rohwer, Treasurer. The original city council was comprised of Jurgen Schroeder, Dr Schneller, Nickolas von Doren, Detlef Wieck, Claus Gottburg and G. B. Fehmerling.

In addition to the commercial and residential building taking place, a number of people both from in town and from the countryside thought there should be a community center, so an association was formed to construct an Opera House. Construction was begun in the spring of 1900, and the building was finished in September being located at the south end of the business district at 305 Oak Street across the street from the Boock Implement Store. It boasted a 20 X 60 foot elevated stage, a curtain that could be elevated, five sets of scenery, three dressing rooms, a twelve-foot balcony, and a hard maple floor for dancing. Chairs, organized with six to a bank so they could be easily cleared from the floor, comprised the seating for the new building. The cost was the extravagant amount of $4500.00. The grand opening was on September 8, with the Eggermeyers Band from Carroll providing the entertainment for the four hundred twenty-five people who attended.

But it wasn't all work in the new town. A number of social activities went on in the community including the organization of several fraternal societies, the first of these being Lodge 17 of the Sons of Hermann. The organization was originally established to honor the ancient German Warrior, Hermann, who had fought with the Roman Legions and learned the art of warfare after which he organized the German tribes to defeat the Roman General Darius in the Battle of Teutoberg Forest. Hermann was held in honor by Germans everywhere. The Schleswig Chapter was organized on April 22, 1900 with a membership including August Rickert, C W. Christiansen, August Braase, Albrecht Boock, Herman Boock, Henry Hahn, Henry Krohnke, Jurgen Schroeder, John Jepsen, Matt Lorenzen, and Bernard Andresen.

Two other fraternal societies were established in Schleswig, both on the same day–May 12, 1900. One was the Pretoria Lodge No. 696 of International Order of Odd Fellows. The I.O.O.F. was a secret society with social and civic interests that had started in England and spread worldwide. Local membership included Adolf Cook, F. W. Gigax, Theodore Rohwer, Hans Baeth, Claus Gottberg, Chris Kruse, William Schmidt, J.D. Naeve, Clause Grill, H. C. Hansen, Dr. R Fuester, and Edward Reimer. A third organization was the Schleswig Camp No. 8087 of the Modern Woodmen of America. Modern Woodmen of America was founded in Lyons, Iowa, in Clinton County, where many of the settlers had ties. It is a fraternal organization that provides life insurance and other benefits to its members, many of whom were also members of the other fraternal organizations. Some of the early members were H. Hoelring, F.D. Naeve, Max Hueschen, C. Kruse, H. Kohlbaum, August Rickert, Sam Fleeger, Alfred Miller, D. Wohlert, H. F. Wieck, Niels Koch, Charles Miller, Dr F. A Burrows, Nick Naeve and Robert Naeve.

One organization that had a strong influence in early German communities, but never succeeded in Schleswig was the Turner Verein. It was an acrobatic club which also engaged in singing, lectures, readings, debates, and stage performances. Davenport had the strongest group of Turners in America. Many of the forefathers of the settlers in this area had come from the area of Davenport and were influenced by them, and while they did not get started in Schleswig, many of the settlements in this area started their own Turners Group, especially Holstein and Manning. The Turners philosophy was ascribed to by many of the German settlers. One of their more succinct statements said the Turners were to fight against church domination, nativism, and for freedom, enlightenment and welfare of all, including women's rights.

Business in Schleswig started with tremendous enthusiasm attracting more and more businesses–four grocery stores, the Brown and Crawford Café and many others. Included among these businesses was a second bank. The officers of the Crawford County State Bank organized a new bank here called the German Bank for which a new building was constructed at 111 Second Street. Emil Krueger was put in charge, and it had a strong business.

Activity was not confined to Schleswig. The towns of Kiron and Ricketts on the rail line on either side of Schleswig were also going through a great deal of growth. Kiron had been established more than thirty years before the railroad and had a post office for more than twenty-five years. They had a solid business district and a growing and well-respected community. When word was first heard in Kiron that the railroad was coming, the merchants and community leaders planned where the rail line would be most beneficial to the community. However, when the railroad surveyors came, they did not agree that the route that the leaders had planned would be the best for the railroad. The community decided not to sell the right-of-way where the railroad wanted it and thus force them to accept the community's preferred route. The railroad would have none of that and surveyed a new route for the rails and did not put down a siding until they were a mile past Kiron. Consequently, the businesses had little alternative but to move to the new site. Norelius and Nordell moved their grocery store from Old Kiron but many others built new. Some of the new buildings were the Peterson blacksmith shop, Mckeever harness shop, Dr. F. A. Burrows' office, and the Miller livery stable. August Reinking and Adam Auchstetter each built a saloon. The Mauritz Brothers built a hotel. The Boyer Valley Banking Company set up a new bank with W. Sandberg as cashier. On the other hand, many of the people who resided in old Kiron remained there. It was new people who built in New Kiron, and gradually over the years Old Kiron disappeared.

Ricketts did not have the impetus of a previously existing town on which to build. In fact Charter Oak was competing with it to get the railroad to change its route and go through their town, but the railroad decided that would be a little too far out of the way, and the siding was dropped at the location of Ricketts. The town started, but it started entirely with new businesses in a new territory. As a result a full range of services were established, but the total size of the community remained modest. Paul Voss, who had worked in the town of Morgan, operated a hotel and saloon. A Green Bay Lumber Yard was established. Baak and Detlefs set up a general store. Max Wulf had a blacksmith shop. The German Savings Bank was organized by James Toy, Charles Robertson E. Springer, John Dolieu, and Adolph Meyer. Because Ricketts was largely a German community, it drew commercial support from a wide surrounding area which was also populated by Germans.

A substantial number of people moving into Schleswig immediately became concerned about schooling the children, so in 1900, the second floor of Jurgen Schroeder's store was used as a classroom. In 1901, a new school district was established for Schleswig, and a school board was elected with Theodore Rohwer becoming its president. The board twice proposed a $5000.00 bond issue. Both times the bond issue was passed but was declared void because the State officials would not accept a bond that size for such a new district. It was the first election in the area where women were allowed the right to vote. The board then tried a new tactic. They proposed a $2500.00 bond which was approved, and then they immediately proposed a second bond of the same amount, and which also approved. They now had the funds to build a new school house; the next problem was where to build it. Theodore Rohwer and some of the first home builders in Schleswig wanted to have the school located west of the tracks so it would be closer to their homes. The site they favored was on the north half of the first block on Ash Street. Most of the people and most of the school board members wanted to build east of the tracks where there was more land available and where the price was cheaper. To head off any movement east, the homeowners from west of the tracks also bought a lot in the east area. They purchased one lot in each block, thus preventing the school from obtaining a full block on which to build. The school board countered that by buying the half-block directly behind Theodore Rohwer's newly purchased lot and built the new school there. The school was a two-story building with four classrooms and an office. F. N. Olry was hired as principal, and classes were started in November of 1901.

Growth and expansion were not only the key features of Schleswig, Iowa, but also of the entire nation. Andrew Carnegie had just merged 10 steel companies into the United States Steel Corporation with assets of more than $1,000,000,000 making it the largest company in the world. Many local residents went to Denison in May to see President McKinley as he passed through, waving to the crowd as the train slowed on its passage through town. A very sad event took place in September of that year when the President was shot and killed at the Pan American Exposition in Buffalo, New York. Teddy Roosevelt became President, and after a period of mourning for Mr. McKinley, the people of Schleswig gave their wholehearted support to President Roosevelt. His "Bully" attitude fit well with the spirit of the times.

The City Council knew how important a good water supply for the community was, and as a consequence, a well ten feet wide and 442 feet deep was dug just off the alley behind the Green Bay Lumber Yard, and a brick building was constructed over the well. Double doors opened to the south from the well room, and the well itself was covered with planks. A meeting room for the city council and one for the fire department was included. A third room was used to house a water pump powered by a twelve-horse-power gasoline engine. The water was pumped into two steel tanks totaling 25,000 gallons placed next to the building and had enough pressure to throw a stream of water 150 feet high from a 3/4 inch nozzle. The entire system cost $6500.00. The public water system was extended to the business district first through a system of lead pipes, and from there it was extended to the residential district starting with those houses closest to the well. Nearly every house in town had a rainwater cistern, and many of them had their own private wells. Even so, it was difficult to keep a good supply of water available. The railroad's policy of staying to the ridge line to avoid having to bridge creeks and steams was having its effect on finding water. In the case of Schleswig, there are four streams each of which started on a different side of town and each ran in a different direction which made it very unlikely to find groundwater veins that would be running toward Schleswig.

The same lure of cheap land that had brought settlers to Crawford County was now drawing people out of the county, the major attraction at the time being Oklahoma. The government had just opened up additional Indian land for settlement, and people from all over the county, including Schleswig, headed south to get some of the available land. But, this new land did not prove to be quite the quality of the land they had left in Iowa.

The first Rose Bowl was held in Pasadena on January 1, 1902. The team representing the Midwest, the University of Michigan defeated Stanford by a score of 49-0. Publicity like this did attract Iowans to California in enough numbers that in future years they were able to host an 'Iowa Day' picnic with all former Iowans.

In spite of the exodus of some people, Schleswig was growing so rapidly that it was difficult to determine how to scale the new developments. For example, the telephone system that had been set up on the second floor of Jurgen Schroeder's store was already too small, and a new switchboard had to be installed, for there was already sixty miles of phone wire connecting the businesses, homes, and farms in the community. The just-completed school house needed an addition to meet the demands for space. Jurgen Schroeder gave up the office of postmaster because his business interests were taking up too much of his time. Max Hueschen, who could no longer keep up with the increase demands of putting out the newspaper, sold it to J. F. Branaka.

Also at this time, a rather interesting character turned up in Schleswig. He was a deaf, mute man, who earned his living as a painter known just as Deafy. He didn't seem very ambitious, however, as he seemed to spend a lot of time in the businesses on Main Street. A rash of counterfeit money circulated at this time and some of the businessmen began to wonder about Deafy. Their suspicions were reinforced when Deafy suddenly disappeared – and so did the counterfeit money. Some months later, however, they were surprised to hear that a counterfeit ring had been arrested in southern Minnesota, and the principal government agent in the arrest was none other than Deafy. He had been a Secret Service Agent operating under cover.

Because the German people had a long ingrained appreciation of and considerable talent for music, a citizens' band was organized. Many of them were quite talented in this area. The band was utilized to support many activities in the Opera House, and to represent the community in public events. Professor Coates from Denison was hired to instruct the band in their weekly rehearsals.

Doctor Richard Fuester was advancing in age, and an opportunity for a new doctor presented itself. Dr. Fuester had set up an office on the intersection of Otter and Prairie Streets at 31 Second St. Dr. Ernest Schneller had come when the town started, but he was more interested in operating a drug store than in a medical practice. Drs. Dresher and Womeldorf were here for a while, but, they had difficulty starting a practice. Then a local boy, Walter Schultz, who had been born and raised on a local farm decided to set up a medical practice. He went to Medical School in Chicago and graduated in 1900. After an internship, he returned to Schleswig to start a practice in 1902 setting up an office on the second floor of Jurgen Schroeder's store across the hall from the telephone office.

Young Dr. Schultz, also, found it was not a simple task to start a medical practice. He just looked so young and wasn't he the boy who had grown up just down the road. He just didn't look mature enough to trust with one's medical problems. Then it was noticed that a couple of times a week Dr. Schultz would come rushing down from his office and jump into his buggy and race out of town–apparently going on a medical emergency. Public opinion began to change, and the people began to think that if he was in that kind of demand, he must be a worthy physician–and his practice began to pick up. Dr. Schultz was careful to be sure his "medical emergencies" were in varied directions from town, so no one would notice that as soon as he was out of sight of town, he would slow down and quietly drive around a couple sections and drive back to his quiet office. His sly ingenuity was what it took to get a successful medical practice started that would last for fifty years.

Dr. Schultz was joined the following year by Doctor Henry Jones who was born in Battle Creek, Iowa, and came to Schleswig as soon as he had finished medical school. Since Dr. Schultz had broken the ice for young doctors, Dr. Jones had an easier time starting his practice. He set up an office in the rooming house near the depot. He also had a successful medical practice that lasted for fifty years.

At this time, Denison decided it needed a new courthouse. The old building was too small and not particularly functional. A proposal was entered on the ballot to finance the new structure, but it was soundly defeated. The people, especially the merchants, with large property interests that would be taxed to pay for the building, thought a less expensive proposal should be developed. Governor Shaw had just completed his term as Governor of Iowa, returned to this hometown and took up the cause of a major and elegant new courthouse. It was thought that he wanted to make the new courthouse a marble and limestone monument to his political career. He was then appointed by President Roosevelt to the position of Secretary of the Treasury. This appointment gave him a great deal of prestige, and when he was able to arrange a visit by the President to Denison, a lot of weight was given to his position. The merchants in Denison were still not entirely sure they wanted to pay for such an expensive project, so a group of people from Schleswig decided to help the merchants of Denison. The Schleswig group offered to build a courthouse and to give it to the county free of charge. It would, of course, be in Schleswig! Instead of being grateful, the Denison merchants, when they heard of the offer, decided to build Governor Shaw his building and keep the offices in their town. They passed a huge $75,000.00 bond issue. Such are the vacillations of politics!!

With all of the developments and progress Schleswig was making at this time, she was one of the few towns that did not have a church. Those settlers who were religiously inclined attended the Grant Township Lutheran Church or the Hanover Township Church, and occasionally circuit riding preachers would hold services in one of the public rooms around town, such as the depot, the school, or a store building. The leaders of the German Evangelical Lutheran Church took note of this and sent in a circuit pastor to organize the area. After some effort he was able to gather a few prospective parishioners together, and a meeting was held in the City Hall next to the well. The result of this meeting was the formation of the Friedens Evangelical Lutheran Church on September 17, 1903. Emil Hanson, the circuit pastor, was selected as their minister. A new Church building was erected at Fifth and

Elm Streets and dedicated on August 15, 1904. The original members included, Christ Kruse, Max Hueschen, Oscar Seaman, Jurgen Schroeder, Charlie Christiansen, Claus Gottburg, Peter Ernst, Hans Baeth, Broder Brueggen, Hans Lohse, and Pay Jurgensen.

Attendance at the dedication ceremony for the church was twice as big as the church could hold. Ministers from surrounding towns conducted the services–Reverend Lorenz from Peterson, Iowa, in the morning; the Reverend Dettman from Remsen preached on Foreign Missions in the afternoon, and the Reverend Niewohner from Buck Grove spoke on Home Missions. An evening service was conducted in English by Reverend Wetzler from Pomeroy. The morning offering was $40.00; in the afternoon it was $17.00; and in the evening it was $8.00. A group of ladies held a basket social–to raise money for a new organ, the baskets selling for 75 cents to 3.75 a piece–and raised $112.50.

In German, the word "frieden" means peace, and for many years the Friedens Evangelical German Lutheran Church was known simply as the "Peace Church," or the Church of Peace.

An unusual commercial building had been built completely around the Baxter Brothers Bank building with one door opening to the east on Second Street and a second door opening the south onto Cedar Street. Unfortunately, the floor on the south section was lower than the floor to the east, so a set of steps had to be installed between the two. The south half was occupied by a drug store and a jeweler's shop, and the east half was unoccupied for some time, but then Theodore Rohwer approached Peter Hollander, a young farm boy working at the Noble and Dessel Lumber Yard, and proposed that if he would take a year's training at running a clothing store at Hollander's cousin's store in Boone, Rohwer would form a partnership with him and provide the funds for a new clothing store. The new store was located in the east side of the building, and in later years also occupied the south half. After a few years Peter Hollander was able to buy out Mr. Rohwer's interest.

The town had two hotels. The first was a wooden frame structure on the southeast corner of Second and Cedar streets generally
known as the "Wooden Hotel." It was two stories high and ran the
length of the lot with an attached saloon. Broder Petersen built it,
but it was operated by Johannas Lorenzen. The second hotel was
built somewhat later, a half a block north at 110 Second Street
and was known as the "Brick Hotel" after the material from which
it was made. It was a two-story building fifty feet wide with two
doors, one leading to a lobby on the south side of the building in
which was a check-in counter and an open stairway to the rooms
above. Behind the lobby were the manager's living quarters. The
door to the north lead to a restaurant which was one of the finer
eating places in the community. Hugo Wiegand, a brother-in-law
to Dr. Schultz, was the manager for a number of years.

One of the early services provided in the town of Schleswig
was a gas generating plant located on a small triangular lot at the
corner of Cedar and Maple Streets. The plant consisted of a brick
building with a door at the corner of the triangle and a chemical
storage building just to the east. Behind the buildings was a set of
metal tanks sunk in the ground in which were placed chemicals
and water. When they were mixed in the tanks, carbonic gas was
generated that was sent through a series of pipes laid to transport
the gas to various business places in the business district and to a
number of homes. Having the fuel now, a series of street lights was
also erected along the principal streets in town. This improvement
placed Schleswig ahead of most towns of its size in this part of the
state.

One of the familiar figures seen frequently on the streets of
Schleswig was Henry Buck. Everyone knew him and depended on
him for city services. For many years he held the office of City
Marshal. His other duties included that of a night watchman during which time he would make the rounds of the business district
to be sure all doors were locked and windows were secured; an
organizer of security for special social activities such as the bi-weekly
dances at the Opera House; of maintaining the city water system

and its water pump and pressure system; of operating the city gas plant and being the lamplighter for the street lights. When the Schleswig Fire Department organized a second company, Henry Buck was appointed its Captain. He also maintained the city's streets with his road grader. In his spare time he operated a dray service delivering packages to and from the depot. The townspeople justifiably felt secure and comfortable when Henry was on the job.

The German Mutual Insurance Association celebrated its 25th year in existence in its annual meeting in 1904. Many farmers had been saved by the Association from the effects of accidents and disasters and, accordingly, it was extremely popular and growing. Its two major centers were in Schleswig and in Holstein, although there were members throughout the two-county area. In the 25-year history of the company, they had not used an office but held each officer responsible for the records and activities of his position, and since they had been so successful, they decided to continue that business practice. The officers at the time were: August Schultz, president; Hans Lohse, vice-president; Carl Wendt, secretary; and Clause Grill, treasurer. Among the adjusters were Henry Bremer, Henry W. Rohlk, Adolph Eggert, and Johanns Preuss.

The arrival of the railroad defined the location of the town
and the depot became the center of activity. On the far side
of the depot is the Cedar Street crossing.

At this time, the Federal Government opened new land for
settlement that had been part of the Rosebud Indian Reservation
in South Dakota, and number of people from Crawford County
applied for homestead grants; however, Schleswig people were not
interested. The farmland in the area was becoming well developed
and provided a good living for the area residents. They didn't need
to go farther for a better living. The produce raised–the milk, cream,
eggs, and vegetables–could almost provide for the daily cost of
living. The major crops and livestock could go to pay off the land,
and the increase in the value of the land could make them wealthy.
Startup costs for equipment and seed would run in the $500.00
range. From there on, hard work would be rewarded.

Alcoholic consumption was a concern throughout the nation
and had been for some time. Many people who could not control
their impulses to consume liquor lead to an ineffectiveness in some
segments of the work force and was devastating to some families.
An attempt had been made to enact a Prohibition law in Iowa in
the 1880's, and it did pass the legislature but was in danger of
being struck down by the Supreme Court. A compromise law was

enacted then called the Mulct Act which provided that the local government could fine a saloon operator for abuses even if he were duly licensed. As a result, the temperance movement was strong in many communities, such as in Denison, which had a strong chapter of the Woman's Christian Temperance Union under the leadership of Mrs. Mary McKim and others. The movement became so influential that every Republican politician had to give lip service to Prohibition if he expected to be nominated for an office.

Of course, this issue was not at all popular in the German communities where beer had long been a part of the cultural scene. In the Fourth of July parade in Denison, the Germans had a float to express displeasure with the sentiment. The float had Gambrinus, the King of Beer, chained, endeavoring to slake his thirst from a number of kegs about him which were chained and padlocked. In Holstein, a vigilante committee was organized to protect their beer distributors from such nonsense. Schleswig did not directly display their sentiments, but they did have four saloons operating in the town—one in the Wooden Hotel, and others operated by William Pipgras, Broder Bruggen, and J. Krohnke. The saloon operated by Broder Bruggen was a modest frame building on the northeast corner of Second and Cedar Streets where he was able to get the Pabst Brewing Company to build an icehouse for him behind the tavern on the north end of his lot. In 1905, he sold his business to Hugo Krohnke who decided to replace the building with a larger two-story cement block building. But rather than deprive the community of one of their sources of libation, he moved the old tavern into the middle of the street and continued to operate it there until the new building was completed.

The towns in the northern part of the county were known to maintain themselves in a quite orderly fashion. Kiron suppressed the sale of alcohol, though it was not eliminated entirely, whereas Schleswig and Ricketts maintained a more liberal attitude but maintained order in their communities. This whole area was relatively crime free which was quite a contrast to Denison where robberies, shootings, and all sorts of criminal activity were conducted on a rather regular basis. The ability of their night watchman, Lou Baer, was tested and challenged often.

When the people in Schleswig did have a problem, they usually found a unique way of solving it. For example, Fred Gigax, the manager of the Green Bay Lumber Company, was one of the first people in town to buy an automobile. He was quite proud of it, but he was not too adept at operating it. One day in 1905, he frightened Fred Jepsen's team of horses whereupon they ran into a ditch. Mr. Jepsen was furious, and he decided to get even with Mr. Gigax, and to do it where it would hurt the most—in his pocketbook. After discussion with some of his fellow farmers, a competing business—the Farmers Lumber and Coal Company—came into being. It was incorporated, but each shareholder could cast only one vote regardless of how many shares he owned. Thus, no one person could get control of the company for his own benefit, and in this way the company was sure to operate in the best interest of its consumers. The structure worked so well that it outlasted all of its competition and continued as long as there was a market for lumber products in the community.

California was the main topic of conversation in Schleswig in 1906. The San Francisco earthquake that year was the most devastating and destructive ever recorded. Then, the Modesto, California, Board of Trade and Commercial Club's three-train-car exhibit came to town. The exhibit included fruits, grains, shells, a live alligator, and a large shark; it was electrically lighted, and the purpose of it was to entice people to move to California. Some nine hundred people paid admission to see the exhibit.

The trains played a major role in a funeral in 1906. The unexpected death of Emil Kruger, the manager of the German Bank, created a great deal of sympathy in the community. Mr. Kruger was a well respected community leader and when he underwent surgery but did not survive the ordeal the entire community felt the emotional blow. When the family decided to have the funeral in Vail and the burial in the family cemetery plot there, a special train was set up to take mourners from Schleswig to attend the services. Seven passenger cars were needed to transport the 230 people who wished to attend the funeral.

Ricketts suffered a major catastrophe on May 14, 1907. A fire destroyed most of its business district. The day had been cold and wet with even some snow in the air that evening, causing everything to close up early. Peter Petersen owned a café, in the rear of which his family resided, and the building next door, which was a harness shop run by Al Kuhlman. Mr. Kuhlman noticed there was a fire in the Petersen residence shortly after midnight, and he rushed over to alert them. He was none too soon, as the smoke was so thick it almost smothered the family. The alarm was sounded, but it was really too late. The fire which had started in the café's washroom quickly consumed the building and the strong winds soon spread it to the harness shop. From there it spread to the Krohnke pool hall and barber shop and to the saloon and hotel owned by Paul Voss. An inadequate supply of water and a chemical fire engine, which was not nearly large enough for such a blaze, could not prevail against such odds. When the fire was contained, there were only four businesses left in the town. The railroad section crew used the water in the water tank which supplied the train engines to prevent the depot from burning. Fortunately, the Nye elevator and the Green Bay lumber yard were far enough away to escape the flames.

It was a devastating blow to the community, but they pitched right in and cleaned up the mess and started rebuilding. Pete Petersen even set up a tavern in a tent so the workers could find refreshment. One of the first items on the agenda was to build a new water system that could handle a crisis before it got out of hand as had happened in their recent fire. The following summer bids were let for the construction of a wooden water tower and a cement reservoir. A water committee was formed by the City Council to monitor the use of water.

The Schleswig Post Office operated by Postmaster August Schultz had grown to the extent that it had two rural mail routes serviced by Herman Schultz and Robert Naeve. The Post Office came out with the order that all postal employees were to wear the regulation grey uniforms, and it also established that postal carriers had the right-of-way on public roads, because the delivery of mail was being delayed when mail carriers were not being given proper respect on the thoroughfares. That would no longer be tolerated.

In 1908, Schleswig too suffered from fire. It was a large blaze, but fortunately it was confined to one business—the Trans-Mississippi grain elevator which burned to the ground. The fire department made a valiant effort to control it, but the blaze had too good a start. However, they were able to save the office building and to prevent the fire from spreading. The company decided not to rebuild the elevator and sold the brick office building to Siegfried Kettlesen, who used it as a carpenter's shop for many years.

October 6, 1908, being the 225th anniversary of the arrival of the first German immigrants to America in 1683 called for a celebration, so a German Day was held. A large celebration in Denison was sponsored by the three major German organizations in the county—the Lansverein Veterans, the German Brotherhood, and the Schleswig Sons of Hermann Lodge. Flags and bunting decorated the entire town. At 10:00 there was a large parade lead by the Denison band, followed by more than 200 Germans who had immigrated, boys on horseback carrying stalks of corn, and a variety of floats. The Reverend Hansen from Schleswig opened the ceremonies with a prayer followed by a number of speeches by the Mayor of Denison and other prominent speakers detailing the history and accomplishment of the German people in America. A merry-go-round operating and a major tug-of-war between two teams of local people were part of the entertainment. In the evening there was a dance that was held in the German Bunderschaft Hall on north Main Street and lasted until the next morning. The hall had been built and donated to the Bundershaft by Herman Grill several years before. The Lansverein Veterans were the owners of the Denison Opera House.

In Schleswig, the Sons of Hermann Lodge held most of their

activities in the Schleswig Opera House which was the social center of the town. Regular dances were scheduled every two weeks and were usually held in conjunction with a special dinner at the Brick Hotel. It is interesting to note that a prominent notice in the dance posters was that the dances would be well regulated and controlled. They were not going to stand for the rowdiness that had occurred in the dances that took place before the town was established.

The opera house was used not only for dances but also for a variety of activities. A number of musical programs ranging from the Schleswig Orchestra to vocal recitals were performed there. Athletic activities, commencement exercises, banquet, wedding, anniversary, and masquerade dances, all types of large group meetings and silent movies were all held there. The Schleswig Drama Club also used it to put on its performances, one of which was "The Country Kid" featuring Eddie Schroeder in the leading role, supported by Julius Rohwer, Sara Hoiten, and Loretta Schmidt. The Opera House also served as the hub for the Children's Day or Kinderfest celebration in the spring and the annual Firemen's Ball in the fall.

A variety of clubs and organizations were begun. The Schleswig Gun Club or Schutzen Verein was having a fair amount of success, and they hosted similar clubs from surrounding communities in competitions. Their best team consisted of Schmidt, Pipgras, Kudel, Stock, and Stegeman. In the early days the only social activity the settlers had was to visit the neighbors, and informal birthday, anniversary and similar types of parties were held to fill the calendar. The main activity at such parties was a game of cards. Many card clubs were organized and named after the location of where they were held. Others were named after the games that were played. Still others were fanciful names such as the MGR club, the CLM club, the Cousin Hugo club or the Happy Hour club. One of the more popular games was Schop's Kopf or Sheep's Head. Whereas the foregoing were social clubs, the Fraun Verein was an organization for women of the church.

The Schroeder dance hall on Birch Street was an active social center. It had been built with a hip roof and resembled the thatch roof buildings that had been popular in Germany. An unfortunate incident took place in the hall about this time. Two men with a long-standing dispute developed an argument over a minor issue involving some stamps. The argument became quite heated and one man pulled out a gun and shot the other man in the head. Fortunately the bullet glanced off the man's skull and went out the top of his hat. At the sound of the shot, the dance hall was evacuated in seconds leaving only two couples on the dance floor. Eddie Schroeder was one of them. He turned to his partner and said, "Everybody must be all right. They can still run pretty good." The other couple remaining on the dance floor was Louie Grill and Julia Kroeger. The shooter, Bill Schroeder, was never charged as he immediately left town. The victim was a man by the name of Booth or Burke. It was not long after this that Jurgen Schroeder closed the dance hall.

The Boock Brothers' partnership in the implement dealership dissolved after having been in operation for some time. Herman Boock, the first mayor of Schleswig, moved to Oregon to try his luck there. Ernest moved to Manila, but Emil stayed and formed the Boysen and Boock Buick and Overland automobile agency located in the former Boock implement building. At about the same time Gus Hollander and Charles Reinking started a competing business in Jurgen Schroeder's former dance hall at 112 Birch Street where they sold Michigan and Metz cars. The City Council was becoming concerned by the number of cars that were careening around town, so to settle things down they passed Ordinance Number 46 which set the speed limit in the city limits at six miles an hour.

The Chicago Northwestern Railroad began promoting the sale of new land that had been opened up in the Standing Rock Indian Reservation in northern South Dakota. Among those from Schleswig who went to check it out were William Kortum and his son-in-law, John Grill, but they decided the land part way across the state looked better. John Grill moved to Ree Heights, South Dakota, that fall which put him fairly near his brother Chris, who had moved to Woonsocket some years earlier. Many families such as the Dahmses and the Petersens either moved or invested in South Dakota land, but many of them moved back to Schleswig after a few years. The productivity of the land just was not the same as they had grown accustomed to in this area.

An organization, the Modern Woodmen of America, had purchased several blocks of land when it went on sale in the northeast part of town to serve as a park which became known as the Woodman's Park. Then, the Naeve family donated additional land to the park as part of a housing development in that part of town, and the name was changed to the Naeve Park.

An awareness of a need for fire protection was obvious, so the Schleswig Fire Department was started almost as soon as the town was organized. It has always been a volunteer department with many of the businessmen volunteering for service. The community has been generous in its support of their efforts, and as a result the organization has always had the latest of equipment. When the department was housed in the brick building next to the city well, it was equipped with two hose carts, 1200 feet of hose and water mains located so every major building in town had protection. In 1909, a new bell was purchased at the cost of $100.00, and it was mounted on a stand near the office. The department was organized into two companies—one headed by John Berndt and the other by Henry Buck. C.J. Claussen was the Fire Chief for a number of years, and Peter Hollander was a longtime secretary.

The Fire Department sponsored a community wide picnic on June 23, 1909 for which the Brick hotel provided much of the food. It was a pleasant day and everyone had a good time but shortly after the event, a number of people became ill, some of them extremely so. The total number of sick people grew to more than fifty, and by July 15, the situation became so serious that Dr. Schultz converted his home at 517 Birch Street into a hospital to which he brought in extra nurses from as far away as Council Bluffs.

Some twenty people were admitted there. Some of the people who were confined for three weeks or more were Mr. and Mrs. Peter Hollander, Misses Rasch and Iverson, Ernest Schultz, Herbert Bendixen, Techla Hollander, Christ Hofer, and Otto Hollander. Some of them actually approached the point of death before they improved. Mrs. Hollander lost all of her hair. There was one fatality—Ella Hansen, a 15-year-old girl, had been weakened by the illness and then developed a gall bladder problem that required an operation. In her weakened condition, she did not survive the operation.

Word began to circulate around town that the problem had been food poisoning, the likely source being the potato salad that Hugo Wiegand had made at the Brick Hotel, apparently in copper washtubs several days before the event. Mr. Wiegand denied any such thing. He even wrote an open letter to the community and published it in the Schleswig Leader saying no food was improperly handled in his establishment. Dr. Schultz, who was Hugo Wiegand's brother-in-law, said it appeared to be typhoid fever, and he sent some tissue samples to the department of health labs in Iowa City. The response was that it could well be typhoid. However, typhoid fever is a water borne disease, and water samples from all known sources showed no signs of typhoid contamination.

Public meetings were held and a lot discussion took place. The business in the Brick Hotel dropped precipitously. On August 12, Mr. Wiegand sold the hotel to Raymond Larrison who changed the name to the Larrison House. But that was not enough to mollify the public concerns. By October it changed hands again, and H.C. Petersen bought it. By this time Mr. Wiegand had purchased some property near Sioux City and had moved there. The last of the hospital patients, Eddie Ebert, was released on October 1, and matters were beginning to settle down. The official word was that there had been a typhoid epidemic of unknown sources, but there were certainly a lot of people around town who would not buy that. If a topic of conversation was wanted with which to start an argument for years afterward, this was it.

Above: Buggies on lower Second Street.
Below: Governor Carroll addressing an interested crowd on upper Second Street. In the background is the Steward Lumberyard, Adolph Hansen Saddle and Harness Shop, and the Bakery.

It was not the only strange thing that was going on that year. Sun spots were more prevalent than they had been for thirty years causing a great deal of disruption on the telephone and telegraph lines. Lineman Lund of the Schleswig Phone Company said messages were being sent great distances without any current being applied. Lights were said to come on with the switch being in the "off" position.

Marshal Buck was informed one day that a team of horses was tied to fence near the railroad crossing outside of town. He stabled the team and began calling around to see if there was a report of missing horses. The Sheriff's office in Denison answered there had been a team reported stolen there. It appeared to be of a more mischievous than of criminal intent. The person who owned the horses had a name very similar to that of one of the ringleaders in the old horse thief ring that had operated here in the old days. It was probably just coincidence, but it had tongues wagging for a while.

By this time the business district had expanded to cover an area from the first block on Second Street into the 300 block of Oak Ave. In an east-west direction, it extended from 100 Cedar Street to the 400 block of Cedar Street. The area that changed the most was the first half of the 100 block of Cedar Street where four two-story buildings had been built along the north side of the street. At 100 Cedar Street, Chris Kruse had a hardware store; at 104 Cedar Street, Claus Gottburg owned a furniture and coffin store; at 108 Cedar Street George Areman operated a harness shop; at 110 Cedar Street August Rickert had a grocery store; at 112 Cedar Nellie Porter had a small millinery shop that was a social center for the young women of the town. Yes! The town was growing.

Albert Schultz had been working as a carpenter since the town started and he was working on a building for Jurgen Schroeder across the alley from Chris Kruse's Hardware Store at this time. Mr. Kruse came out while he was working and asked if Albert was mad at him because he was doing all that building in the area and had not bought any materials, not even a nail, from his store. Albert explained that Mr. Schroeder had bought all the material from the Farmers Lumber Yard to which Mr. Kruse replied if the Lumber Yard was going to start selling hardware, he was going to sell out. After considering that statement through the evening, Albert went to see him bright and early the next morning and by 7:00 A.M. on August 8, 1909 Albert Schultz was in the hardware business. Three years later he bought Fred Mohr's saloon on Second Street and moved his business there remaining in the hardware business for nearly sixty years.

As times changed, so did names. The Nissen Cemetery underwent a name change when the cemetery board decided to have the cemetery known as the Morgan Cemetery. It had grown beyond the original two-acre donation. The Farmers Lumber and Coal company also changed its name and would now be known as the Farmers Lumber and Grain Company when it bought out the Nye and Snider Grain Elevator. John Claussen, brother to Peter Claussen, the Bank cashier in Ricketts, was to be the manager. John Claussen had been managing a small elevator in southern Minnesota when this opportunity came up, and he turned the position of manager into a dynasty.

Automobiles were becoming more and more common. A lot of action was occurring with the dealerships, too. The Boock and Boysen Agency split up and in the process they loss the Buick and Overland dealership. Gus Hollander's father, Thomas Hollander, bought part of the old Krohnke livery barn and built a new block building at 205 Cedar Street. Gus dissolved his partnership with Charles Reinking to go it on his own in the new building. He was able to pick up the Buick and Overland car dealership and added Republic Trucks. Boysen formed a new partnership with William Pipgras. They constructed a new garage at 106 Second Street, and they picked up the Michigan and Metz dealership and added the Avery line. This activity created interest. Max Kropf came all the way from Kiron to buy an Overland. But they could not please everyone. Gus Schuman and his son Rudy went all the way to

Sioux City to get a hot new Appleton "Jackrabbit." But the most interesting car in town was Barney Boysen's 18 passenger Avery. It was rigged so it could also power a threshing machine or a corn sheller.

Boysen's Avery was put to heavy use transporting the local baseball team. The Schleswig Wildcats played an active schedule and they had a strong local backing. It was said that nothing promoted a town better than a good ball team and a good band. However, the Schleswig band had dissolved, but now there was a movement to reorganize it. With little effort, they had more volunteers than they could use. There were other new organizations that were formed at his time as well. A Commercial Club was organized to promote the business interests of Schleswig. The German American Liberal League was formed. It took positions on the issues of the day to promote the interest of German immigrants, and also endorsed political candidates and political activities.

The largest construction project in the history of the county was taking place in 1910. It was the straightening of the Boyer River, and it was a massive effort. Huge dredging cranes were ripping out a straight, deep river channel, and in places, dynamite was used to speed the process. It did stabilize the route of the river and reclaimed some farmland, but its environmental impact was very questionable.

Water was on the minds of the people of Schleswig, too. The old water system based on a pressure tank system was no longer adequate. The City Council decided to erect a steel water tower for $9000.00 on September 16, 1910, and a thousand dollars more to improve the system. It was debated whether to have an 80-foot tower or a 100-foot tower, and the decision went for the taller tower which had a 65,000 gallon capacity. The fire bell was supported by a section of railroad rail which was suspended in the tower.

The fire department was put to the test at Christmas time in 1911 when the school house caught fire. Unfortunately, the fire had too good a start before it was noticed and the building was a total loss. As a result, classes were spread out around town with the high school classes being held in the City Hall and Well House by the water tower and the elementary classes were held in various rooms available in the business district. A new brick building was built to replace the school, and the contractor used the same floor plan that had been used in the old school building.

The town was growing rapidly in size and in prosperity. The population had nearly doubled in the first decade of its existence, and the people were proud of their many accomplishments. Many of the residents had also done quite well financially. They had not only built a substantial set of buildings but also developed a sophisticated and diverse society which, too, was always in a state of change and development.

One of the areas of change was in the town's churches. The Church of Peace, the Friedens German Evangelical Lutheran Church, had served the entire community for a number of years. It had an open and accepting policy that welcomed all comers. Some dissension began to arise among the congregation, however. Some people did not think this policy really reflected their status and position. They thought it was time to start a new church, and so, at a meeting on August 12, 1912, in the city building under the new water tower, a new congregation was organized. The principal participants were Otto Stegeman, Andreas Hollander, George Brodersen, Franz Keller, and William Baak. They felt more comfortable with the very conservative and restrictive doctrines of the Missouri Synod of the Lutheran Church. Here worldly position was dependent on God's Grace and selection. Communion was closed until one had proved his worthiness by obtaining full membership status in the congregation, and there would be no modern foolishness such as women suffrage in church matters. In the following year, 1913, the Immanuel Lutheran Church was dedicated.

Of course, the Church of Peace was strongly affected by these actions. A significant block of the believers with a strong Lutheran inclination left for the new church. The remaining members of the congregation decided to continue their open and egalitarian policies. They also began to look favorably at the other strong Protestant movement in Germany and northern Europe–the Reformed Church–which followed the doctrines of John Calvin and Ulrich Zwingly. In time, they dropped all affiliation with the Lutheran Church and became the Friedens Evangelical and Reformed Church. They became the repository of spiritual belief of all Protestants who came to the community who were not Lutherans.

A truly revolutionary event took place when the businessmen decided they were no longer going to be open on Sundays. With some pressure they were able to extend the rule community wide, and their next step was to extend the closing hours to evenings, except for Wednesdays and Saturdays. Many businesses, except Cafes and Taverns, accepted this. The City Council also passed regulations on the sale of liquor in town, and they passed an ordinance requiring that all new buildings or major remodeling in the business district had to use brick or fireproof materials. (All small towns that started in Iowa began with wood frame buildings and many of them did not get beyond this style of architecture.)

The pace of construction was fast in Schleswig. There were at least a dozen building projects, either commercial or residential, going on all the time. Some of the major ones were Dr. Jones' office, the August Rickert grocery store at 116 Cedar Street, the two new auto dealerships: Schleswig Auto Co. at 205 Cedar and the Boysen and Pipgras Garage at 106 Second St. The Christiansen Grocery Store at 202 Cedar Street had a fire which was contained in the building, but Mr. Christiansen decided to rebuild with brick taking one shortcut by attaching the roof to the Krohnke Building next door without a supporting wall. One interesting change took place when Chris Kruse's hardware store, which was a two-story building on the north side of Cedar Street on the west end of the business district, was to be moved to the south side of the street. Part way across the street, the building collapsed. Unfortunately, one of the workmen was fatally injured in the accident, and what was left of the building was picked up and moved to the new location. By now though, it was a single story building.

On the land vacated on the north side of the street, Dr. Schultz built a new home at 100 Cedar Street and a new office building next door at 108 Cedar Street.

Much change was taking place among the business combinations in town. Emil Boock, who had been part of the Boock and Boysen Automobile Agency, left to be replaced by William Pipgras, who had been operating a John Deere implement dealership. Mr. Boock then formed a partnership with Charlie Jurgensen in the Boock and Jurgensen John Deere dealership . They set up shop in the "new" single story building on the south side of Cedar Street and mounted a John Deere horse-drawn walking plow on the top of the false front as an advertizement. This building was later used as a produce station. A new Postmaster, John Nickolsen, took over, and this necessitated a move of the Post Office to the east side of Second Street. Both mail route men were also replaced with appointments by the new Postmaster. Hans Kroeger had only been on the job for a few months, but he had to make way for a new man. Many workers came to town and only stayed a short time and moved on. For instance, Roy Rogers moved in from Minnesota and worked several weeks in the Stock Barber Shop and moved on to Dakota where prospects looked better. Motion pictures were in their infancy but were quite popular whenever they were available. They were first shown in the Opera House and then in various buildings that were available at the time.

Along with other growth, some manufacturing was starting in the area. Johan Kirsch set up a cigar factory at 204 Cedar Street. Detlef and Henry Wieck began a wagon works in the alley behind 210 Cedar Street. A saw mill was set up on the north side of Birch Street across from the dance hall. A cabinet shop was placed in a former photography shop on Birch Street. Albert Schultz opened a tin works in his hardware store where he made specialty pots and pans, such as "Groten Hans" pudding pans and other hard-to-get items. Martin Godbersen set up a cement works behind the Farmers Lumber Yard. Beneficial as all of these projects were, none of them grew beyond individual efforts and did not outlast the owner's participation.

Railroad activities had increased to the point where there were four regularly scheduled trains through town each day. There was a passenger train and a freight train coming through each morning and each afternoon and special excursion trains were also scheduled to take people to the resort at Lake View or to a special event, such as a train from Denison to Schleswig when the German Day celebration was here. The fares were quite reasonable—one could ride to either Ricketts or Kiron for 26 cents.

Crawford County received another distinction in 1913. It received a great boost when the first Transcontinental Railroad laid its tracks down the East Boyer River Valley in 1869. The Transcontinental Railroad was the technological achievement that transformed the entire nation. Then in 1913, Crawford County received the distinction of having the first Transcontinental Highway, the Lincoln Highway (U.S. Highway #30), come through it. The Automobile was the new technological achievement to transform the country, and Crawford County was part of it. The Lincoln Highway was a partially graveled road full of ruts and mud holes, but it grew to become the most direct and accessible route from New York and Chicago to San Francisco.

Festivals were universally popular. These joyful celebrations of the community's way of life and of their accomplishments were anxiously anticipated. The oldest of these festivals in Schleswig was the traditional German Kinderfest held in the Spring. The day was filled with children's activities and dances that were home grown in that the adults organized, supervised, and enjoyed watching. Large communal dinners were common, and in the evening an adult dance was held lasting until the early hours of the morning. Carnivals were not scheduled on a regular basis in Schleswig, but they occurred about once every three years. In 1908, and in 1911, and probably at other times carnivals were here during this period. Unscheduled traveling shows and tent shows came through from time to time and drew a large crowd.

In 1912, the new Commercial Club organized a highly successful two-day Harvest Festival for which two bands and 34 free attractions were hired. The central attraction was a hot air balloon which could rise high over the community. Parachute jumps from the balloon when it was at a 2000 foot level were among the attractions as was a trapeze performance, high wire acts and a contortionist. On the first day, there was a parade of business floats. The wind came up in the evening, however, and rain began to fall. As a result, the evening activities were somewhat curtailed, but the next day the attractions were still there and an automobile parade was held. That evening there was a dance that lasted until morning.

In 1913, a Harvest Festival was again planned. To be sure it would be successful, the Commercial Club organized a series of booster trips to advertise the event. Fourteen carloads of people, including the German Band, visited Battle Creek, Ida Grove, Arthur, Kiron, Deloit, Denison, Charter Oak, and Ricketts. The Festival was again very successful.

The German Day celebration, which was held in October, had always been held in Denison where the Denison Lansverein German Veterans, the Denison German Brotherhood, and the Sons of Hermann in Schleswig where the sponsors. However, in 1914 it was held in Schleswig. The Sons of Hermann Lodge was in charge, but they had the help and support of the Odd Fellows and the Woodmen as well as other community organizations. A special excursion train brought a large number of people from Denison. It was very successful.

Christmas Eve of 1914 brought one of the larger catastrophes the community had experienced thus far. It was a cold and windy night, and the steam heating plant in the pool hall owned by Jurgen Schroeder overheated and caught fire. The fire had a good start before it was noticed. By the time the Fire Department got to the scene, the fire had spread to all three of Schroeder's buildings on the north end of Second Street. Charles Schnoor had a second floor apartment, and he had to be evacuated through a window. The heat from the flames was so intense it cracked windows in the Brick Hotel across the street. Fortunately, the Firemen were able to contain the fire to the buildings that were already on fire, but three buildings were destroyed, leaving a large hole in the business district.

The fire marked the end of an era in Schleswig, but while it was still a growing and dynamic civic center, a new generation was taking over. Albrecht Boock, who had started the town of Morgan, had died in 1908. Jurgen Schroeder was retired. Now, of all the buildings he had moved from Hohenzollern only his house and a horse barn in the alley remained. Many of the early settlers who developed the area and retired to Schleswig were disappearing from the scene.

A new century is starting. There is promise in the air. New ideas, fresh approaches, and interesting inventions are coming faster and faster. No one would have thought it would have turned out this way. Many of the old things will be left behind. Some things that were so well established slipped away while other things that did not seem so important grew large. It might be good to see what is coming, but that is not so important. There are so many interesting things that are happening right now. Who would have thought things would have developed in such strange ways and still worked out? The trick is to keep the good things coming.

VII. OUTSIDE INFLUENCES

1914-1932

A person or a community can exist for years doing its own thing and not be influenced by the outside world. Regional, national, or world events have little if any effect on daily life. Those are just events happening somewhere else. But that can only continue for a certain length of time. Outside events are bound to come tumbling in and change the whole course of events. It is times like this that decisions have to be made and positions taken that can change the way everything will be done, and whole communities are affected in such circumstances. Big events call for major actions. "When, in the course of human events, it becomes necessary for one people to dissolve the bands which have connected them with another, and to assume, among the powers of the earth, the separate and equal station to which the laws of nature and of nature's God entitle them . . . " Old bonds and understandings can change on many levels.

One of the things that seemed very remote and far away in 1914 was the assassination of a minor prince in Sarajevo, Bosnia, and the squabble between the interrelated royal families of Europe. All that had little to do with the price of corn at the Farmers Lumber and Grain elevator or with the value of a good work horse at the livery stable down the street from the bank in Schleswig, Iowa, U.S.A.

In spite of this remote event, there were still numerous local things going on that attracted attention. Dr. Henry Jones, for example, stirred up some local interest when he installed a gasoline-

powered electric generator in the basement of his new office building, giving him the first electrically lighted building in the area.
Unintentionally, he created even more discussion when he struck a
match one day to see what was on a shelf on the stairway only to
discover the basement had filled with gas fumes. The resulting
explosion knocked him back through the doorway and singed his
eyebrows and hair.

There was a general discussion at this time about the old car-
bide gas plant owned by the town. People thought it was just not
adequate and should really be replaced with a new electric power
plant. The Commercial Club was especially in favor of this proposal because they wanted the town to be on the cutting edge of
technology. It was the kind of publicity from which their business
could benefit. They even sent a delegation to the City Council to
initiate the process of making the change, which, of course, eventually did occur.

Despite how much they wanted to ignore them, international
events were intruding into local events. The people of Schleswig
were very much aware of what was happening in Europe because
the *Schleswig Leader* had a regular weekly column entitled "News
from the Fatherland" and many features on national events which
were popular columns and were widely read. Fairly regular arrivals
of new immigrants from Germany explained the current situation
in Europe. That, together with the regular media of the day which
consisted mainly of papers from major metropolitan areas and travelers on the railroad, provided a good survey of world events.

Schleswig residents were cognizant of the fact that the last
three Presidents of the United States–Roosevelt, Taft and now
Wilson–were all strong promoters of the Hague Conferences which
were set up to avoid future wars by providing arbitration to settle
world problems. Building their businesses and farms in a peaceful
and stable situation was their goal in life. But it was not to be. On
July 28, 1914, Austria declared war on Serbia. Within two weeks,
every country in Europe had declared war on each other. Considering the colonies, possessions, and alliances of these countries, it

very nearly became a world wide war. The United States was one of the very few countries that was not involved and was remaining neutral.

The people of Schleswig with their strong ties to Germany wished the German armies well but strongly supported the United States' position of neutrality. They watched the activities closely but did not want to become directly involved. In these early days of the war, the only direct action on the local front was that a fund drive was able to raise nearly $1000.00 for the German Red Cross by the end of 1914, the money to go for the benefit of the German casualties of the war. Similar efforts were made for the next several years.

The mood in the United States shifted back and forth between the two sides in the war. The United States, since it was neutral, was free to trade with both sides and with other neutral countries. Great Britain, which had been acknowledged as the dominant sea power in the world for the last generation, declared a boycott of all militarily useful material to its enemies. It planned to enforce its boycott by stopping ships at sea and inspecting the cargo or requiring ships to stop at British ports for inspections. The U. S. protested this violation of its neutrality position causing a great deal of tension between the United States and Great Britain.

Germany, on the other hand, since it could not match the strength of the British Navy, began developing a fleet of submarines. The rules of sea warfare required a warship to give warning and to allow a ship carrying contraband to evacuate ship before it was sunk and afterward it was to pick up survivors. A submarine could not do so. If it surfaced to give warning, it could easily be destroyed by a war ship and its effectiveness would be annihilated. It had to attack by surprise with torpedoes from below the surface, and it did not have the room to house survivors.

On May 7, 1915, a German submarine sank the *Lusitania*. More than a hundred of the 1200 casualties were Americans. President Wilson and all Americans were outraged. The President demanded that all attacks on ships carrying Americans be stopped and reparations be paid for the damages, but Germany was slow to respond. Harsher and more restrictive measures were then demanded. This movement was headed off by Secretary of State William Jennings Bryan, who resigned rather than put the U. S. in a position that would force it into the war. William Jennings Bryan was a frequent visitor to Crawford County, especially in the home of J. B. Romans in Denison.

In Schleswig, everyone was keeping an uneasy eye on the happenings in Europe. Nevertheless, the rapid rate of local development continued. The International Order of Odd Fellows lodge announced they intended to build a huge new meeting hall on the site of the former Schroeder store building on the corner of Birch and Second Streets. It was going to be a two-story, $10,000.00 building with an entire second story to be used as a large open meeting room, and the first floor was to be utilized as commercial rental property. It would be an impressive improvement since it would cover in part the hole in the business district created by the massive Christmas Eve fire. This stirred interest for additional building. The Palace Movie Theater was constructed at 105 Second Street by John Krohnke. Between the Odd Fellows Hall and the Theater, Will Schroeder constructed a brick building which became a pool hall. The concept of attaching a roof to an adjoining building without a supporting wall was again tried for the theater, and it worked for some time.

The City Council let the contract for the building of an electric power generating plant and a brick building to be constructed at 114 Ash Street next to the alley. The construction was under the direction of Superintendent Herman Fust. When it was completed, a specialist was brought in for final testing. John Jakso, a recent immigrant from Austria, had been working his way up in a major New York electrical firm. Concerns for his health forced him into an open air environment, so when the plant was tested and operational, Mr. Jakso agreed to stay and accepted the position as plant manager.

The plant began operation on September 23, 1915. It had both a 50-horsepower and a 75-horsepower generator which operated smoothly and efficiently. Thirty-five electric street lights were erected in the business district and surrounding area. The rates were relatively high, approximately 20 cents per kilowatt hour and, as a result, electric use was reserved for lighting purposes only. Coincidentally, the Palace Theater opened the same week.

The newest thing in criminal activity was the theft of harness. A number of farmers in the area were victims of these thefts. Marshal John Berndt went to Dunlap to confer with the Sheriff of Harrison County where there also had been a number of thefts reported. Notes were compared, and it was concluded that a young drifter by the name of Logan Maxin had been in both communities at about the right times. An alert for him was sent out, and he was arrested in Norfolk, Nebraska, and returned to this area. He was put on trial, found guilty, and sentenced to the penitentiary for five years.

Normally, though, the people of Schleswig were quite forgiving of their fellow citizens who showed evidence of repentance. The horse thief in Goodrich township was tolerated as long as he stayed on the straight and narrow. The Schroeder who was the gunman in the shooting at the dance hall returned to town after a few years and lived a quiet life. Hugo Wiegand, the hotel manager, who left town at the time of the firemen's picnic returned some years later, held the office of City Marshal for a time, and was even elected Mayor for a term.

But not everything that happened was of a serious nature. Earl Hart, a local farmhand, took his best girl to a dance one night and while they were occupied with the festivities, someone tied the reins to one of the buggy shafts, making them ineffective in controlling the horse. When the young couple came out and Mr. Hart was helping his lady friend into the buggy, the horse began walking off. He quickly grabbed the reins and hollered which only spooked the horse, which ran off and soon dumped the buggy in a ditch, throwing the young lady out. Fortunately, no one was seriously injured. Mr. Hart spent the next several weeks closely checking out his "friends."

Several additional recreational activities were started. In addition to the Palace Movie Theater, a bowling alley was set up, and a roller skating rink was opened on Cedar Street, probably at 206 Cedar. It became one of the more popular attractions in town.

An action by the Iowa State Legislature was not popular in Schleswig. The legislature repealed the Mulct Act which controlled saloon operation. With the Mulct Act overturned, the law reverted to the 1884 Prohibition Act which it had amended. The result was that all saloons in the state were to be closed down on January 1, 1916. Iowa entered the Prohibition Era years before the rest of the country! The Krohnke Saloon was the last to close, closing at 8:00 P.M. on December 30, having exhausted its inventory. The dejected clients quietly went home. After the first of the year, the Krohnke saloon was remodeled and opened as a Candy Kitchen.

The Schleswig baseball team, managed by Jimmy Schultz, was a popular and widely supported activity. They had an active schedule and a spirited attitude, although their record was not entirely perfect. Some of the main players were Eddie Schroeder, Ed Lehman, Julius and John Rohwer, and young George Pipgras in center field. A large number of young men played on the team at one time or another and many residents enjoyed the games. Barney Boysen's 18-passenger Avery car was the team bus for many years.

Rudy Schuman, generally known as "Schumy," was one of the players on the ball team, but his regular occupation was that of being a crank artist in the projection room at the Palace Movie Theater. After one ball game in which Schleswig played a team from Fort Dodge at the Cottage Grove field near Lake View, Schumy wrote his name and address on a slip of paper, enclosed it in a bottle and cast it far out into Black Hawk Lake. He soon forgot all about the note, but several months later he received a letter from a farmer's daughter from near Carroll. She had found his note and wrote to him giving her name and address. He showed the letter to several of his friends, and, in no time, the entire town knew about the incident, and everyone was offering him advice on how to proceed with this romance. Embarrassed by the attention, he ignored all of the advice.

Another star ball player was Eddie Schroeder. Being no slouch with a pool cue, either, he was known as Schleswig's boy pool shark. He seemed like an ordinary player until there was some action on the side. Then his game improved dramatically. He was given the nickname "Slick" Schroeder. Some people said the nickname came from the fact that his clothes were often slick from paint which he had acquired in his day job of house painting. Those were the people who had not seen him run the table at eightball.

Other happenings at the time included: the City Council approved a public water fountain in front of the Baxter Brothers Bank; in Grant Township, Will Rogers trapped a wolf northwest of town, the first seen in years, and when he turned it in to the county for a $20.00 bounty, it created quite a stir for a while; Henry Boysen broke open a chunk of coal and found a fossilized fish inside. It was quite detailed and also created quite a bit of interest. The speed limit in town was raised to 15 miles per hour. To show they really meant business, the Council put the penalty for speeding as a fine of up to a $100.00.

The Council contracted to have the water tower cleaned and checked hiring Albert Schultz, a local hardware dealer, as the contractor. He hired a crew to do the work, and when they were finished, he climbed into the tank at the top of the tower to inspect the work. He slipped and fell into the tank, breaking his hip in three places, fractured three ribs, injuring one arm and cutting his head. He was not in good shape, and it was very difficult to get him down. John Schmidt from the blacksmith shop across the street helped to attach him to brace boards. He was hoisted out of the tank with blocks and tackle and then lowered to the ground, a process which took five hours. He survived and healed, but it was an experience he never forgot.

The old city gas generating plant which had been replaced by the electric plant was dismantled and sold to Albert Schultz who bought the equipment for salvage. The office building and storage building at 401 Cedar Street was sold to the telephone company which used the buildings as a service center for their linemen.

One of the most active businessmen in Schleswig, William Pipgras, sold his business on April 25, 1916, and moved his family to Anthon. In the more than ten years he had been in business in Schleswig he had run a saloon for three years, an implement dealership for three years, a car dealership for a year, managed the Brick Hotel for two years and operated a meat market for a year and a half. The Pipgras' had four sons—George, Henry, Fred and Ed, and a daughter Amanda. Their active life style was missed.

By now, Germany resumed its submarine warfare. It did so cautiously, but casualties were inevitable, and a few of them were Americans. Anti-German sentiments mushroomed across the nation. In February, President Wilson severed diplomatic relations with Germany. In March, the U.S. Secret Service set up a nationwide network of offices. Their purpose was to identify and track any aliens or foreign-born citizens whose loyalty may be suspect. Of course, our German community was very apprehensive. One such office was opened in Des Moines, and their investigations were conducted in complete secrecy.

At the end of March of 1917, the Cabinet advised the President to request a Declaration of War from Congress. On April 2, he made the request and within four days it passed both houses of Congress, and the President signed it on April 6, 1917. We were at war with Germany.

The Declaration of War included provisions which made it a crime to give aid, comfort, or information to the enemy. It entreated the population to maintain a high standard of patriotism, and it made a call for volunteers. It also provided for the issuance of War Bonds to help support the effort.

In Iowa, Governor William Harding issued an edict requiring only the English language be spoken in public and private schools, in conversation on trains, in all public places, and in all telephone conversations, in public addresses and in all church services. Those who could not speak English could worship at home. Using the

English language was a sign of patriotism. The edict was denounced by fair-minded people everywhere and was declared unconstitutional by the Supreme Court, but that took time.

In Schleswig, there was a great deal of concern with the turn of events. The German people were very proud of their heritage, were also very patriotic and took their vows of citizenship to the United States seriously. They resented the implication that because they wished to maintain their cultural heritage they were in some way unpatriotic. They also realized it was difficult to express this position. Any attempt seemed defensive and counter productive. But overtly expressed or not, there was a stubborn pride in maintaining as much of their German background as possible.

The first person from Schleswig to volunteer for the Armed Services was Rudolf Schuman; "Schumy," the son of Gustav and Theodora Grill Schuman. On April 26, 1917, he enlisted and was assigned to the Sioux City Ambulance Company Number One. His act was 'hitting home' and War Bonds were readily subscribed to in the community.

A number of people were arrested in Iowa for making subversive statements. One of them was from Manilla, but none were from Schleswig. The anti-German sentiment was intensifying. German names on public places were being changed to more Anglicized identification. Even the royal family in England changed its name from the House of Hanover to Windsor, but Schleswig resisted such changes. One exception was the German Bank which was owned by the Crawford County State Bank in Denison. One of the officers was former Congressman and Judge James Conner, who decided to change the name to the Commercial Bank of Schleswig. The News from the Fatherland column also disappeared from the Schleswig Leader. In Scott County, where many people in this area had friends and relatives, five housewives were arrested for speaking German on a country telephone party line, and they were fined $225.00. A number of people around the state were forced to salute the flag or to kiss it.

A draft law was enacted and a registrar was assigned to each voting district. It was a criminal offense not to register, and the sign-up went without a hitch in this area. The enlistments were going very strong. Some of those who enlisted were John Rohwer, Herbert "Hap" Peters, Lawrence Bly, and Ted Lohse. A few people like Henry Iwen needed the inducement of a draft notice. Dr. Jones spent much of his time in Denison serving as one of the doctors providing military-induction medical examinations.

Campaigns were initiated to save materials of all kinds to increase the resources available for the war effort, and a concern about a possible food shortage caused farmers to be given preference for a number of scarce materials. Farmers were encouraged to put every possible acre into production. Commodity price supports were being considered, and the demand for many products increased significantly. Farm products especially saw a sudden surge in demand and in price. Corn went from 60 cents a bushel in 1916 to $1.02 in 1917, $1.40 in 1918, $1.80 in 1919. Hogs went from $9.00 per head in 1916 to $15.00 in 1917, $24.00 in 1918 and $27.50 in 1919. All other commodities had a similar rise. In future years, when farm programs were discussed, these years were the standard to which the new programs aspired. They were known as the parity years.

At this time, Iowa Senator William Kenyon sponsored a bill that would exempt liquor from the protection of interstate commerce laws meaning that liquor could not legally be sent from a wet state into a dry state by train or other public conveyance, nor could private individuals order liquor for their own personal consumption. A proposed amendment to the Constitution of the United States on this issue was slowly working its way across the country. When put to a vote locally, Schleswig voted 200 nay to 15 in favor of the amendment. The national movement would curtail the consumption of liquor, but in Schleswig many people continued to brew their own beer.

The Crawford County National Guard was called up and ordered to report to the Ida Grove Armory to be regrouped and sent on for training. Some ninety cars of supporters conducted them to their destination and when they paused in Schleswig they were greeted by Theodore Rohwer, Peter Hollander and some 300 other citizens. An additional 24 carloads of supporters joined the procession and arrived at Ida Grove, unannounced and to the surprise of the residents, putting on a parade of 114 cars of cheering patriotic supporters, the Denison band, the Schleswig band, and National Guard performing a close order drill. Such shows of support for those military inductees being sent off to fight the "war to end all wars" became fairly common place.

Schleswig's resistance to denouncing its German heritage generated resentment in other parts of the county. For instance, one man from Charter Oak filed a complaint against the Schleswig school, saying they were flying the German flag under the American flag on the school flag pole. County Superintendent of Schools Olry had been the Superintendent of Schools in Schleswig for years and had many friends here. He absolutely could not believe the report but had to check it out. He found there was a flag under the American flag, but it was the Class of 1917 pendant. There was also a report in Ida Grove that the German flag was being flown on the City flag pole which was located in the center of the intersection at Cedar and Second Streets. That report, too, had no merit. However, there was one flag in the county that did create a controversy. The German Landsverein Veterans Society in Denison had for years proudly displayed a special flag presented to them by the German government. It was very ornate and displayed some intricate needle work. A number of highly patriotic citizens wanted passionately to find that flag and burn it, but somehow it had disappeared. Repeated attempts could not locate the ensconced article which did reemerge after the war. It had been a mattress liner in several sympathetic homes during the hostilities.

Massive efforts were made to put the American economy on a war time status. Governmental agencies were given extraordinary powers to regulate whole industries. Daylight-saving time was introduced to save on electrical energy. Military training programs were put into high gear. The Axis Powers, at the same time, were putting out extra efforts with Germany disseminating the Russian and Italian forces, thus freeing up the troops on these fronts. Their next step was to make a massive effort to break through the western front before the American troops could arrive there.

On the home front, a meeting was held in Schleswig in 1918, in the Palace Theater, to discuss the question whether Schleswig should change its name. Former Congressman, Judge Conner, was there to explain the procedure should the community decide to take the step. The meeting had been precipitated by several recent occurrences. Several weeks earlier, Marshal Maurice Nielsen from Denison, acting for the County Council of Defense, came and posted signs against the use of a foreign language. A large crowd gathered, and he was told to take the signs back down. He refused. No action was taken, but tensions ran very high until he left for home. The other incident was that the Chicago Northwestern Railroad, which was under governmental control, issued a new time schedule in which Schleswig was not named but merely identified as No. 18. Holstein had also not been named but designated No. 16. Mayor Jimmy Schultz opened the discussion by saying it looked like the government did not like the name Schleswig and wanted to know the feelings of the people. A spirited debate resulted, and the outcome was an overwhelming consensus to keep the name. No official vote was taken, so the critics would not have a peg on which to base an argument.

Word of this decision was not well accepted in some parts of the county. A group was forming in Dow City, a town across the county, to make a raid on Schleswig in which they were going to change the name, stop the speaking of German, and make the people into good Americans—all in one fell swoop. They had already forced the *Denison Herold* to stop printing its paper in German. They came in a caravan of a dozen Model T's with each car carrying four to six determined men in dark hats and overalls, holding a shotgun or a rifle. As they drove up the main street, there was no one in sight, with the exception of one man. On a stand by the new 60-foot flagpole that had just been erected in the main intersection stood Jimmy Schultz, the mayor of Schleswig, waiting for them.

When the men pulled up, the mayor gathered them together and began to speak. He welcomed them to town and said he understood their concerns, but he wanted to explain some things. He said that while the people here were proud of their German heritage, they had come to start a new life in this country and were loyal Americans. To demonstrate this, he listed the young men who had enlisted in the armed services. He then listed the names and number of people in the community who had invested in war bonds. He challenged them to produce as good a record in their communities. As the Mayor spoke, the men from Dow City began to notice that from every window, every doorway, over every fence and from every alley, there was a gun barrel pointed at them. As the mayor finished, he thanked them for their visit and wished them a pleasant trip home. The men from Dow City thought that was a good idea and quietly left.

The community had been warned about the arrival of the delegation. Dr. Walter Schultz, the mayor's brother, had received a phone call from a friend in Dunlap warning of the intentions of the raiders. He had alerted the community. In Grant Township, a twenty-four-hour watch was set up to protect the Grant Church. The Ernst family played a large part in this effort.

One incident did not turn out well, however. Elmer Watson had been the mail carrier on Rural Route 2 out of Schleswig for five or six years. He also ran a popcorn and peanut wagon on the streets of Schleswig when there was any kind of activity going on. He was well known and generally well liked, but when the war progressed, he became very strongly patriotic and took strong stands against the use of the German language and was strident about changing the name of the town. He lost many friends and over time became ostracized. As he became more and more opinionated, he began to be harassed. It was thought he had been making negative reports to the County Council on Defense. One night his house, his barn and the mail wagon were all splashed with yellow paint. When his complaints were not received with much sympathy, he decided for the safety of his family to get out of the community. He moved to Denison and ran the Railroad Express office there for many years.

Not all of the activities at this time involved the war, however. Chris Lafranz and Barney Boysen built a new automobile showroom and garage for the Schleswig Auto Company, located on the corner of Birch and Second Street. It was a huge brick building that could hold up to 50 cars. Clarence Chamberlin of Denison came to set up an extension of his agency to sell Diamond tires. Mayor Schultz could be seen on Sunday mornings grading the streets in town with a road drag attached to the rear of his car.

The Spanish influenza epidemic of 1918 was the most serious health problem in the memory of most people in the community. It was a worldwide epidemic of catastrophic proportions–was very contagious and serious enough to cause a large number of fatalities. More than 400 people in the Schleswig community were afflicted with the disease. Some families were hit harder than others by the epidemic; for example, in the Hans Lohse family four adults, Carl, Johannas, Anna and sister-in-law, Mary Tamm, all died within a two week period. Carl Lohse left a wife and three small children: Elvera (Hollander), Mary Ellen (Marquardt), and Elwin. The exact number of deaths is not certain because a number of the people who died were buried in the countryside in family grave plots on the farm, an action taken in an effort to minimize the spread of the disease. The location of many of these graves has been lost, although it is known that there was one in Section 12 of Morgan Township, and there were at least two in Section 27 of Otter Creek Township and many more. A number of business places were restricted in their operations or were quarantined to keep the spread of the disease under control. While much concern was directed toward our boys serving in Europe, the disease was causing a great deal of devastation on the home front.

American troops began to trickle into Europe in late 1917. Their numbers grew quickly in 1918. The plan was to provide additional training behind the lines and to have the Americans fight as a separate army. The tremendous pressure of the German army fouled these plans, and as a result, Americans were rushed to help hold the battle lines as soon as possible. By May of 1918, the Americans were making major contributions to the war effort. By the end of July, the German advances were stopped and, gradually under heavy fighting, they were being pushed back. They retreated grudgingly, and it was a long, hard series of battles, but by November they had given up much of their gains. By then, the German nation was demoralized and rebellious. A naval revolt in Kiel triggered widespread demonstrations which lead to the collapse of the German government. The Kaiser was forced to flee, and the new government agreed to an armistice on November 11, 1918. The World War was over.

There were celebrations all over the country, for everyone was happy the hostilities were over. Our boys were no longer being killed. The relief and exhilaration were double in Schleswig. Not only were the boys safe but also the pressure on the home front was over. Four Schleswig boys had lost their lives during the conflict—Henry Braase, Erhard Michaelsen, Emil Bendixen, and John Jacobsen. As it turned out, the loss of lives from the Spanish Flu was much greater than that of the war. Dozens of people had lost their lives to the disease.

The new national income tax that had been enacted in 1913 had not had much impact on this area in the first years. As income grew, however, due to the wartime increase in prices, more and more people found themselves subject to a tax. Anyone with more than $2000.00 net income had to file an income tax form. For example, the following figures were taken from the 1917 tax return of a farmer tilling a quarter a section of land.

Income from sale of Livestock and Grain	$6815.25
Expenses: Labor	$400.00
Livestock bought for resale	$926.25
Interest	$141.30
Taxes	$129.00
Insurance	$37.00
Threshing	$75.00
Casualty Losses	$100.00
Depreciation	$489.00
Total Expenses	*$2297.55*
Net Profit	$4517.70
Less Contributions and Exemptions	*$2260.00*
Taxable Income	$2257.70
Tax Due at 2 percent rate	$45.15
Plus Wartime Surtax of $5.15 = Total Income Tax	$50.30

This was at a time when a living wage was considered to be $600.00 to $700.00 per year. What is also interesting to note is the ratio of income to expenses. The costs of operating a farm were only a third of the income it produced. Many farmers had a banker or a lawyer help them fill out their tax returns, and the Internal Revenue Service also provided agents to help fill out the returns. An agent was available in the Courthouse in Denison, and, in 1919, they even had an agent in Schleswig at the Schultz Pharmacy. Farm profits were huge and staying high.

There was a movement to start a third bank in Schleswig. Both banks here now were owned by out-of-town interests. The Baxter Brothers Bank was owned by people from Ida Grove, and the Commercial Bank was owned by the Crawford County State Bank in Denison. It was thought that a locally-owned bank should be organized because it would better reflect the interests of the local community. A bank was organized, the stock was sold, and capitalized at $60,000.00. Building an office was considered but before construction could begin, the new bank had entered a deal to buy out the Baxter Brothers Bank. Business was continued in that building under the new name–Farmers State Bank. Theodore Rohwer, who had been the cashier for the Baxter Brothers Bank, stayed and became the president of the new Bank.

A committee was set up to organize special homecoming celebration for the return of the servicemen. When they received word that the last serviceman, Sailor Ben Naeve, was scheduled to return, the dates of September 3 and 4, 1919, were set for the festivities. It was a gala celebration starting with a very long parade including the Westside Band and 150 service men in uniform providing a demonstration in close order marching. There were speeches by Mayor Jimmy Schultz, by a well-known speaker, Carl F Kuehnle of Denison, and by several others. Balloon ascensions and parachute jumps took place during the day, but an evening ball game was rained out. On the second day, The Des Moines Concert Band preformed and a second parade was held. There was ring riding, and a tug-of-war between Ida County and Crawford County(won by Crawford County) and a ball game between Denison and Ida Grove (Ida Grove won). Mayor Jimmy Schultz pulled off a surprise attraction. He had proposed to Alice Miner, a nurse from Omaha, and when she accepted, he asked if she would mind getting married during the celebration. She assented, and he quietly made the arrangements. At 3:30 in the afternoon he added a new feature to the program. He announced his wedding and brought forth the parties. Jimmy and Alice were married on the stage in the middle of the main intersection by the city flag pole before a surprised and delighted crowd of 8000 people. That evening there was a magnificent display of fireworks including many special feature display groupings on which well over a thousand dollars had been spent. The service men had been welcomed back in grand style. The good spirits lasted for some time after the event.

Nick Vollersen had been the manager of the Green Bay Lumber Company for a number of years. He was well liked, and a good operator, and he had always been an active promoter of the town. In November of 1919, he and his brother Chris bought out Herman Grill's huge Independent Lumber Yard in Denison and moved to Denison to operate it. Needless to say, he was missed in our community. This was also the year that Hans Behrmann and his father-in-law, Johannes Lorenzen, bought out the August Rickert grocery store, renaming it Behrmann and Company. Three major grocery stores in town–Behrmann's, Stoltenberg's and Christensen's–as well as, a variety of meat markets and produce stations were able to keep our citizens well supplied.

John Bendixen and Bernhard Evers had bought Claus Gottburg's furniture store known as the Store Next Door at 119 Second Street several years before. At this time they had a Christmas promotion in which a large part of the lower floor was converted to a children's section displaying a large number of toys. On a Saturday several weeks before Christmas, Santa Claus would come to visit with the children. He would arrive by way of a rope-operated freight elevator from the upper reaches the building. Each child would receive a box of animal crackers from Santa. The event became so successful they became concerned about the safety because of the pressure from the crowd in their building. The owners approached the Commercial Club to see if they wanted to participate in the promotion and to move it outside. The Commercial Club was glad to be involved in such a successful promotion, so in approximately 1920, Santa Claus arrived by coming down Second Street in a Model T truck to a stand by the flag pole in the central intersection. The crowd of youngsters and their parents blocked the streets in all directions. The original gift to the children of animal crackers expanded to a paper bag filled with peanuts, fruit, candy and Cracker Jacks. It has become a tradition to which the children of the community have looked forward with anticipation ever since.

Above: Dr. Henry Jones by his office and his driver Rudy Schuman.
Below: Veterans preparing for WWI Homecoming Celebration parade in 1919.

Wedding of Jimmy Schultz and Alice Miner on the City
Square before a crowd of 8000.

For entertainment a number of the young men of the town
began gathering in the Wood Hotel on Sunday afternoons where
they enjoyed a good game of cards and some lively conversation.
Gradually the card games took on a more sporting air, and gambling became the central activity. Some of the more prudish citizens heard about it and complained to Mayor Henry Boysen who
thought it was his civic duty to send the Marshal in to shut the
games down. The young men including Ted Lohse, Rudy
Schumann, the Peters brothers, and the Backhaus boys were in-
censed, and as a result spent the next several days telling everyone
what a rotten person Henry Boysen was and no one should do
business with him. The boys got very little sympathy, and no one
paid too much attention to their complaints, but the games did
not continue–at least, not in the hotel.

Residents of the young town who had relied on a system of
outhouses were beginning to agitate for a sewer system for the

town, so the City Council contacted an engineer to see what could be done. Without a natural outlet like a river to drain it into, it was determined to be too expensive for the current city budget, so outhouses continued to be in existence.

Farm income was so high that even medium-sized farms were making their operators wealthy. Farmers were proud of what they had accomplished and lived better than anyone would have imagined. They loved to display their position with new cars, new equipment, and new buildings. A long tradition in the area evolved that if one wanted a quick start on the road to wealth, inherit a farm. It also made farmers' daughters very popular because they came with a sizeable dowery.

In addition to the demands of the war, there developed the needs of the millions of people in Europe whose lives had been disrupted by the warfare. Wide spread famine and starvation were taking place, so President Wilson set up the American Relief Administration to alleviate the suffering. He appointed former Iowa boy, Herbert Hoover, to head the effort. He did a fantastic job and saved thousands of lives. He accomplished the feat with American food products, thus helping to keep farm prices up.

The increased farm income was also reflected in what interested people were willing to pay for farmland. Prices went on an upward spiral that matched the earlier rise in farm income. Before the World War, the price of farmland had been $100.00 per acre or less. By 1919, farms were selling for $200.00 an acre–then $300.00. In the early 1920's, the prices went to $400.00 and then to $500.00. There was even some land that went for $600.00 an acre and more. It was claimed that this was a new era. There was a new basis for valuing land, and the prices would continue to go higher and higher. The old rules based on productivity did not apply anymore. After all, there was a limited amount of land, and God was not making any more. What there was would just keep growing in value.

Warren Harding and the Republicans won the 1920 elections. They balked at ratifying the peace treaty, would not accept the

League of Nations, proposed crippling demands on Germany and wanted to impose heavy tariffs which would restrict trade. Herbert Hoover was appointed to be Secretary of Commerce, and without his leadership the relief effort floundered, and with it, the demand for food products. Price supports that had been in effect during the war were also discontinued and the other markets in the world were still in disarray. On the other hand, farm production was running in high gear, putting out massive amounts of food. Supply began to outrun demand, and prices for farm products were dropping faster than they had gone up. Corn went from $1.68 in 1920 to .47 cents in 1921 and .41 cents in 1922. However, land prices remained strong.

When there are problems in farm country, a new farm organization usually comes into being. It seems to happen every fifteen years or so. First there was the Grange, and then the Farm Bureau. This time the Farmers Union became the dominant group. Its first efforts were to try to help market farm products. Commission-selling services at the major livestock exchanges such as the Omaha and Sioux City Stockyards were established. John L. Lewis, the noted labor leader, spoke to the farmers in Schleswig encouraging them to form such a union. Farm supply services were set up, one such outlet being located at 103 Second Street in Schleswig. It was not well managed, however, and was relatively short lived. The Farmers Union was more successful at some of their lobbying projects. They sponsored some laws favorable to agriculture, and pressured the railroad to grant more favorable rates for livestock transportation and to provide equal rates for small producers and large operators. On many of these boards Schleswig was allowed two representatives. The farmers west of town were represented by Andrew Clausen, Sr. and those east of town by Louie Grill. The rail rates issue was an especially important issue to the farmers around Schleswig, for our farmers had always been strong exporters of livestock. It was not uncommon for Schleswig to send out, in season, from ten to twenty-five train cars of cattle and hogs a week—an obvious reason for better rail rates.

Prohibition had created a new industry but not a legal one—the distillation of liquor. The demand for alcoholic beverages was strong, and where there is a need, there is going to be a supply developing. Federal agent Sumner J. Knox was assigned to combat the problem in this area. He had some success in the Denison area closing down several small bootleg operations. He did locate one substantial operation southwest of Schleswig operated by an immigrant farmer who had run a distillation operation in the old country. Strangely, the illegal nature of alcoholic consumption made it more appealing to many. A number of people who would have otherwise been moderate consumers in ordinary times became compulsive addicts and alcohol was not that hard to obtain.

The *Schleswig Leader* changed hands in 1923. The new publisher, Percy Lyon, came all the way from Cedar Falls to take over the paper. He was running into some new competition because at this time a new media—radio—was becoming popular. New stations were popping up everywhere. Market news could be obtained from WNAX in Yankton, South Dakota; music from WOI in Ames, Iowa; audio homemakers from KMA in Shenandoah, Iowa, and it wasn't long before the airways gave rise to a new form of entertainment—the soap opera. The early radio stations were not stand-alone operations—they were sponsored by seed companies and nurseries to promote their products or by large city newspapers to expand their reach.

This was also the year, in which the Daughters of the American Revolution decided to commemorate the fact that Abraham Lincoln had once owned a farm in Crawford County. The land—five miles south and one mile east of Schleswig—was owned by Jurgen Jepsen. A large boulder was moved to the roadside, and a plaque commemorating the fact of Lincoln's ownership was mounted on that boulder.

The school system was operating smoothly. Athletics was rather low key. Games were scheduled between local schools of similar size—Kiron, Deloit, and Charter Oak. One basketball game of note occurred between Schleswig and Kiron. Kiron won, which was good, because when young Bob Lyon was sent in as a substitute, the kid he replaced did not realize it was he who was supposed to leave the game. For most of a quarter, a six-man team was playing a five-man team, and no one seemed to notice. When Kiron won anyway, no one protested.

At the time of the twenty-fifth anniversary of the town in 1924, Schleswig had a set of statistics of which it could be proud. In the history of the town, they had never had a single person go on welfare. No Schleswig citizen had ever been confined in the county jail. No one from Schleswig had been granted a petition for divorce. It was a record in which they took pride and which reflected well on the local social controls. There were interesting times ahead, however, and this peaceful reputation would prove difficult to maintain.

Word was received that a former resident was making a name for himself. George Pipgras had been a promising baseball player on the Schleswig ball team. We have noted that his father, William Pipgras, moved to Anthon, and the family moved with him. From there they moved to Slayton, Minnesota. George had served in the war, and after it was over, he played ball for a local team being good enough to attract the attention of professional scouts. He played for a regional team in Sioux Falls, and his contract was picked up by the Boston Red Socks. He had made it to the major league professional teams!!

By now more problems were developing on the farm. The new rules governing the value of farmland did not seem to work well when the commodity prices were not there to support them. People just could not afford to pay the high prices for land when they were barely getting break-even prices for their products, so land prices started to slip and the speculative bubble in land prices burst. The value of land eventually dropped to below $100 an acre, and it took more than forty years for it to recover its record levels. Fortunes that had been made in the war years were now being lost. The speculators were the first to feel the pinch. Dr. Schultz was one who had speculated in farmland, and he lost a fortune. He practiced medicine in Schleswig for another twenty years, but he was never again considered a particularly wealthy man. He was not alone in this fate. Many people lost a lot of money when the land values dropped.

In 1923, the Teapot Dome scandal broke and revealed massive bribe-taking in handling the nation's oil reserves. When that scandal broke, even more fraud was uncovered. Charles Forbes had taken $250,000,000.00 from the Veteran's Bureau. Thomas Miller authorized $7,000,000.00 in illegal payments. Attorney General Harry Dougherty took bribes from organized crime in prohibition cases. There seemed to be no end to the graft. The Harding administration was the most corrupt government since the days of the Grant administration. The Republican Party was saved only by the death of President Harding on August 2, 1923, before the election, and by the appearance of the fresh, clean face of New England conservative Calvin Coolidge.

The falling land prices and the low farm commodity prices were taking their toll on Denison banks. The McHenry banks–the National Bank of Denison, the Traders Bank of Vail and the Bank of Dow City–closed and went into receivership. Over a dozen additional banks in the county were in serious trouble for they had made loans on the high values of land and crops, and now the values had dropped below the loaned amounts. However, it was thought too many banks were closing too easily and too soon, thus cutting off depositors to maintain bank assets. The most prominent banker in Denison was C.L. Voss of the Bank of Denison. When that bank failed, Mr. Voss was indicted for forgery and convicted and sentenced to ten years in jail. When there was a run on the Crawford County State Bank, they were able to find the cash to meet the demands. There was a brief threat to Commercial Bank in Denison, but the bulk of the worry was past. The Schleswig banks had remained strong through this crisis and enjoyed the support of the community.

The Fraternal scene in Schleswig was changing. The Sons of Hermann Lodge did not survive the anti-German sentiment prior to the World War and the Woodmen of America had waned. It was the International Order of Odd Fellows that came on strong. Their lodge hall, which dominated Second Street, became the social center of town. Their women's auxiliary, the Rebekahs, was formed July 23, 1925, with Elma Stoltenberg as Grand Noble, Emma Behrmann as Vice Noble, Edith Kroeger as Secretary, and Augusta von Doren as Treasurer. The men's group had over a hundred members in 1927 under the leadership of Hugo Kroeger as Grand Noble. Both organizations had very active social schedules.

The American Legion had been founded by American soldiers during the occupation of Europe after the war and had grown rapidly in this country. Many of the towns in Crawford County had developed chapters—Chapter 179 was started in Schleswig in 1919 with John Rohwer in charge. The first military funeral was for Henry Braase, the first World War I casualty from Schleswig, who had died in France in 1918. He was returned home in 1920 and was reburied with full military honors in the Morgan Cemetery. As the years passed, interest in military affairs diminished, and the Legion Post surrendered its charter in 1926.

Traveling carnival shows provided much of the entertainment during the summer months. They came in all sizes, large and small, providing all kinds of attractions and moving on in a few days probably never to be seen again. There were freak shows, animal shows, circus type acts and, occasionally, even a girlie show. Usually there was very little reaction to these visits, but on one occasion it was noted that several prominent young businessmen soon thereafter visited the Mayo Clinic to consult about the medical implications of social interaction.

In Schleswig, the pressure for a new sewer system was making itself felt again, and this time the City Council was willing to look seriously at the matter. The more they discussed it, the more they came to the conclusion that if they were going to dig up the streets to put in the new sewer lines, extending the water mains and hard surfacing the streets at the same time would only be logical. It would be a massive construction project that would affect the entire town. Engineers were hired to develop plans for the project.

Building a sewer system would have to overcome a number of problems. Water drains away from town in four different directions, and not one system could accommodate all the drain areas. The larger drain area was to the southeast, and since there was no river or stream to carry away the discharge, a treatment plant would have to be built. It was decided that the best place for one would be a quarter of a mile downstream from the city well which was in the southeast corner of the town. This plan would accommodate the part of town east of the tracks almost as far north as the town was currently developed.

The business district was on the west side of the tracks, however, as well as a significantly sized residential district. To connect these residents to the sewer system, a crossover main would have to be buried forty to fifty feet deep at the point where it went under the railroad tracks to provide the right degree of drop. A difficult project, but that was the only way it could be accomplished.

The decision had been made to hard surface the whole town at one time. What type of surface to use proved to be a problem. A number of towns had used paving brick–a traditional and durable material. Some advocated using concrete which was less costly and smoother. Then the Council heard of a proposal that advocated the use of a new system call Warrenite Bithulictic Compound. It was composed of a concrete pan set well below street level. The pan would be filled with a compound composed largely of coal tar pitch and an aggregate composed of 3-inch chunks of Sioux Quartzite. It had the advantages of being soft enough to be easy on horses' hoofs and to be quiet enough to make the rumble of a farm wagon easy on human ears and to be very long lasting. Convinced that it was the best product on the market at the time, the Council decided to give it a try.

The bids were let and the Western Asphalt Company from Sioux City got the contract. The company began the project in

1925 and would take at least two years to complete the work. They brought in a crew of largely Negro workmen. The only Negro who had ever lived in Schleswig before was a chef who worked for a short while in the Brick Hotel. Now suddenly, Schleswig was the most integrated town in Iowa.

Deep ditches, six to eight feet deep, were dug down the middle of every street, and travel was disrupted all over town. When the main lines were laid, they had to be connected to each building and house. The crossover main that connected the west side of town to the sewer system was so deep that the workers had to use lanterns even on a sunny day, to see what they were doing at the bottom. It crossed approximately where Fir Street would be if it were continuous.

The work crew was a hard-working lot. They were friendly, sporting people who lived in boarded shacks near the stockyards. A good game of chance was their entertainment, and that put them in good stead with a number of local residents. It was heard there were some interesting games in shacks. Ed Jepsen was one of the local guys who would engage in a game now and then. One night he was participating in a game in one of the shacks and was substantially ahead financially. As the game was about to break up, he noticed a couple of the workmen slip out of the room ahead of time. He suspected they may be waiting to relieve him of his winnings. When he had gathered up his money, he suddenly lowered his head and rolled over straight backward and kicked the wall behind where he had been sitting. He kicked through the shack wall and took off in a direction where they were not expecting him to go. He made good his escape. On the whole though, relations between the workers and the town people were quite good.

The street work began in 1926. First, the streets had to be graded to the proper level. Many of the streets had been lined with concrete drainage ditches, so the old concrete had to be broken up and buried alongside the streets. Years later, residents were sometimes puzzled by these curved pieces of cement buried in their lawns. The next step was to form a new concrete pan at the bottom of the street, then the tar had to be heated to a liquid, the rock mixed with it, and then transported to the streets.

The streets would be filled with 12 to 18 inches of the compound. It would be leveled and let cool. Next a seal coat would be applied. Brass medallions were imbedded in the compound in the alley approaches where they would be out of most of the traffic. The medallions explain the nature of the streets. A huge processing plant for all of the activity was located next to the tracks a block south of Cedar Street.

The street construction ran into a problem, however. The problem was with the plans. There was a great deal of dissatisfaction in the community with the way the engineers had drawn up the plans. Many of the businessmen, especially those on the east side of Second Street, did not like the plan. It would result either in a very high curb on their side of the street or the necessity of re-building the entryways to the buildings on the other side of the street. A number of residents east of the tracks toward the north end of town were also dissatisfied with the plan. Various property owners, including Theodore Rohwer and John Claussen and others, thought the street was designed to be either too low or too high near their property. It would cause their lawns to slope down sharply to the street which they thought would detract from the beauty of their homes.

When the construction crews were ready to begin work on the streets, the engineering plans for the upper end of the business district were nowhere to be found, and part of the plans for the residential district was also missing. But construction had to begin, and when Second Street was to be graded, the businessmen demanded that it be done the way they wanted it, with standard curbs on both sides. This meant that the street had to slope sharply downward to the west which was not a problem in dry weather, but in winter snowy conditions, it meant the parking area on the west side of the street was virtually unusable. However, that is the way the businessmen wanted it, and that is the way it was laid.

In the residential area, the homeowners, in the areas from which the plans had disappeared, also demanded the streets be laid the way they wanted them. As a result, the eastern part of Cedar Street is higher than the engineers had intended as were the portions of Date and Elm Streets where the plans were also missing. Strangely, the remainder of the plans were there. When the workmen finished the project with the plans, the result was that a number of the streets in the southern part of town were laid out too high which seriously disrupted the natural water flow in a number of streets and alleys. (The problem remains today.)

Years later there had been an attempted break-in at the Farmers Lumber and Grain office. In the process of inventorying the contents of the safe to see what, if anything, had been stolen, the missing street plans were discovered under some old records in the bottom of the safe. John Claussen, the manager of the company since it had been formed, said he had no idea where they came from, since he had never paid much attention to the old records in the bottom of the safe. Since a number of influential community leaders had been in favor of the outcome of the missing plans, no farther action was taken.

The work crews left after the completion of the project. A good job had been done, and their relations with the community had been good. Friends had been made, and there was a farewell party. One of the Negro workmen stayed on in town to start a dry-cleaning business which he operated successfully for some time, but it failed when a bank closing wiped him out financially—as it did to a number of other people in town.

The community was glad to have the commotion over and to have more order in their routine. Rightfully, they were proud of their new civic improvements. Schleswig had a better street, water, and sewer infrastructure than any town its size in the state. Many much larger communities had a hard time matching it. Schleswig was now a modern city.

While the farm economy was slowing down, other parts of the country were going strong. Investments in the stock market were doing well, and the country elsewhere was generally prosperous. Prohibition had inspired a whole new subculture in the country. The entertainment crowd went underground where the world was of speakeasies, blind tigers, and flappers. If one wanted to have fun, it had to be done clandestinely. To go to a dance and have a drink, one had to go to strange locations and knock on locked doors, stand before a peep hole and know a password before being permitted to enter. And, of course, there was always the apprehension of a police raid. It was the era of short skirts, loud music and bad whiskey.

Homebrew beer had a tradition in Schleswig, but now home-made "hard stuff" was also coming on the local scene. There was some production, but it was on a small scale. Means of distribution, however was a different matter. Certain houses in town were open to visitors and, for a fee, a drink could be had. One such place was in the 400 block of Hickory Street and another was in the 500 block of Birch Street. Some places even permitted a pint to taken out. One such place had a circle drive on Maple Ave where one could drive up near the house, make the purchase and be gone in a minute. Another such place was in the 100 block of Elm Street. However, these operations were not limited to the town. Many places in the country side were known where such nefarious activities were taking place as well. Certain places, where, if one left a certain amount of money and returned in a few hours, there would be a bottle of "hootch." Sometimes a fencepost would be left loose in a hole and under it would be a transfer box. Law breakers had to be ingenious!

The illegal nature of the whole Prohibition scene, and the tremendous amounts of money that could be generated, soon lead to an invasion of organized crime. The corruption crept into the highest levels of government. As was mentioned, even Presidential cabinet members were accused of accepting bribes to cover such crimes. The demand for liquor in the larger cities was so great, that the tentacles of criminal organizations reached far out into the countryside to get their supplies. The most famous of the crime kings was Al Capone in Chicago.

While there are not many really large operations in our vicinity, just to the east of us in Carroll County, there were a number of good-sized producers who were even developing their own recognized brand names. Templeton Rye was the most famous of these, for it was well known as far as Chicago. Several things permitted their growth and sustenance. They were not only culturally homogeneous, but they were also bound by a single religion, and they had a tolerant and supportive county law enforcement structure. In other words, they were tightly organized groups in every sense of the word. Government agents did their best to shut them down but with little success, never being able to find the stills since the stills were not tied to one single location. In the making of liquor, a mash of grain, sugar, water and yeast was allowed to ferment for several weeks. Then it was run through a still to concentrate the alcohol. At Templeton, it was not a single-man operation with a single still, as it was in most operations. There, when the mash was ready, the farmer put out a call, and that evening a group of men would arrive with a still on a truck. They would operate the still all night, and in the morning the still would go in one direction and the alcohol in gallon bottles would go in another direction or be buried in the grain in a granary. Government agents might raid a farm, but all they could find was a batch of mash, which the farmer would say was a tub of hog slop that he had let spoil. There was never any equipment that could be tied to a distillation operation. When a shipment was ready, the gallon bottles would be placed in the bottom of a grain truck, and the box was filled with grain. The driver would be given a specific route to get to Chicago, the route being different every time. The truck was to be parked on the street at a certain address; the keys were to be left under the seat, and the driver was just to walk away. He could have a fun time on the town that night, and the next morning the truck would be parked at a different location. The box would be empty, and the gas tank would be full. He would head back for Iowa, and the money for the grain and booze would be delivered later.

An interesting story about events that happened in this era involved a farmer near Templeton. He noticed one evening that a car stopped down the road from his farmhouse. Two men in dark coats went out to a haystack, spent a few minutes and returned to their car and drove off. He was rather inquisitive and went down to the haystack to investigate. He discovered two cases of pint bottles of liquor. He thought he would take that liquor and sell it. After all, what could those guys do? They could not turn him into the police. So he did sell it. Then, one night a week later there was a knock at his door. When he went to answer it, he found two large men in dark hats and heavy coats. They asked if he had been down to his haystack lately. He thought he had better not lie to these guys, so he said, yes, he had been down there. They asked if he had found any bottles there. He said yes he had. They asked what he had done with them. He admitted he had sold them, but he was willing to give them the money. They said, no, he could keep the money. Next week, though, there would be two more cases of bottles by the haystack. He should sell those, too, but this time they would be back for the money. On the way out, one of the men said, "Mr. Capone appreciates a good salesman." From then on, the farmer was in business.

In the Ricketts and Ute area, one of the more popular night spots was the one run by Ann Casey which usually went by the name "Casey Ann's." It survived the prohibition era and lasted a good many years after that.

Schleswig, too, had its interesting little story. The grocery stores in Schleswig were wary of anyone who bought large quantities of sugar. Hans Behrmann was especially concerned about one farmer. Martin Knutsen would buy sugar by the 50 pound bags. There was little doubt what that amount of sugar would be used for, and Mr. Behrmann did not want to be implicated. He had little to be concerned about though. Mr. Knutsen was indeed operating a still, but the sugar he was buying locally was only a small amount when he was running short. He had converted a large hog house into one huge moonshine operation which was large enough that he was bringing in sugar by the truckload from Sioux City. The still was one of the largest ones made being over six feet tall, and was equipped with an oil-fired evaporator and a water-cooled condenser, and could produce a gallon of 100 proof whiskey every six minutes. A large network of mash tanks had to be established to supply it. He was raided, but it had nothing to do with a Schleswig connection. He had a load of sugar coming down Highway 141 from Sioux City when it started to rain. The truck driver was not sure how tight the canvas was over the load, so he stopped in Holly Springs to ask if he could park the truck in a garage until the rain stopped. The attendant at the service station became suspicious and sneaked a peek under the tarp. When he saw it was a load of sugar, he contacted the authorities. When the truck took off to complete its run to the farm, a government agent was on its tail. The raid was made at 5:00 P.M. one evening. Martin Knutsen was a large, heavy, hard-working man with a large farming operation. He was milking cows when agents under the direction of head revenuer, "Crooked-Neck" Anderson, came in to serve the papers. Mr. Knutsen was so shook that the milk stool had fallen over, but he had not moved. He was still in the same position—just shaking. He had not sold any liquor yet. The plan was for a huge shipment to go out the very next day. Tens of thousands of dollars worth of alcohol was in the hog house. The bottles were all broken, and so was the equipment. There was a stream of alcohol running down toward the creek which the hogs lapped up and there were drunken hogs wandering all over—or so the story goes.

It was the largest raid in western Iowa. It was so large that it even made the Chicago newspapers. Martin Knutsen was put on trial and found guilty. He was sentenced to six months to a year in the Ida County jail. Since he was hardly a dangerous criminal, he was allowed some privileges. Mrs. Knutsen could bring in home cooked meals. She also brought in curtains and tablecloths to make the cell more comfortable. For exercise, he could often be seen walking with the Sheriff down to the Post Office to get the mail. He said the only benefit he had gotten from his operation was when he traded some liquor to a neighbor for a young bull for his cow herd. The raid had come just too soon. He later retired to a house on east Fir Street in Schleswig and peacefully lived out the remainder of his life.

Many years after Prohibition had been repealed, some old timers were discussing the old days. One of the questions was where did all of the knowledge of distilling and all the equipment come from. Before Prohibition no one knew how to make liquor. After it was made illegal, there were stills everywhere. One old timer from the part of Carroll County where the product produced was generally known as "Carroll County Thunder," said he did not know where the knowhow came from, but he did know where a large part of their equipment came from. It was from a town to the west of them–the town of Schleswig. If you needed a high quality still, you would go to one particular businessman and put in your order and you would be given a date on which to pick it up. On that date, you would go to town after dark and go up main street and down an alley and knock on a side door and the equipment would be handed out. You would load it and slip out of town as quietly as possible.

It would not be good to glamorize this time too much, though, since these activities were illegal. A great deal of crime and violence was involved in a lot of cases. Big money deals went bad and there were retributions. Thefts and territorial protection problems occurred. There is a farm building between Schleswig and Mapleton that still has bullet holes in it. Organized crime escalated to huge proportions, and people were blinded and died from consuming bad booze. Many good people became alcoholics because of the lure of a forbidden fruit. The social consequences were devastating.

The farm economy at this time, which had begun to slip a number of years ago, continued to decline. The times began to be called a depression. Businesses that depended on farm income were also beginning to suffer. Farmers and businessmen are generally optimistic, and in bad times they tend to be in denial for as long as possible. The facts, however, could no longer be denied when a major financial institution failed. The Commercial Bank of Schleswig closed its doors and went out of business on December 16, 1926. There was no insurance on deposits in those days. If one had money in a bank that closed, it, for the most part, was just gone.

A lot of people angry about the bank failure were searching for a reason for this calamity. The Commercial Bank seemed like such a solid concern. There had been confidence in the officers of the bank, such as Judge Conner, who had been a frequent visitor in Schleswig. Judge Conner had died, however, and many of the former officers were no longer on the scene. The men in charge now were no-nonsense executives who were going to make hard decisions based on the facts. Not everyone believed this, however. Word on the street was that the parent company–the Crawford County State Bank–was in trouble with bad loans. In order to save that organization, the bad loans had been transferred to the Schleswig Bank, and the good notes in the Schleswig bank had been transferred out. Albert Baker said he was asked by one of the bank officers if he would like to ride along on a trip to Denison one evening. There were boxes of papers in the back seat and later he thought they may have been the negotiable notes being transferred out of town. It was said that the Schleswig bank could have made it if it had been on its own. In any case, the strategy did not do any good, because the Crawford County State Bank also failed.

Positive news was a little on the scarce side, but a few good happenings did occur. For one thing, the county had agreed to gravel the high road from Denison to Schleswig. During the Spring rains the railroad had been the only link Schleswig had with the outside world; secondly, the Fire Department had purchased a new electric siren and mounted it on a stand. It would replace the fire bell in the tower which had served the town well when it was small and growing, but as Schleswig began to spread, the old bell became less effective.

At this time, Sheriff Art Greene was an effective law enforcement officer and was popular with the people in the county. When he was involved in a shootout with a couple of criminals in Denison, he was wounded in the wrist. His pay being modest and there being no such thing as medical insurance, he found it difficult to take care of his medical bills. Because he was so well respected, many people around the county contributed to help with the medical bills. The people of Schleswig liked the job he was doing, and the local contribution was well over half of the total medical bill.

Coincidental things can occur at strange times. Such was the case when a near tragedy occurred on the streets of Schleswig. A number of children had been playing on the sidewalk and in the adjoining parking area, when a car rolled forward and pinned a young boy under it. A crowd quickly gathered, but the owner of the car could not be found, and the car could not be started without his key. There was not time to get jacks and blocks to move the car, since the boy could not get his breath. Johannes Gosch, the blacksmith, seeing the dilemma, crouched in front of the car, grabbed the front bumper, and lifted the car off the boy. Bystanders quickly pulled the boy to safety and Mr. Gosch let the car drop back to the street. The boy was scared and shaken but survived in good shape. After the excitement was over, there was no way Mr. Gosch could lift the weight of a car, but when it was needed, he found the strength to do so.

Germans love their music, and their proficiency in it was demonstrated when in 1927 the high school sent a mixed chorus to Iowa City to enter statewide competition. School had been dismissed for the occasion, which showed the support the school and community gave to the mixed chorus under the direction of Ingeborg Nielsen. They won first place in the state making them—and Schleswig—very proud.

1927 was a year of personalities around Schleswig. Actually, two of the men attracting attention were not directly from Schleswig but had connections here. Clarence Chamberlain had operated a bicycle shop and automobile garage in Denison and had been in Schleswig numerous times. He had even set up an outlet for tires here at one time. However, his real passion was aviation being one of the pioneers in the field. Now a large eastern newspaper was offering a large cash award for the first person to fly across the Atlantic Ocean. Clarence decided to make a try for it, but he could not afford the huge expense. A financial backer was found, but unfortunately, the backer held Clarence back in order to squeeze a little more publicity out of the event. In the delay, an unknown flyer from a small town in Minnesota, Charles Lindbergh, took off and won the prize. Chamberlain took off a few days later and easily made the trip and flying farther than Lindgergh had flown, landing in central Germany. Chamberlain did win the record for flying the first passenger across the ocean and for flying the first mail over there. Great as his accomplishments were, he is relegated to a footnote in history. Not, however, before Denison gave him a resounding homecoming with a huge parade. Schleswig sent a prominent entry–a float in the form of a large biplane mounted on a Model A frame. It was entitled the Spirit of Schleswig.

The other man attracting attention was a former Schleswig native, George Pipgras. The boy, who used to throw stones at a box in the alley back of the Brick Hotel for practice, had made it "big time". Now, he was a starting pitcher for the New York Yankees in one of the biggest years in the team's history. He had always been one of the hardest throwing pitchers anyone had ever seen, but he had some control problems early in his career which he had worked out, and now, he belonged a team that included Babe Ruth, and Lou Gehrig. In 1927, he had a 10-3 win record with a 4.12 earned-run average, which was the best of any pitcher on the team. George pitched the second game of the World Series that year giving up a triple to the Pirates' first batter, Lloyd Waner, and a sacrifice fly to Clyde Barnhardt, before settling down to win six to two. He allowed just seven hits over nine innings. Every radio in Schleswig was tuned to the game. There wasn't a conversation that didn't include a reference to this favorite son.

George led the American League in games won in 1928 making the magic number of twenty-four games. In his career, George Pipgras started three World Series games and won them all. He was pitching for the Yankees in game three of the 1932 World Series when Babe Ruth hit his famous "called shot" home run off Cub's Charlie Root. Unfortunately, George's pitching career ended when he threw a pitch so hard he broke his arm. He was quoted as saying he would rather play baseball than eat. His determination had carried him far.

Vanity created a new profession for Schleswig at this time with the opening of Emmy Lou's Shop in 1928. Emma Louise Braase (Struck) had opened the first beauty shop in town. Until this time, most of the women in town took care of their own hair with occasional help of a friend or relative. This service was now available professionally. It took some time to establish a need for the service, but with the advent of the "Marcelling" style, a professional touch was required. She was followed in business by Marie O'Meara (Lyon) and Rose Kallin (Friedrichsen/Wellendorf). Once the struggle to establish the new profession had succeeded, the early founders were followed by a number of practitioners.

Hard times were beginning to be felt more and more. The Brick Hotel that the Pipgras family had run at one time had ceased to operate as a hotel. Jimmy Schultz bought it and converted the second floor rooms to apartments. He operated a hatchery in one half of the first floor. and the other half, which had been the restaurant, was rented to Hans Behrmann who moved his grocery store into it.

There was no doubt that times were bad and getting worse. A ray of hope emerged in the national elections that Fall. Former Iowa boy, Herbert Hoover, was running for the Presidency of the United States. As Head of the American Relief Administration, he had prolonged the wartime farm prosperity, and as Secretary of

Commerce, he had not directly affected the farm economy, but he had been one of the few Federal executives of the time who was not involved in corruption. Many people in Schleswig felt that if anyone could help the situation, Herbert Hoover was the man who could do it.

Herbert Hoover won the election. He was inaugurated into the office of the Presidency on March 4, 1929. Six months later on October 24, the stock market crashed. Billions of dollars were lost. The entire country felt the pain that the farm country had been feeling for a number of years. The economic leaders said there was nothing to worry about because the economy was basically strong. President Hoover put in higher tariffs restricting foreign trade even farther, which, he said, would help farmers, but farm prices declined even further. Appeals were made to have the Federal government intercede directly in the economy and put strong stimulants in place. President Hoover, however, was a conservative Republican, and all of his training was against governmental intervention in the domestic economy or society. In time, his well-known humanitarian instincts were beginning to get the better of his political policies. In the last year of his administration, he began to initiate some policies directed at improving the overall situation such as starting the Reconstruction Finance Corporation (RFC) and the Federal Home Loan Act (FHA). Unfortunately, they proved to be too little and too late.

The people in Schleswig were not sympathetic. They had placed a lot of hope on President Hoover. When things got worse, and it appeared that Mr. Hoover was resisting effective action to correct the conditions, they turned against him. He was not at all popular by the end of his term.

A person or a community can exist for years doing its own thing and not be influenced by the outside world. Regional, national, or world events have little if any effect on daily life. Those are just events happening somewhere else. But that can only continue for a certain length of time. Outside events are bound to come tumbling in and change the whole course of events. It is times like this that decisions have to be made and positions taken that can change the way everything will be done. Whole communities are affected in such circumstances. Big events call for major actions. "When, in the course of human events, it becomes necessary for one people to dissolve the bands which have connected them with another, and to assume, among the powers of the earth, the separate and equal station to which the laws of nature and of nature's God entitle them… " Old bonds and understandings can change on many levels.

VIII. REPETITIONS

1932–1949

It was once said that he who does not learn from history is doomed to repeat it. That surely cannot be the case in Schleswig. A community that has gone through a severe economic downturn, persecution by its neighbors for its cultural heritage, and the humiliation of having to fight a war against the country from which the ancestors of many of its residents came, would certainly have enough in its past. Even though many of the problems were caused by outside influences, they would not be the kind of issues that could be allowed to repeat themselves. There are new things, better things, to be accomplished. We must look ahead to forthcoming possibilities rather than to dwell on past problems.

Schleswig lies on some of the richest farmland in the world; yet, for most of its existence it has been an importer of grain due to the strong history of livestock production in the area—cattle, hogs, and sheep were the main large animals that were raised, but chickens, ducks, and geese were also abundant. Every farm had cows to milk and the cream was separated from the milk, or it was processed into hard cheese and cottage cheese. The excess cream was sold to a produce station, and the excess skim milk was used to prepare hog feed. Chickens supplied both eggs and meat. Ducks and geese provided down for insulated clothing and bedding as well as meat for special meals. If there was an excess, it would also be going to the local produce station. The produce used in the home and the income from the sale of excess was almost sufficient to provide for the day-to-day operation of the household. An interesting event for a number of years was a special Rooster Day sponsored by the produce stations and merchants . This usually took place long enough after the spring hatch that the sex of the birds could be determined, at which time the excess roosters would be sold off. The special Rooster Day was to accomplish this in an organized fashion and to have some fun doing it. A small premium was paid on that day for the birds and there would be a number of contests in which the birds could participate as well. There would be a rooster race, for which the bird's wings would be tied so they could not fly and then set to race down a track. Sometimes the birds would cooperate, and some times they would not. There would also be a handsome bird contest, an ugly bird contest, the heaviest bird contest, the longest spur contest, and for the ladies, a chicken calling contest. It was an activity in which almost every farmer could participate and thousands of pounds of poultry were sold. At other times during the year, the produce man would come out to the farms and cull the birds removing the nonproductive hens from the egg-laying flock.

The larger livestock sustained the farming operation. Some of the first settlers in Otter Creek Township were the Lehfeldt Brothers, Rudolf and Henry, who raised thousands of sheep. They had a large sheep ranch in Montana where the sheep were bred, and then shipped here to be fed out to maturity and sent on the Chicago stockyards. Through the years the numbers of sheep raised in the Schleswig area have fluctuated greatly from time to time. Hogs have been the mainstay of most farming operations. Their prolific reproduction rates, relatively short time to gain maturity, and high feed conversion rates made hogs highly profitable. The hogs provided income to pay off many farm mortgages. Year in and year out, it was hogs that provided a steady and predictable income flow for many farm operations.

Cattle was the glamor end of livestock production. Beef has long been prized for its flavor, but cattle took much longer to raise and finish, and it was a costlier process. To be a cattleman, however, was a mark of distinction. High profitability with equally high risk financially was the challenge. Cattle finishing operations have always been here. The routine was to bring feeder cattle from western ranches which were fed to a finished weight, and shipped to the Chicago Stockyards or in later years to the Omaha or Sioux City Stockyards.

Since the time the railroad started operation, Schleswig originated from six to ten train cars of livestock a week in season. In the years leading into the World War, livestock production increased extending into the 1920's, when there were many times when twenty or more train cars of livestock left the Schleswig stockyards in a week. It was during the 20's that local cattle-producers began to participate in major stock shows.

When livestock was shipped to a major livestock terminal such as the Chicago Stockyards, it was consigned to a commission firm where it was the firm's job to broker the sale to buyers from the various packing plants in an effort to get the highest bid possible. For this service and for maintaining yard space for the arriving livestock, the firm would receive a percentage of the sales price as a commission. In the early days, the commission firms would, at times, sponsor young farmers in getting started in the livestock business. The Ingwersen Commission Company in Chicago sponsored several farm families in this area and helped some farmers obtain feeder cattle. As a promotion for the industry, they, also, sponsored livestock shows.

The most famous of these shows was the International Livestock Show in Chicago. Schleswig farmers began entering the competition in the mid 1920's and began winning some of the prizes—in 1927, John D. Moeller, who farmed a mile east and half a mile north of town, won second place at the show and interest in the competition grew. In 1926, Schleswig farmers sent 14 train carloads of cattle to the International Show, by 1930, it was up to 23 carloads, and in 1931, 22 farmers sent a total of 50 carloads. In that year John D. Moeller was named King of North American Cattle Feeders, and he received a Grand Champion Award for his carload of Hereford cattle. John Turin of Kiron was awarded best load of two-year-old cattle, and Horace Westcott of the Crawford County 4-H Clubs was awarded 1st place in showmanship.

Schleswig held a Cattle Feeders Barbeque in Mr. Moeller's honor on December 17, 1931, in the Opera House with over a 1000 people in attendance. The Farmers State Bank had purchased some of Moeller's beef to serve at the occasion. The speakers included Theodore Rohwer, and B.M. Anderson from the American Hereford Association, who presented Mr. Moeller with a $600.00 award. There were reporters from as far away as the *Des Moines Register* in attendance.

A relatively new concept in the cattle-feeding industry called Baby Beef was becoming popular. The feeder cattle being brought in were very young usually weighing 500 pounds or less, and they were fed out to a finished weight of 1100 to 1200 pounds which produced a tender, lightly marbled meat product, which was in contrast to earlier standards in beef production. When the first beef producers in the Schleswig area bought feeders at about 1000 to 1100 pounds, they feed them up to about 1500 to 1600 pounds producing a heavily marbled steak with a wide ring of fat around the edges.

The feeder cattle were brought in from the western ranches. Many of our farmers made direct contact with the ranchers and developed personal friendships as well as business relationships. During the 20's and 30's many of the cattle came from the Nebraska Sandhills. Later they came from the Dakotas and then from Montana. They also came from some of the regional sales barns and from stock shows. In 1932, Schleswig farmers bought over a thousand head at the Denver Stock Show. In 1933, the numbers were increased to 36 train carloads from Denver and more from Kansas City.

While the prestige was with the cattle-feeder, the price was not always there. John D. Moeller's prize winning pen of cattle sold for $20.25 per hundredweight, the lowest price on that type of cattle since 1923, and John Turin received only $14.25 per hundredweight for his young cattle. The depression was making its effects felt throughout the area, but fortunately, for the farmers, the Farmers State Bank came to consider itself as a cattleman's bank and continued to finance such operations. In 1932, the bank directors formed the Schleswig Cattle Loan Company to secure funds from the Federal Intermediate Credit Bank to finance feeder cattle in the area, the Schleswig Cattle Loan Company was an affiliate of the Bank but made loans, specifically and only, for cattle feeding.

In a depression, there is a general lack of confidence in the economy. People all over the country quit buying products because they are not sure where their next dollar is coming. As a result, businesses slow down, people are laid off, and business failures increase. The prices on all products come down, since even people who have money are slow to spend it, because the longer they wait the better the prices might become. The whole business cycle spirals downward to a smaller and smaller base.

Franklin Delano Roosevelt was elected President in 1932 and in his inaugural address he said the people had "Nothing to fear but fear itself." He said they should have confidence in their country and its businesses. To help instill confidence, he declared a "bank holiday." The bank failure rate in the U.S. was phenomenal–there had been over a dozen failures in Crawford County alone. The "bank holiday" ordered all remaining banks closed, and when the officers could show to Federal officers that their institution was solid and solvent, they could reopen. The ones that did reopen were ones in which the people could have confidence.

Theodore Rohwer, the president of the Farmers State Bank in Schleswig, and H.A. Klotz, the cashier, went to Des Moines to meet with Mr. Bates, the Federal bank examiner. They were told that based on their records they would have to increase their cash position by 25 to 35 thousand dollars, put in a service charge system, and reduce salaries by 25%. If they complied with those demands, they could open their doors again. The officers readily agreed, that would not be difficult to do at all, and the bank was open and operating normally again within a few days.

However, matters were becoming desperate, economically, on the farm, especially on the smaller farms. As is usual in such situations, a new farm organization was formed. This organization was called the Farm Holiday Movement, organized by an Iowa boy, Milo Reno. The idea behind the movement was if people were not going to pay a decent price for farm products, the farmers were going to take a holiday from delivering them. Products would be held off the market. Members would not only stop delivering products, they would create roadblocks to prevent others from delivering their products, too. Milk was dumped in ditches and eggs were broken, etc. At times the clashes on the road became violent. Times were desperate!

Many small farmers were being "sold out" to pay their debts. The Farm Holiday movement was not only instrumental in commodity prices but also wanted a holiday from foreclosures–a delay to give the farmer a chance to get past the current financial crises. One of the Farm Holiday's answers to this problem was a "penny sale." When there was an auction to sell out a farmer, the Holiday members would intermingle with the crowd and "discourage" bidding. As a result everything the farmer had to sell would bring only a few cents an item. All the equipment and supplies would then be left for the farmer to start over, and the creditors would have to be satisfied with the few dollars that had come from the sale. The debts were cleared, and the farmer had no title to any of the equipment that had been "left" for him, so no more could be recovered from him. Certainly, the non-farming community was not happy with this arrangement.

Such a sale was to take place on the Joe Shield's farm near Denison on April 28, 1933, when the District Court ordered a foreclosure sale to satisfy a judgment secured by the landlord, John Houlihan. The authorities learned there would be trouble and called in reinforcements. Six state police officers and two officers from the State Militia were brought in, and a number of unofficial vigilantes were deputized and armed with axe handles. The sale was called to order by Sheriff Willey with his deputy acting as the auctioneer and a crowd of about 500 in attendance. Shortly after the sale started, a truckload of 25 to 30 additional "farmers" arrived. They joined farmers already there and attempted to gain control of the situation, but the authorities moved to prevent that from happening. The scuffle soon turned into a full scale riot in which the authorities were outnumbered and overcome. Two of the State agents were badly injured. Jack Hess, from Schleswig, an unofficial deputy, was badly beaten and dumped into a horse watering tank. Hugo Jensen, a spectator, went to the aid of a State agent he thought was in danger of being killed, only to be knocked down himself. Ben Bielenberg, a golden glove boxer, ran into a big farmer whose anger more than made up for any lack of skill. When Sheriff Willey realized he was losing control of the situation, he called the sale off and returned to Denison to report to County Attorney Andrew Bell. A large number of farmers stayed on the sale site to be sure the sale would not be started again after things quieted down.

County Attorney Bell and Sheriff Willey decided to call in extra help. Wanting as much help as they could get to return law and order to the situation, they made a frantic call to Governor Herring. Normally a moderate response would have been appropriate. After all, the violence was over, and the scene was peaceful. It was not a normal weekend, however. In Le Mars, a group of farmers roughed up a newspaper editor, forced an attorney to convince his client, an insurance company, to refrain from foreclosures for the time being, and then, worst of all, they stormed a courtroom and kidnaped a judge, and, with a noose around his neck, attempted to force him the salute the flag and pledge not to foreclose on deserving farmers. Other incidents occurred in Denison as well. Max Kropf, a real estate agent who had sold land that resulted in tenants losing their operations, had been visited by night stalkers who rattled his windows and attempted to intimidate him. Attorney G. L. Gilchrist answered a knock on his door one night only to be confronted by a group of farmers intent on kidnaping him. Saying he wanted to calm his wife, he stepped back into the house far enough to retrieve a double-barreled shotgun he had stashed behind the door and held the crowd at bay and escaped any farther harassment. The incident earned him the nickname "Shotgun" Gilchrist for some time afterward.

In the face of all these events, the Governor decided to take dramatic and decisive action. He activated the National Guard and declared Crawford and Plymouth counties to be under martial law. By 7:00 P.M., uniformed troops from Council Bluffs, Red Oak, Glenwood, Shenandoah, Neola and Des Moines arrived in Denison. In all there were 248 enlisted men and 28 officers under the command of Major General Matthew L. Tingley, who set up a strong defensive perimeter around the Courthouse and placed machine guns at strategic points. The troops bunked in the Courthouse halls for the night.

The next day it was announced that the sale which had been the cause of all the trouble would be rescheduled for 10:00 A.M. Some 400 people showed up and were required to park away from the sale site and were checked for weapons before they were allowed to enter. Troops were on hand to keep order, and a machine gun was mounted next to the auctioneer and pointed at the crowd. There were no problems. The bids were low but reasonable, and the tenant's son, John Shields, was able to buy much of the property.

This was not the end of the incident, however. The proclamation of martial law was in effect for the whole county until all the law breakers and rioters were arrested and tried. The National Guard set up a military camp south of Highway 30 near the railroad tracks, naming it Camp Macrae in memory of Donald Macrae, a veteran of the first medical detachment in the Spanish American War and World War I. Under martial law, when more than two people stopped to talk in any public place, they would soon be confronted by soldiers with bayoneted weapons and encouraged to move along.

The next step was to apprehend the law breakers. Some of the first to be arrested were Frank North of Vail, the local leader of the

Farm Holiday organization, and H.C. and Fritz Blume, the sons of
the State Representative. In all 47 people were arrested. The jail
was too small, so a barbed wire "Bull Pen" was erected on the
Courthouse lawn to hold them. Since they were arrested under
the rules of martial law, the law breakers were not allowed bail nor
consultation with an attorney. Each man was brought before a
preliminary military tribunal to verify that the correct men were
identified and accused. All parts of the county were checked by
the militia, and people were arrested from the additional communities of Woodbine, Logan, Glidden, Harlan, Shelby, Carroll, Little
Sioux, Onawa, Moorhead and Walnut.

The Chief Justice of the Iowa Supreme Court appointed Judge
Martial law was lifted on May 11, 1933, but a contingent of
soldiers was to remain to help maintain order at the upcoming
trials. Camp Macrae was dismantled. In spite of the commotion,
the Denison merchants were happy with the way things were turning out. The militia bought all of its supplies in town, and there
were thousands of sightseers who came to see what all the commotion was about. Reporters from all the major newspapers came to
gather news for their papers. It was a very active time.

The Chief Justice of the Iowa Supreme Court appointed Judge
Homer Fuller, a no nonsense judge from Mt. Ayr, to try the cases
against the men. The rioters were convicted and fined $50.00 and
sentenced to an additional 24 hours in jail. When the case was
being presented against Frank North, his brother was in the
spectator's section. He thought the activities being described were
so funny he could not restrain his laughter. He was removed from
the courtroom, and at the next break, he was arrested and charged
with contempt of court, and he was also fined $50.00. He had
brought $50.00 to pay for his brother's fine, but now he had to
use it for his own fine, and his brother had to wait in jail until he
could scrape together another $50.00. After the trials, things settled
down to some semblance of order. Assistant State's Attorney Leon
Powers from Denison was appointed as prosecutor in the trials in
Le Mars.

Milo Reno was a dedicated and forceful speaker, but his mes-
sage was not always openly received and accepted. When he was

speaking in Schleswig, Stanley Baker, a local farmer with quite conservative views, began making gobbling noises to distract the speaker. Mr. Reno was not disturbed, however, and in the portion of his speech where he referred to his opponents as "dirty skunks", he pointed out Mr. Baker as a prime example of what he meant.

In 1932, the Schleswig Chapter of the American Legion was reorganized. The chapter had been allowed to dissolve half a dozen years before. The new chapter was renamed Schleswig Post No. 645, and the more matured veterans were now ready to take their organization more seriously.

A human tragedy caused Schleswig residents to be shocked when they heard of an accident that occurred near the community. Two young boys and their cousin were digging a cave in the soft road bank near their home at 1531 260 Street. They had excavated a hole large enough to hold all three when the soft, sandy soil collapsed on them. Two of the cousins, Ronald and Lester Jensen smothered to death before they could be rescued. The wholehearted sympathy of the community poured out to families.

President Roosevelt had been getting his new activist administration off to a rapid start. A whole number of new agencies were created. The National Recovery Administration (the NRA) set up a series of price and wage controls to ensure fairness in the marketplace. Merchants who agreed to comply with its rules were allowed to display its blue eagle symbol, and many Crawford County merchants made a sincere effort to comply with the program. Other programs included the Agricultural Adjustment Administration (AAA) to help farmers, the Civilian Conservation Corps (CCC) to provide workers for environmental improvements, the Civil Works Administration (CWA) and the Public Works Administration (WPA) to provide jobs for the unemployed in civic improvement projects. The Federal Deposit Insurance Corporation guaranteed individual bank deposits up to $10,000.00 even if the bank failed. While the German tradition around Schleswig was one of strong independence, it was affected by each of these programs to its benefit.

The program with the strongest impact for the Schleswig territory was the Agricultural Adjustment Administration with its
purpose of helping the long-suffering farm economy. Several approaches were made that were intended to be used to improve the
situation. The program that had the most immediate impact was
the corn–hog program which provided for direct payments to farmers who agreed to restrict production in these commodities. This
would have the effect of first infusing money where it was needed
the most, and second of decreasing the supply of these commodities so a stable market price could be established. It proved to be a
very popular program with ninety-three percent of the farmers in
Morgan and Otter Creek Townships signing up for the program in
the first year. Another part of the program provided for lending
operating money to farmers using the excess grain they already
had as collateral. When the grain was identified as collateral, it was
considered under "seal," and the farmer could not feed nor sell it
without first making arrangements to protect the loan. The farmer
could either pay off the loan and use the grain, or forfeit the grain
to the governmental agency and the loan would be forgiven at the
farmer's option. The decision was based on the market value of
grain at the time.

Other programs such as the CCC, the CWA, and WPA were
also put into effect. A number of young men were able to obtain
work and, at least, a subsistence wage. A large CCC Camp was
brought into being just outside of Denison. WPA projects were
organized in a number of communities including a project by the
CWA to improve the Schleswig Park in which new sidewalks were
installed, trees were planted, and the buildings and the tennis
court were improved. Several of the local men were also sent to
other states to work on projects there.

All this activity was extremely new to the nation as past conservative administrations had strong policies of keeping hands off
business practices and letting individuals fend for themselves as
best they could. In good times, such a policy could work in most
cases as it did in the 1920's. The general economy was growing,

and the stock market was strong. Only a few groups such as the farmers and the wage earners were having problems. When the depression spread nationwide, the conservative policies were of no help, and the nation went to the liberals for new ideas and experimental programs. They injected money and helped at the grassroots level with the underlying idea being if consumers had money to buy, then markets would be established, and business would respond. It was a new and novel idea for governments to try. The prior conservative policies not only crippled and stifled our economy, but also their extremely high tariffs disrupted international trade, and their crippling reprisals on the Axis nations put their economies in chaos. Germany went into a hyper inflation in which it took a wheel barrow of money to buy a loaf of bread. Politically, they went the opposite direction from the U.S. especially when they elected the extremely conservative NAZI party to power, and Adolph Hitler became Chancellor in January of 1933, a few months before Roosevelt was inaugurated.

This set up one of the largest scale economic experiments in the history of the world. On one hand was the liberal experiment in this country attempting to help the individual citizen and put him in a position where he could build up the structure of the economy. On the other hand was the extremely conservative Fascist and NAZI approach of a rigid structure imposed from the highest levels of government, and extremely tight controls were placed on individuals. Over the next decade the competition between the two systems would play itself out.

In Schleswig, the people were distracted by local events. The first murder in the history of the town had taken place. Louie Hamann, a local 18-year-old youth, had discovered his Grandmother's body in her house. Mrs. Charlotte Evers had been bludgeoned to death in her bedroom. The people were in an uproar, and Marshal Jim Davis, who had kept order in town for the last ten years, took charge of the situation. He immediately brought in Dr. Jones, Coroner John Gottberg, and Sheriff Hugo Willey. After a brief survey of the scene, they called additional help from the Iowa Bureau of Criminal Investigations which sent fingerprint expert, J.S. Gladstone, a photographer, and special agent, Paul Gruber. Very little evidence was found. The house had been ransacked, but $140.00 in cash lay undisturbed in a drawer. There were no unknown fingerprints, and the only thing they found was a beer bottle opener under the body. It seemed unlikely that a passing stranger would have picked Mrs. Evers' modest house at 23 Fir Street as good picking for a robbery. They also found out that, unlike many homes in Schleswig, Mrs. Evers always locked her doors at night, yet there was no sign of a break-in; the killer had walked right in. Things were not adding up right.

Louis Hamann, Mrs. Evers' grandson, was living with her since his father had died two years before, and his mother had taken a job as a housekeeper for a family in town. Louis had difficulty holding a job, but he had spent the afternoon working for John and Magnus Jacobsen butchering a hog on their farm southeast of Schleswig. He had been in the house during the entire investigation and was quite distraught. He kept nervously putting more and more wood in the stove until it was so hot in the house it almost drove the investigators out. When they could find no more clues, they began looking for a motive, and the more they put things together, the more they looked at Louis.

The authorities decided to take Louis to the Sheriff's office where he would not be in familiar surrounding and question him some more. In the meantime, Marshal Davis began asking around town about him, and he discovered that Louis owed a substantial amount of money at the local pool hall and that the owner had been putting pressure on him to pay up. Marshal Davis also asked Mrs. Hamann, Louis' mother, to check to see if any of Louis' things were missing. She did so and said there was a set of clothes including a white shirt missing. With this new information, the authorities began in earnest to question Louis.

After hours of questioning, in the wee hours of the night, Louis Hamann broke down and confessed. He needed the money he knew his Grandmother had in the house, and he felt humiliated that his Grandmother would never give him a key to the house. He always had to waken her to get in at night, and thus he never had the opportunity to look for the money when she was gone. That night his frustrations had gotten the best of him, and he had grabbed a piece of firewood and beat her to death. He then ransacked the house in the dark but could not find the money. When he then took a chance and turned on the lights to look for it, he saw in the mirror how much blood had been splattered on him. He forgot about the money and was consumed with how to cover up the crime. He changed clothes and cleaned up, throwing the old clothes and the bloody piece of firewood in the stove to burn them. He then went uptown and met his cousin and his girl friend coming out of the theater and had them accompany him back to his Grandmother's house where he "discovered" the body. He had kept throwing wood in the stove earlier to be sure all the evidence was completely burned.

The murder had taken place on Sunday, March 11, 1934, and on Tuesday, Louis Hamann appeared before Judge Peter Klinker. Within 48 hours of the crime, Louis was found guilty and sentenced to life in prison. Before the end of the week, Mr. Hamann was on his way to the Fort Madison Penitentiary.

Special Agent Paul Gruber wrote up his version of the investigation which appeared in *True Detective Magazine*, a popular source of such stories. It was not the kind of publicity that Schleswig appreciated, but it could not be avoided.

A variety of other things were happening on the local scene, too. Lawrence Welk and his famous Honolulu Fruit Band played a long series of engagements at the Playmor Ballroom, formerly known as the Bowery, a mile east of Schleswig. Mr. Welk had a music program on radio station WNAX out of Yankton, South Dakota. Ted Hollander and some local promoters had heard him and went to hire Mr. Welk to play here on his open days.

Other things of interest were the Schleswig Elks baseball team which was having a good season and drawing large crowds. Talk about building an improved highway across the whole state from north to south that might go through Schleswig was becoming more frequent. Julius Rohwer was appointed to the committee which was to discuss the building of the road which would be called Hwy. # 21. The Iowa Power and Light Company moved the store it had been operating to sell electric appliances for the last nine years from the side of the Stoltenberg Grocery building at 121 Cedar St. to their plant on Ash Street. Mr. Stoltenberg converted the electric store into a frozen food locker plant, a relatively new concept in preserving food. Gus Hollander had taken the wooden hotel building down and built a gasoline service station on the lot several years before. Now the Standard Oil Company bought it and leased it to Walter Petersen. Rudy Schuman had been working at the station and would continue to do so. Next to the gas station was the bowling alley at 203 Cedar Street. A record game was bowled there. John Sucksdorf bowled a 299-point game. On the last ball, one pin denied him a perfect game. A local girl was also making a name for herself. Elvera Lohse (Hollander) was elected president of the Women's Athletic Association at Grinnell College, Grinnell, Iowa.

With the growing influence of the automobile, as well as trucks and farm tractors, the sale of gasoline was becoming a large and profitable business. The first gasoline pump in town was located on the sidewalk outside Albert Schultz's hardware store, with additional sidewalk pumps located at the car dealership at 206 Cedar, where an office on the east side of the building was used for the attendant, and at the car dealership at 34 Second Street. Full service gas stations in addition to the Standard Station at Second and Cedar Streets were the Community Oil Company operated by Rudy Schuman and Ted Lohse at Second and Date Streets; Peter Boysen's Sinclair station at Cedar and Hwy 59; John Evers and John Clausen's Texaco station at Birch and Hwy 59; and many years later Beep Sonksen and Milt Wasgren's Standard Oil at Hwy 59 and E-16.

Farm prices were starting to come back up a little. This was partly due to the effect of the corn–hog program and partly due to a long dry spell that had reduced the amount of the crop. The irony of the situation was that while the prices were better, there was less crop to sell. The prestige of the cattle feeders was helping to keep the spirits of the farmers up. For the fifth year in a row, the local cattle producers held a feed lot tour. A caravan of cars would go around the countryside to the various cattle producers and see how their operations were set up. The tours attracted not only a number local people but also cattle-feeders from various places throughout the Midwest as well as stockyard commission men, ranchers, and reporters. These tours have been the object of feature stories in a number of publications. That Fall the cattle train to the Stock Show was as full as usual and Louie Reimer took first place at the International Livestock Show. Farming may not have been paying well at the time, but the Schleswig cattle feeders certainly knew what they were doing.

The dry spell that produced a short crop on the farm also put strain on the town's water system. The old well by the water tower had been discontinued and a new well had been dug in the southeast corner of town and a second larger one next to it. The town had grown, however, and even the new wells were not adequate, so a shallow well was dug in a low spot a mile west of town, near the site of the old town of Hohenzollern. It would do well in normal-to-wet times, but in the drought it, too, fell short. The town fathers continued to look for an answer to the water problem and decided they wanted to dig a deep well by the water tower. The State Health Department, however, vetoed that plan as there had been too many outhouses and horse barns in the vicinity to guarantee a fresh water supply.

A major concern in town was the new railroad schedule. The number of trains on the punkin vine line had been reduced to two passenger trains and two freights a week. The City Council protested the decline in service, but the depressed economic conditions had hit the railroads, too. Kiron was hit even worse. Their depot was closed down permanently, but to try to keep their spirits up, they started a new celebration, which they called the Play Days.

One titillating little story was making the rounds at the time. Some people went out to gather walnuts in the woods north of Deloit. What should they find way back in the hills and woods but a nudist colony. There were at least fifteen participants, mostly from Denison. Their little secret was embarrassingly out.

For a town that had little crime for most of its existence, Schleswig seemed to be making up for lost time. In 1935, a number of houses had been burglarized—some of the victims included Albert Reimer, Roland Stuck, and Julius Else. Albert Phiel, a local farmhand, was caught red-handed and confessed to all of the burglaries. Within four hours of his arrest, Judge Klinker sentenced him to ten years in the State Penitentiary. Judge Klinker just did not believe in delaying justice. He was a Crawford County boy—only the second county resident to become a Judge. James Conner, the first, had been appointed in 1886.

The City fathers decided to bring in a civil engineer to help solve the water shortage problem. A firm from Webster City was contracted. After a series of tests they recommended a deep well at the site of the shallow well west of town, and the Rasmessen Well Company was hired to drill the well. They were able to accomplish the feat although they had equipment failures and lost drill heads down the well and all kinds of other problems, but in the end they had a good well. In the final test, the well was pumped for three days continuously, and the water level had not dropped. They had succeeded in getting into the Dakota Aquifer! The water was quite hard, but there was a lot of it. Word got around that the water had medicinal qualities, and people from towns all around came to fill their jugs. If one was not accustomed to it, it could well serve as a tonic.

Hugo Reimers and Ben and Bart Bielenberg bought the old Tie Barn or livery stable from the Butler Brothers who had been using it as a sales barn. The new name was the Schleswig Sales Pavilion, and Ben and Bart practiced their skills in the auctioneering trade here, which led to their future success as the premier auctioneering team in the region.

In 1935, a tragedy rocked the community. Theodore Rohwer, the President of the bank, died. It was an unexpected shock to the community. Mr. Rohwer had been depressed partially because of the general economic situation, and partially because of the death of his son, John, in a mine accident in California. One July day, he worked all day in the bank, drove home, and put his car in the garage where he took out a revolver and shot himself in the chest. He died later that evening. He had been a community leader for many years, and he prided himself in the fact that in the thirty-five years he headed the bank, he had not foreclosed on a single farmer.

Farmers were going out of business, though, for the drought of the year before was continuing. A new trend was occurring in Schleswig–a number of retired farmers were moving back to the farm. They had retired and moved to town where they were living on the rent from the farm. The renters were no longer able to make the rent payments–thus, in order to live, the retired farmers had to go back and start farming again. Many of them were 50 or 60 or even 70 years old.

Mother Nature had her way of adding insult to injury. Schleswig had a close call from a tornado in 1935. It came from the southwest and did extensive damage to the Eric Pagel home at 628 Glad Street and continued northeast just missing the rest of the town. It did a large amount of damage at the Play-Mor Dance Pavilion on the corner of Ave D and 230th Street and, also damaged the Ray Bielenberg and Henry Schroeder farms. The winter of 1936 was the worst winter since the black blizzard of 1888. Huge amounts of snow were whipped into gigantic drifts by strong winds. Schleswig was the most isolated town in Crawford County in January of that year, and a storm the week of January 10 closed not only all the roads but also blocked the railroad. The town was running low on groceries–there was no meat to be had except what could be freshly butchered. Mail had not arrived for a week, and the schools had been closed to save fuel. If the town ran out of coal, it would be a major crisis. When the winds did die down after four days, the railroad tried to send a train through with a snowplow blade in front, but it barely made two miles an hour from Kiron to Schleswig.

The cut in the hills that the railroad tracks went through west of Schleswig was buried under thirty feet of snow. No plow could make it through that obstacle, so a crew of a hundred men set out with shovels to dig the tracks out so the train could get to Ricketts. By the time the tracks were open the wind was starting to drift it shut again creating a constant battle to keep the tracks and the roads open for the rest of the winter.

At this time the farmers' problems were largely the fault of the weather. There was very little the Farm Holiday organization could do about the weather, but they were able to keep busy, anyway. The Crawford County chapter founded its own underground newspaper called the *Spotlight*. It printed scathing articles about local politicians and anyone they considered pompous or predatory. Actually, there were plenty of targets for their attacks. The paper was distributed by hand. A man would walk through a café or tavern or some other public place and quietly whisper "Spotlight, Spotlight, get your *Spotlight* for a nickel." If you gave him a nickel, he would slip a copy of the Spotlight out from under his overcoat. Charles Speck, one of the activists at the Shields Sale, was thought to be one of the main sponsors of the paper.

A very talented cartoonist on their staff by the name of Ted Baer could clearly express the most biting and sarcastic concepts in his images. Many people could not wait for the next issue of the *Spotlight* to come out. Baer and the staff thrived on printing exposes' about the Board of Supervisors and the elected county officials. For instance, when they were all caught having a party in Omaha, possibly at county expense, the *Spotlight* had a field day. The establishment was outraged by the attack, but the general population was delighted to see the pompous upper crust being needled.

It was not always the upper crust who were attacked, however. A case in point was that of Gustav Schmann. Gus had come from

Germany as a very young man and spent the rest of his life farming in the Schleswig area. (His son, Rudy, was very active in town life.) After Gus retired, he worked as a part-time bartender where he always wore a white shirt and highly polished shoes. When he worked, he would run the beer from the tap right down the middle of the glass creating a large head of foam on top of the glass. "A good German always likes a good head on his beer," he would say. Not everybody was so sure about that, but when he would set up a free round of beer every third or fourth time, they thought he was O.K. Actually, when all that foam was taken into account, he never gave away any free beer.

Gustav loaned some of his savings to a farm family by the name of Bielenberg, and as the depression grew deeper, they were not able to make the payments. This went on for several years and Gus was becoming concerned, because he was depending on that loan income for living expenses. He would forgive the interest and delay part of the principal, but he needed some money coming in on the loan, so he approached them on that level. They said no they could not afford anything and reluctantly, he took them to court. He was awarded eighty acres of land that had been put up as collateral for the loan.

The Holiday movement thought it was terrible to see a farmer lose part of his farm because a lender had wanted a loan payment. They wrote a full-page article denouncing Gustav Schumann as one of the worst people in the county. This did not affect Gustav while he was in Schleswig where everyone knew him, but when he left town, he had to be careful of what he said and to whom he said it for quite a while.

Because of the influence their organization had in the farm country and wide readership of the *Spotlight*, the Farm Holiday found they were in a position to arbitrate a number of disputes. If a farmer had a problem, he could bring it before the Holiday organization, and, if they agreed, he would have the full backing of the organization and their paper. Many an individual and organization backed off in the face of that pressure. Farm Holiday backing was not automatic, however. Louie Grill and his brother-in-law, Hans Kroeger, both farmers themselves, had lent money to another farmer southwest of town. He refused to make payments, too, even when Louie and Hans were willing to accept part payments. His contention was that he did not have to make payments, and if they kept bothering him, he would go to the Holiday and cause trouble for them. Louie and Hans kept after him, and he did go to the Holiday. The Holiday investigated the case and determined the borrower not only had the money for a part payment, but he also had enough for a full payment and required him to make it. The Farm Holiday did not like to be used!

The County Sheriff Art Greene spent much of his time trying to locate the mimeograph printing press the Holiday used to print the *Spotlight*. The authorities would have liked nothing better than to find that press and bust it to "smithereens," but they never found it. It was moved from location to location under the cover of darkness and with the help of the general population.

On the Fourth of July of 1936, the temperature rose to over the hundred-degree mark, a phenomenon that was repeated every day for the next week with the temperatures ranging from 105 degrees to 110 degrees. The open pollinated corn that was available at that time cooked in its own juices. The heat caused crops to be so badly damaged there were a number of fields that were not even harvested—there was not enough grain to make the effort worthwhile. What had not been withered by the heat was eaten by a grasshopper plague. Air conditioning was not available, so the heat was equally hard on people and livestock. With the vegetation burned off, the dust would be blown up by the wind and dark drift-like banks of dust were created.

In November of 1936 the cattle train to the International Stock Show in Chicago was able to accumulate 100 cattle cars from the towns on the Punkin Vine Line, Schleswig accounting for 63 of them. The Chicago Northwestern Line provided the fastest engine it had available and two Pullman cars for farmers, and it was given the right of way, thus making it possible to make the trip in record time. The farmers appreciated the service but were concerned over the fact that the company had abandoned the portion of the Punkin Vine Line from Denison through Deloit. Rail service was still available in Schleswig, however.

Denison was the scene of an abnormal number of unusual incidents during the 1930's. In January of 1937, the unemployed and some of the poor farmers were becoming irritated with the treatment they were receiving from county officials. Assistance was supposed to be available, but the needy were getting a runaround, being sent from one office to another and always having to obtain additional forms. Finally they decided to react and went to the court house to see the Board of Supervisors. The Supervisors contended there was no problem in the county and refused to meet with a committee of the discontented. Individual appointments could be made, but the Supervisors would not recognize an organization, so the group settled down to a sit-down strike in the courthouse hallways. However, the Supervisors still refused to talk with them. At closing time Deputy Sheriff Cavett and Police Chief Eldor Lehfeldt ordered the protestors out of the building, and when they refused to go, the officers set off tear gas bombs in the courthouse. The peaceful demonstrators poured out of the building. One man, Loyal Johnson, was arrested and charged with defacing a public building when a window was broken on the second floor to let in fresh air. The Holiday Organization loved the action. Frank North, the head of the local Holiday chapter, posted the bail for Mr. Johnson who was later found not guilty. Write-ups of the incident were in all the news media from the *Spotlight* to the *Des Moines Register*.

A group made up of local ministers and WPA people approached the Board of Supervisors to see if a solution could be found to the problem. In the face of all the bad publicity, the Supervisors decided to take steps to settle things down and by agreeing to meet with a delegation from the protesters. They answered the questions that were posed and explained how the system was designed to work. A number of misunderstandings, which had been perpetuated for some time, had to be clarified. Finally, when proposals were made to make the system function, the protesters disbanded. One of the facts that resulted from the attention that was focused on the situation by the newspaper stories was that the public assistance programs in Crawford County had administrative costs about three times higher than in the neighboring counties.

The Farmers State Bank in Schleswig and its companion organization–the Schleswig Cattle Loan Company–were proud of their reputation as an agriculture supportive bank. There was certainly no doubting this. Farmers of good reputation could go out west to buy train carloads of feeder cattle and write a check for them without first bothering to secure a loan to cover the check. They would stop at the bank after arriving home to explain what their needs would be. The necessary credit was there for them. This applied only to farmers, however, and only those farmers who had a good reputation with the bank. Merchants in town had a more difficult time. If they needed money to expand their businesses, they would be likely to be told to put some of their old inventory on a sale to raise money rather than go into debt with a new loan. When a new merchant wanted to start up, as when Bill Wollenhaupt wanted to start up a sausage operation in connection with his new grocery store, he had to talk long and hard. Only then did he receive part of what he wanted, but he was able to get started, and his Schleswig Sausage brand wurst became highly profitable and widely known. He was able to buy the old stagecoach station and rebuilt the stable into a slaughterhouse for his meat processing operation, and he was later able to show the bankers his books and gloat a little. A number of other merchants, however, did not have the same opportunity.

The First of March was traditional moving day on the farm. Farm leases expired on March first and tenants who were moving had to wait for the new place to be vacated and new tenants were waiting to come in. Everyone moved on March 1st.

Most of the merchants in Schleswig were immigrants from Germany. Bill Wollenhaupt had come to Schleswig in 1935; Johannas Gosch had come in 1925; and Hans Behrmann had come ten years before that. A steady stream of immigrants had come from Germany who had become farmers, merchants, farm hands, laborers, and workers of all kinds. They provided a constant source of renewed vigor and energetic creativity. It was only interrupted briefly by the World War, after which the injection their energy continued and was a source of strength for the community. Many of the immigrants worked for businessmen who were already here before launching on their own. Hans Petersen came in 1927 and worked for Ted Jepsen, the boy whose hand had been crippled in the Blizzard of 1888, before starting his own construction company in 1944. These immigrants all added a great deal to the community.

The railroad brought a whole variety of interesting people to town. There were visiting relatives, travelers passing through, salesmen dealing with merchants, and bums riding the rail. Sometimes some of them were not always happy to be here. One incident involved several salesmen who had come through, and after they had finished their rounds, had a fair amount of time until the next train out of town. They were bemoaning the fact that now they were stuck for hours in such a quiet, dull place. They bragged about the fancy places they had seen on their travels and the sharp deals to which they had been a party. They thought it was a shame to be stuck in such a town full of hicks and where they could not even get a good card came organized. A bartender helped out by suggesting a few local men who might be willing to play. The salesmen were not sure it would be much of a challenge to play with some local yokels, but they had nothing better to do at the time. A game of poker was organized with "Sport" Korner, "Slick" Schroeder, and Andy Paulsen and within short order the salesmen were broke–completely cleaned out and were much humbler when they were ready to go to the train station. As they were heading out, the Schleswig boys called them back. Our boys said from the way the salesmen had talked they must have been sophisticated gamblers. To test them out, our boys said they stacked the deck, palmed cards, signaled hands and engaged in every trick they could think of, and the salesmen had not caught on to any of it. Being "honest" cardplayers, our boys did return the money to the salesmen with the warning that if they played cards again, they had better be sure they were dealing with amateurs.

George Pipgras appeared in the record books one more time. When his major league career as a baseball player ended, he accepted a position as an umpire. His no-nonsense approach helped him to maintain control of the games he worked, as was demonstrated when he ejected seventeen players from one game–nearly enough for the starting line-up of both teams. Bill Zuber, the New York Yankee from the Amana Colonies, nearly fifty years later could reminisce clearly about his game action under Pipgras' watchful eye. Zuber also related that the team would occasionally attempt to harass George after a close call by having someone call out, "Pipgras you have the eyes of a cat," which would by followed by a chorus from the dugout saying in unison, "Yeah, a POLE-CAT!" This would, of course, encourage George to be even more vigilant.

President Roosevelt had put into effect a wide variety of new and experimental programs, many of which were having a strong effect on the economic depression that gripped the nation. After retreating so far, it took the economy some time to revive. A great deal of uncertainty in society was eased by the passage of the Social Security Act and the Federal Deposit Insurance Corp., but, not everyone was happy with these developments. The conservative faction in the country was wondering with all this tax money going to the farmers, the poor, and the elderly, what would be left for them? Their strongest tool was the Supreme Court which declared a number of the new deal programs unconstitutional. The President struck back by proposing to pack the Court with more members to change its direction. The proposal was not popular with Congress, so the President went directly to the people with his Fireside Talks. The pressure was on the Court, and the outcome was to allow the new programs to operate, and, as vacancies were filled, the complexion of the court became more moderate.

Philosophically, the Farm Holiday was changing, too. It had started in response to the problems being suffered by a large segment of the economy, and when it became a very successful organization, it was courted by several other groups. One of these was the American Communist Party. The Communists were a legitimate political party in the 1930's having people like Hal Ware, Mother Bloor, and Lem Harris who worked with the Holiday and, in some instances, used them. The Communists wanted to get rid of the whole economic system and set up a new, fairer one. On the other side, the Holiday was being wooed by Henry A. Wallace and the *Wallace's Farmer* group who wanted to use the government to make long term improvements in the current economic system.

When he was appointed as Secretary of Agriculture and given free rein by President Roosevelt, Wallace's movement was successful. The bulk of the Holiday organization wanted neither approach. Long term changes were not what they wanted. Instead they wanted short term reprieves from foreclosures and repossessions—just enough time to get back on their feet after being knocked down by forces beyond their control. The Holiday movement began to fade after the founder, Milo Reno, had died in 1935. As farm problems began to fade from the headlines, many chapters were beginning to dissolve. The *Spotlight* was one of the features that helped to hold the Crawford County chapter together—it had changed though. It had become a cell of the American Communist Party, and the stories in the *Spotlight* began to reflect this change.

On the world scene, the forces of power were aligning themselves for another conflict. Unfortunately, for the second time in the lifetimes of many of the residents of Schleswig, the winds of fate were aligning them against their cultural traditions. Germany and Italy were grouping themselves against England, France, and Russia in a strong ideological conflict. It would be the conservative forces of Fascism and Nazism against democracy and capitalism.

The first clash of the two systems occurred in the Spanish Civil War in 1937. Francisco Franco's fascist forces were trying to overthrow the monarchy which was supported by an international coalition of fighters led mainly by the Russians. The conflict was described elegantly by Ernest Hemingway in his prize wining novel *For Whom the Bell Tolls*. The Americans who went unofficially to fight in the conflict were known as the Lincoln Brigade. The Communist Cell in Crawford County was so strong, they sent their own fighting contingent to Spain. Included in this group were Maynard Schuler, Clarence Schuler, Fritz Grell, and Harry Smith. They and the others formed a link between the Lincoln Highway and the Lincoln Brigade, and the *Spotlight* was printing stories from the fighting front in Spain!

Incidental bits of news in the area were also being published. In Schleswig, the Rebakah Lodge hosted the regional convention of their organization–a large undertaking for such a small group. There was a large attendance, and it was a successful event with much of the town supporting the activity.

Hugo Kroeger, the rural mail carrier, developed one of his series of unusual vehicles in which to deliver the mail. He developed the first snowmobile in Schleswig–a car frame in which a second set of rear wheels was mounted in front of the originals and a set of caterpillar-type tracks was then mounted over them. A set of skis was mounted by the front tires so they could be lowered when the snow was deep enough. The problems of covering blocked rural roads were overcome when the machine was in working order.

The first high school band summer concert in 1938 was on the evening of June 1. The Schleswig band would put on concerts on Wednesday and Saturday evenings when the stores were open and the farmers would come into town. In the early evening the band would play a concert on a mobile bandstand that would be wheeled into a vacant lot or in front of an alley. A number of benches were set up, and many spectators brought their own chairs. After the concert, the farmers would attend to their business with the merchants and then socialize a little in the cafes or taverns before returning home near the bewitching hour.

If Wednesday and Saturday nights were town nights, then Sunday afternoon was visiting day on the farm. Grandparents and aunts and uncles from town would go out for a leisurely afternoon on the farm. In this way, family identities were strengthened and support groups were available for the young and the troubled. It was a good way of life.

The Schleswig cattle-feeders did not take the top prizes in the Stock Show in 1938 but did get quite a bit of publicity. Strong, favorable articles featured our feeders in both the *Hereford Journal* and in the *Farm Bureau Spokesman*.

In Europe the Fascist powers were making advances. Francisco Franco won the civil war in Spain and was mopping up the liberal forces. Germany annexed Austria and part of Czechoslovakia. Mussolini was tightening control on the population in Italy. Japan was making inroads into China. Consequently, the world situation was making many people nervous.

Late that season, Mother Nature put on a spectacular display of Northern Lights in which the Aurora Borealis glowed and leaped high in the northern night sky. Usually it is faint if it is visible at all. It is a rare year when a strong display is seen this far south.

Lights of another kind were on the mind of many farmers. The Rural Electrification Administration was bringing electric lines into northern Crawford County. Completion of the lines was scheduled to be June of 1939. A few farmers didn't see the need for such an expensive and dangerous service, but most farmers, and especially farm wives, could not wait for the lights to be turned on.

Several local people were doing well for themselves. Burness Kastner was going to play his accordion on KSCJ radio station in Sioux City. Ray Kolbaum bought the Kiron blacksmith shop. Broder Petersen was hired to operate the Texaco service station on the highway. By the way, the number of the highway had been changed from #21 to #59, and it had gone from a main highway across the State to being a main highway across the country from Canada to Mexico, giving an extra bit of prestige to the project.

In the local high school, the band was becoming the desirable organization of which to be a part. Over the years good showings in regional contests had been made. Miss Mable Fritz–a tough taskmaster–was the band leader who conducted the show. She called practice meetings at 7:00 A.M. and expected everyone to be there and to perform–there was no messing around. Her approach paid off in 1939 when the Schleswig High School Band won not only every local and regional competition, but also they were invited to participate in the Minneapolis national competition from which they emerged with a third rating–very prestigious, indeed.

Girls' softball was becoming a popular sport and, although the Schleswig team wasn't bad, the real power house was the team from Boyer. The core strength of their team was a group of girls from the large Kropf family which was known as the "Kropf Battery." The star in this group was the pitcher, Arlene Kropf (Miller). An interesting game was sure to result when they came to town.

The Schleswig Gun Club was quite active, but target practice was about all they could get in since wildlife was very scarce. Intensive farming had destroyed much of the habitat and what had been left dried up in the drought. There were so few wild animals left that when a deer was killed by a car near Onawa, nearly 40 miles away, the story made the local newspapers.

The war situation was growing worse daily. Germany signed a peace pact with Russia and turned its blitzkrieg loose on Poland. Britain and France immediately declared war on Germany and Italy. President Roosevelt was maintaining a position of neutrality, but the national sentiment was in favor of Britain and France. It was difficult for the Germans in Schleswig to be placed in this position again although the persecution was not as blatant this time around. However, it was not a comfortable position in which to be.

Some of the boys from the Communist Cell in Denison had gone to some of the bigger cities to help the Communist Party organize, and a number of them were arrested in Sioux City and charged with aiding a foreign country. The five from Crawford County were cleared, although among the mounds of propaganda literature was a fair amount addressed to Crawford County addresses. These boys also discovered there was some very violent opposition out there, so they decided to low key it for a while.

The most popular head wear in Schleswig was a white hat with the number 40 across the front as the fortieth anniversary of the town had arrived. There had not been a community wide celebration since the Veterans homecoming twenty years before. It was a three-day event, and the crowd in attendance approached ten thousand people. It was a gala time, and many of the participants reminisced about the beginning of the town–although Schleswig certainly seemed to have gone through a lot in a relatively short period of time.

John Jakso, Sr. was elected mayor of the city. His favorite phrase was, "That be right." Soon it became the favorite expression of the whole town. Whenever there was agreement on a point, it was acknowledged by the phrase, "That be right."

Losing one of the town's long time landmarks when the old Tie Barn or livery stable on south Second Street burned down was a sad occasion. A produce station next to it also burned. The sense of loss was amplified when it was discovered that Hugo Kroeger's "snowmobile" had been in the building and was totally destroyed. The REC was also storing its excess poles in the building.

Losing a feature of the past only urged progress for the future. A literary group had been campaigning for a city library in Schleswig and were now taking their effort a step farther by featuring a book drive. Six hundred books were accumulated and now all they needed was for the city to authorize a place to store them.

In the Fall, John D. Moeller was given the honor of judging the International Livestock Show in Chicago. He was certainly the preeminent cattle-feeder in this part of the State. The following year in 1940, he sent 124 head of cattle to the Omaha Stockyards where he obtained the top price for his cattle. He had fed them out from 500 pounds to an average 1246 pounds. It was a rather remarkable feat.

In Europe, Germany continued to take over more countries. Most of the Scandinavian countries fell under the NAZI control, and Italy was invading northern Africa. Britain attempted to send troops to reinforce France, but they were forced to retreat and to make an emergency evacuation at Dunkirk. Schleswig was not the only place that was uneasy about the international developments. On the other side of the world, Japan was invading China.

In Schleswig, a number of aliens who had not bothered to obtain citizenship decided this would be a good time to complete the process. If the United States was drawn into the conflict, they thought it would be better to be considered a citizen of the United States rather than a citizen of Germany living here.

Once again Mother Nature reared her head. A massive invasion of chinch bugs destroyed crops very rapidly. The only defense was to put a strip of creosote around the fields. It, however, had to be renewed after each rain. In all over 15,000 gallons of creosote was used in Crawford County alone. The chinch bugs were offensive little creatures; they not only eat crops but when they were crushed they gave off a very offensive odor.

The town was growing and an addition to the schoolhouse was proposed, including a new auditorium. Schleswig had been using the Opera House which did not have a shower room for athletic events nor an adequate stage for other school programs. Events and the number of spectators who wanted to attend them were becoming too large for the old Opera House. A new auditorium was badly needed and the plans were to include additions for several new classrooms, a new kitchen, and a new heating plant for the whole school. The school administration suggested that Federal help be obtained through a WPA grant—a suggestion that was soundly defeated. The farmers appreciated the Federal farm program when they were really down and needed it, but economic conditions had improved, and they could build their own school. They did not need Federal aid. The school addition was proudly built with local funds!

That was not the only improvement in Schleswig in 1940. The Schleswig Library opened in the City Hall with a series of low shelves that were built along the wall in the front room. The Literary Society, which had initiated the library movement, had accumulated 600 volumes and continued to raise funds by selling doughnuts and coffee. The Library was well supported and was frequently used by many of the residents.

The military draft was re-instituted even though the country was still at peace. The first person from Schleswig who was drafted was John Stewart who worked at the bakery. The CCC Camp was turned into a camp for conscientious objectors and was to serve not only Iowa but also all of the surrounding states.

Though Schleswig was progressing, it was sad to see one of the oldest operating businesses in Schleswig close. The auction service run by Col. Fred D. Reinking held its first sale before the town of Schleswig began, but after 42 years in the business he had decided to quit the operation. His familiar cry would be missed.

Several changes were also happening in the business district as Charles Jurgensen sold his John Deere dealership to Stern and Gempeler. The old car garage on Second Street (106 Second) was converted to a bowling alley. The dirt work involved in the conversion caused the oven in the bakery next door to break.

The High School Music Department pulled off the coup of the year in 1940. Because of the prestige they had earned in prior years and the record that Miss Fritz had established, they were able to bring in Karl King from Fort Dodge to conduct a week-long musical seminar. Mr. King had a national reputation as a band leader and composer, having started his career with Buffalo Bill Cody's Wild West Show. Later he became the Musical Conductor for the Ringling Brothers, Barnum and Bailey Circus. During this time he composed dozens of very popular musical pieces for large bands, and he was at the time conducting the Fort Dodge Symphony Orchestra. He was the preeminent musical personality in Iowa. Mr. King rehearsed the high school band all week on music that he had composed, and, at the end of that time, the band put on a public concert. The entire evening was devoted to Karl King music conducted by Karl King. It was the cultural highlight of the region.

Most of the world was at war by this time. President Roosevelt and his Vice President, Henry A. Wallace, were able to keep the United States out of it from the time it started in 1939, but our neutrality came to a sudden end on Sunday, December 7, 1941. On that day the Japanese made a surprise attack on the U.S. Naval Base at Pearl Harbor, Hawaii. Suddenly, we were in the war full time and our entry clearly made it a Second World War.

Schleswig supported the national effort wholeheartedly. The farmers were asked to shift gears once more. During the First World

War, the farmers had been asked to produce as much food as possible to support the war effort. Then during the depression the farm programs were put in place to limit production to eliminate the surpluses. Now the government was asking them to produce all they could again. They did respond. In the towns victory gardens were promoted. Every piece of scrap metal—housewives even being asked to flatten all cans—was saved for the war effort. Rationing coupons were issued, and, without them no commodities nor food could be purchased regardless of the price. Schleswig beat all the quotas for the purchase of War Bonds that had been set for them.

This would not be a short, quick war as it had been in 1918. The Axis powers had a similar strategy, however—defeat the Allied powers before the United States could get involved. By the time the United States became engaged in 1942, Germany and Italy had occupied all of continental Europe and northern Africa. Japan had defeated the Pacific Rim of Asia and occupied over half the Pacific Ocean. Britain was under near constant air bombardment, and Germany had attacked its one time ally—Russia. The U. S. first stabilized Great Britain and then began air attacks on Germany. Generals Patton and Montgomery began pushing German General Rommel out of north Africa in 1943 and fought their way up the Italian Peninsula, while Russia attacked from the east. In 1944, the Allies invaded Normandy and began to reconquer western Europe under Generals Eisenhower and Bradley. In 1945, the Allied armies from the west and south and the Russian army from the east closed in on Germany and forced a surrender on May 6, 1945.

On the Pacific front, however, the Japanese continued to gain territory for the first half of 1942 including some islands in the Aleutians off Alaska. The turning point came with the battle of Guadalcanal. The distances were tremendous, and the only allies we had in the area were Australia and New Zealand, and they were not heavily populated. It was a long hard fight back, but our troops took the key points and jumped to the next major area, and by

1945 we were ready to attack the Japanese mainland. Admiral Nimitz and General MacArthur directed the operation. To save the many casualties that an invasion would cause, President Truman ordered the dropping of the atomic bomb, and as a result, the Japanese surrendered on August 10, 1945.

A large number of young men had entered the military services. How many came from Schleswig depends on where you draw the boundaries for the Schleswig territory. In 1942, Hans Behrmann had posted pictures of 48 area men in the armed services in the window of his store. In the following years, double, triple and more young men were called to service. They were represented in almost every major campaign, and they all conducted themselves honorably and with distinction. There were so many of them they would run into each other in odd places such as when Herbie Reissen ran into his brother, Ernie, in Australia, and Magnus Johansen found John Witt in Italy. There were innumerable individual stories of sacrifice, heroic effort, and of pain and suffering—entirely too many to report here—but many of these men or their families are in the area and can be contacted directly for individual accounts.

Not everyone made it home. A number of casualties including Vernon Gluesing, Delbert Schoenfeldt, Leroy Maas, Kenneth Stoltenberg, Tom Schlimgen, Martin Wellner, John Kuehl, Hilbert Janssen, Bennie Boysen, and Willie Kuehl caused a great deal of sadness in our community. Difficult times in prisoner of war camps were experienced by Glenn Johannsen and Milt Wassgren. Women were also doing their part by taking jobs to allow men to serve. Lois Kastner ran the Post Office so Herbert Rickert could join the Navy. Mrs. John Witt joined the WACs and Theresa Hordeman became a nurse overseas. Others, such as Irmagard Boettger went west to work in defense plants. Leslie Grell named a B-17 bomber after the *Schleswig Leader* which flew 82 consecutive missions over Germany. Many of the boys wrote letters to the paper telling of their experiences.

On the home front, the shortage of materials and rationing prevented many changes from happening, and yet life continued. In 1942, John Claussen retired as manager of the Farmers Lumber and Grain Company and his son, Claussy, took over the position. An unusual event, a short in the phone lines, caused all the phones in town to ring from continuously 5:00 A.M. to 9:00 A.M. one day. All kinds of materials were collected for the war effort, even old phonograph records. In the county, guards were posted at railroad interchanges, water towers, and major plants. A practice blackout was held on Dec. 4 during which all the lights went out at once on schedule.

The following year, the Play Mor dance hall was sold to the Crawford County Sales Co. It was dismantled, and the materials were used to build a sales barn in Denison. Conscientious Objectors assigned to the old CCC Camp were working on local farms. They had to pay for their own keep but were good workers, many of them being Mennonites from the colonies. Italian Prisoners of War were working on Adams Ranch at Odebolt. War restrictions caused the Ida County Cattle-feeders to serve chicken at their annual banquet. State agents and the Sheriff raided some beer-only taverns in Schleswig where some whiskey and a few illegal punch cards were found but nothing serious. A new veterinarian, Dr. John Hurd, moved in from Pawnee, Nebraska.

War planes could be seen in the skies as they were moved to disembarkment points or as crews were trained. One B–17 bomber had an engine catch on fire over Wayne, Nebraska, the crew bailed out, and the plane flew on to the Schleswig area. The crewless plane circled this area for several hours before it crashed on the Neil Vogt farm eight miles south of town.

Bits and pieces of news made life more interesting. In town, the Opera House was sold to the Farmers Lumber and Grain Company and in the Summer of 1944 it was torn down. Milt Winters built an oxygen tent to save the life of his infant son, Garry. Mayor John Jackso and Skeets Reinking started a series of annual Coon feeds. Nurses Elizabeth Rock and Lillie Hollander who had owned and operated the hospital in Ida Grove for several years sold it and moved to Schleswig. The tin shed that had been brought in from Hohenzollern was used as a depot for the collection of waste paper. New shelves which were taller and could hold more books and had doors that could be locked when the librarian was not on duty were built for the library. Percy Lyon, the editor of the *Schleswig Leader*, died on April 19, 1945, and his son, Robert, took over the paper. There was an attempt to change the route of Highway #59 before it was paved. The proposed route would go through Kiron and Arthur which caused concern since much effort had been put into having it go past Schleswig. A hired hand who worked for Hugo Jensen was arrested by the F.B.I. Byron Thompson was an escaped fugitive from a military camp in Louisiana. One *good* piece of news was that county officials said the ground water level was back to normal for the first time since the drought years in the early 1930's.

Once the war was over, life did not return to normal immediately. It took some time for the military to return the soldiers to America and to muster them out, returning our boys, one by one, over the next year and a half. Many families waited anxiously, but thankfully, knowing that the boys were out of harm's way. The economy had been geared completely for war production, so it also took some time for it to convert to civilian production. As a result, there were many shortages, and, in some areas, a black market was the only way to obtain some products. If one was willing to pay enough, most things could be bought. Farm equipment was a prime example of an area of strong demand and short supply. The war had killed the last remnants of the depression, and the economy was back on solid ground—even in farm country. One sure sign of changing times was the demise of the *Spotlight*. It went out of existence in 1946, since no one was interested any longer in stirring up controversy. It was time to get on with life.

The Commercial Club had been very active in promoting business interests in Schleswig for many years where countless promotions and celebrations had been put on over the years. Julius Rohwer, the president of the bank, was not satisfied with this, however, and thought the principal organization in town should be comprised of both businessmen and farmers. In his view, farming was the largest business interest in the area, and an organization that did not include their interests was not truly representing the entire community. He had to do a lot of talking, as the businessmen looked upon the farmers as customers rather than as fellow businessmen. Eventually, Mr. Rohwer was successful and the Community Club was organized. On alternating years the presidency of the organization would be from the farm community and then from town. Not all of the community was represented, however. It was a men's organization. As a show of its support, the bank has provided a full-course dinner at the December meeting of the club in each year since. The businessmen were not entirely comfortable with this situation and developed the Schleswig Business Club to promote their strictly commercial interests and to include women.

The Highway #59 committee had successfully restored the original route through Schleswig, but the paving project had to be delayed as the cement and equipment were in short supply. It was promised, though, that as soon as it was feasibly possible, the work would begin. Another area where the shortages were having an effect was in the development of a new community center. Since both the Opera House and the PlayMor dance hall were torn down during the war, there was no sizable hall for meetings or social activities. The Community Club had already organized the Schleswig Enterprises Incorporated to solve this problem and had been selling stock and developing plans for a new building, but the materials were not available on the regular market and were far too expensive on the black market. Work on both Highway #59 and the new community center would come, but it would be slow.

In Germany, the Allied Forces set up a special court in the city of Nuernberg to try war crimes. The brutality of the NAZI party had shocked the world, and it was thought the leaders responsible for the atrocities were to be held accountable for their actions. One of the Judges was Denison attorney Leon Powers.

The returning servicemen set up a new organization in town—
the Veterans of Foreign Wars—which was a more active group than
the older American Legion. The energetic young veterans wanted
to do more than the American Legion charter allowed, and one of
the things they established was a social club. The basement of the
Rickert building at 116 Cedar Street became the selected location, the first floor of which was occupied by the Post Office and
the *Schleswig Leader*. Whip Langholdt was hired as manager, and it
was developed into a first rate club room which had been organized as a private club but was operated as being open to the
public. It became one of six retail beer distributors in the community.

Beer was the only alcoholic beverage that was available on the
retail level. Since the repeal of prohibition in 1933, Iowa limited
the sale of whiskey and hard liquor to sales through state owned
liquor stores. The sale of hard liquor by the drink was strictly prohibited. As is the case with laws that are not popularly supported,
a number of violations can occur without serious consequences. It
was said that on occasion a drink of liquor could be obtained in
Schleswig, and it was also said that it made more difference if the
bartender knew you than the location of where you asked. There
were occasional raids by the county or state authorities, but the
good old-boy network had the word out quickly, and the damage
was usually minimal. Gambling was also strictly prohibited by
Iowa law. In Schleswig, there would occasionally be money bet on
a public card game, and the bartenders usually had a punch card
with a cash prize (in some low, dark corners, one might even be
able to find a slot machine or two). Schleswig was not without sin.

This all happened even with Jim Davis as City Marshal. He
had been Marshal for longer than many people could remember,
and he had the respect of the young and old alike. Always there if
needed, he was not a man to be taken advantage of though. If he
signaled from the sidewalk that he wanted you to pull your car
over, you had better be pulling into the parking space. He could
control traffic better from the sidewalk than most officers could

with the newest police cars and equipment. Schleswig being relatively crime free could be attributed to Mr. Davis, but the years were taking their toll. He had been marshal for over twenty years, having started in 1925, so retirement was due. Otto Keller, a World War I veteran, farmer, and truck driver, took over the position.

Cement blocks were the first building material that became available in any quantity. Consequently, it was used for several buildings. Ralph Koepke bought the old wooden building which had been the first Doctor's office at the corner of Birch and Second Streets next to the Green Bay Lumberyard. Koepke moved the building to the south part of town and set it up as a garage. He then constructed a new café building on the site and called it the "Stucco Inn." Not long afterward, John Gottberg constructed a block building at 211 Cedar Street to be operated as a dry-cleaning business.

Many first generation, second generation and third generation families in the community still had family contacts in the Old Country. Word had been coming from Germany, ever since civilian communication had been reestablished after the war, that the war-ravaged country had been suffering severe shortages of the most common items. The people in the Schleswig area, as well as in many other areas, responded with humanitarian aid. Many special packages containing such things as soap, coffee, cooking lard, thread and needles, etc. were sent to individual contacts in Germany. The gratitude of many of the recipients was expressed in numerous ways over many years.

The inflow of immigrants started again as a number of very highly talented people arrived from Germany. The difficult conditions in Germany were solved for a number of people by opportunities offered them by relatives and contacts here. They did a great deal to help our community grow and develop. Included in this group were Heinz Benke, Fritz Berger, and Hans Detlefsen, as well as a number of others.

Schleswig was known as a neat little town with well-kept homes—all of which were painted white. When the town started, not a tree was growing in the place, and it took years for there to be any shade for the houses. Many of the trees that lined the streets were white birch trees which added a distinctive appearance to the town. Sadly, a disease for which there was no cure struck the white birch in the late 40's, and they began dying. Over a few years almost all of the birch trees had to be taken down. The lone survivor of this epidemic stands on the corner of Birch and Sixth Streets.

Halloween had always been a time for mischief around Schleswig. Trick or treaters would go around and really mean it. Some young people would be waiting until the marshal would retire for the evening, and then all manner of junk and garbage would be used to "decorate" the streets, windows would be smeared with soap (homemade lye soap worked the best), outhouses would be dumped, farmers would find their lanes blocked with a pile of hay, animals were slipped into the gymnasium. A bicycle was even hoisted to the top of the town flag pole, but the ultimate prank was when school officials discovered a wagon on the school house roof. John Spahn's entire huge farm wagon was perched forty feet up on the very top of the school house roof! No one could imagine how it had gotten there, and it took a crew of men a considerable amount of time to get it down with blocks and tackle and all manner of equipment. For years it remained a mystery, but when the details did come out, it turned out that a precocious young high school student, Harris Grill, had disassembled the wagon entirely, pulled the parts up to the roof, and reassembled them there–all under the cover of darkness and without being heard.

Progress continued. Bill Wollenhaupt constructed a huge new grocery store and meat processing plant at 100 Second Street, built entirely out of shiny glazed blocks. It would be 50 feet wide and over a hundred feet long, the north half of the building was to be a grocery store, and the south half would be a frozen meat locker plant. For the time, it was a state-of-the-art building. Part of the locker plant would be the usual walk-in type of locker, but the other part would be an automated system that would bring an individual locker to the freezer door, and the patron would not have to enter the cold locker room. In the back of the building and in the basement was the meat processing department with built in smoking rooms, curing tanks, grinders and mixers. Farmers could bring in their animals, and they would be processed and packaged and stored in a frozen food locker. It was the most modern design and technology available and was featured in an article in "Food Dealer" magazine. Iowa State College rated it as the best operation in the State. Bill would also make his own Schleswig Sausage products.

Jack Hess built a new garage for his Schleswig Motor Company at 206 Cedar Street made of cement blocks with a roof of curved steel which was coming on the market from the manufacturers of military quonset huts. The building was finished just in time to display the new 1949 Chevrolet cars.

At long last, or so it seemed, construction on the new community building was starting. Glazed blocks and a curved steel roof were the building materials. It would be 60 feet by 80 feet and have a full finished basement and would be the finest dance hall and community building in the county. Petersen Construction was the general contractor, but there was a great deal of volunteer help to get it finished.

A need for a new fire station was evident. The old fire station in the basement of the City Hall would only hold two of the department's three vehicles and not much equipment. A new fire station was proposed to be built just south of the new Community Building which would hold all of their vehicles and equipment and also have room for some of the City's equipment. The same materials as had been used for the Community Building would be used for the fire station, although the roof would curve from foundation to foundation with no side walls.

Construction was booming all over by 1949. Not only were all the new businesses going up, but Highway #59 also was being paved past town and fifteen new houses were under construction. Charlie Franzek sold the City Café and put in a tavern at 107 Second Street. Schleswig was on a roll.

On the home front we were still winning honors. Herman and Leonard Schrenbeck had won the Malt Barley Contest where they had beaten out all other farmers in a seven-state area. On the annual cattle-feeders tour, Herb Kilder from Iowa State College had declared Ed Reimer as the "Dean of American Cattle-feeders." Bill Petersen and "Beep" Sonksen earned safe driving awards for driving school buses. Elaine Marth had a part in "Calling All Stars" in the Orpheum Theater in Sioux City.

The big story in 1949, though, was Golden Jubilee Celebration. The Community Club had decided to make it the best celebration any community this size had ever put on. The first step was to organize a Calf Club for the young people since they were not satisfied with the 4-H clubs. The local farmers had long been recognized as some of the premier cattle-feeders in the nation, so they went about designing a program that would demonstrate the real world values in cattle feeding. The plan was for a group of the fathers to go out west and buy a whole herd of calves which would be brought back and divided evenly into pens of five calves. Lots were then drawn by the youngsters to see who would get each pen, giving them all an even starting point. The youngster would then have to go to the bank, negotiate a loan for the calves, and sign the loan papers. The cattle would be fed until the celebration, and careful records of their costs and conditions were to be kept. At the celebration the pens of calves would be judged by commercial cattle buyers using the standards for buying commercial cattle at the time and on the last day of the celebration, an auction of the cattle was held in which only buyers for packing plants could bid. Later, awards for special features and for the best set of books would be made, and the youngsters would have to see that their loans were paid off. The fathers felt very comfortable that the kids who went through the program could learn the right way to feed cattle.

Planning for the celebration began in January when committees were set up and began operating. In July, it was announced that the renown Karl King Orchestra had been contracted to perform, the well-known Herb O'Connor would be the master of ceremonies, a firm from Omaha would do the street decorations, and twenty-five thousand pounds of watermelon had been ordered to give away during the celebration. Jubilee license plates were selling fast. The German Band, that had been reorganized, largely through the efforts of Milt Winters, was used heavily on promotion tours to other towns in the area. Eight acts were booked to preform on the open stage without charge. Some of them included Ethel D'Arcy on the high wire, the Connor's rolling globe act, a clown band, the Ballantine family act, etc. and the Iowa State Conservation Exhibit would be displayed.

The schedule of events during the celebration involved the following:

Thursday:

9:00 A.M. The Calf Projects were judged. The Best of Show Prize was provided by the Chicago Livestock Exchange and was won by Marie Wollenhaupt.

10:00 A.M. Business and Farmers Large Float Parade. There were 74 large floats, four bands and other smaller entries. It was over a mile long. Johannas Gosch won first place with a float entitled "Under the Spreading Chestnut Tree." Betty Bielenberg crowned Queen.

1:30 P.M. The Karl King Orchestra performed.

2:30 P.M. Free Attractions would perform.

5:00 P.M. Barbequed Beef prepared by Bill Wollenhaupt in special pits behind his store. Free watermelon was distributed.

7:15 P.M. The Karl King Orchestra performed.

8:00 P.M. Free Attractions.

10.00 P.M. Fireworks display with $1500.00 worth of fireworks.

Bobby Mills dance band will play in the newly finished Community Building.

Friday:

10:00 A.M. Children's Parade.

Displays

1:30 P.M. Karl King Orchestra performed.

2:30 P.M. Free Attractions would perform.
Free Watermelon.

7:15 P.M. The Karl King Orchestra performed.

8:00 P.M. Free Attractions.

Bobby Mills dance in the Community Building.

Saturday:

9:00 P.M. Calf Auction.

1:30 P.M. Karl King Orchestra performed.

2:30 P.M. Free Attractions would perform.

Free Watermelon.

7:15 P.M. The Karl King Orchestra performed.

8:00 P.M. Free Attractions.

Brownie Walters band in the Community Building.

12:00 Drawing for new Cadillac car.

The committees had done their work well as the events took place as scheduled. The barbequed beef was especially delicious. The only thing that did not work quite as anticipated was the firework display. The fire department was in charge and the staging area was in the field at the west end of Cedar Street. There may have been a short in the wiring or some of the firemen may have been so involved in other parts of the celebration that they weren't paying close enough attention to this activity, but the entire hour-long display went off in five minutes! Those who were there early enough to see the show said it was quite spectacular.

The average daily attendance was estimated at 10,000 people and was considered the best celebration of its size in the state. When the books were tallied there was a profit of over $12,000 which was saved for future celebrations.

Later that Fall, the first varsity football game was held under the direction of Coach Top. It was a six-man team that required a lot of running to complete the plays, and there were not a lot of team members to conduct a defensive game.

The Immanuel Lutheran Church announced they were going to begin construction of a new Church building. The architect's drawings revealed a magnificent stone structure to replace to old wooden frame building.

A number of young people were advancing their educations, including Bob Hess, who was head of the Yearbook at Simpson College, Bob Reimer, who was to debate before the Supreme Court,

Joyce Jensen (Petersen), who was at Grinnell, and Lorenz Ipsen, who was completing a forestry degree at Iowa State College.

There was a sense the whole world was changing. The United Nations was giving hope that wars would be more difficult to start. The United States was the dominant country on earth, Iowa was a very proud state, and Schleswig would glow in the developing new society.

It was once said that he who does not learn from history is doomed to repeat it. That surely cannot be the case in Schleswig. A community that has gone through a severe economic downturn, persecution by its neighbors for its cultural heritage, and the humiliation of having to fight a war against the country from which the ancestors of many of its residents came, would certainly have enough in its past. Even though many of the problems were caused by outside influences, they would not be the kind of issues that could be allowed to repeat themselves. There are new things, better things, to be accomplished. We must look ahead to forthcoming possibilities rather than to dwell on past problems.

Prominent businessmen of the day. Bill Wollenhaupt inspecting his Schleswig Sausage. Julius Rohwer pontificating on the economic situation. Ed Claussen and Leonard Hollander discussing events. "Hap" Peters in the Drug Store and Byron Behrmann with a mischievous look in his eye.

IX. PROGRESS

1950–1974

Progress comes in waves like the tides. It will wash well inland, and then recede. The tide will raise all ships, and when the tidal wave recedes, riptides are created just under the surface. The riptides carry the unwary deep under the surface and far out to sea. Somehow, analogies from the sea seem appropriate to an area whose ancestors lived not far from either the North Sea or the Baltic Sea. Many of the old adages even survived, for example one is about the sky, "Red sky in the evening, Sailor's delight, red sky in the morning, Sailor take warning." The tides of economic progress provide a profit for all businesses, but when the backwash comes, the weak and inefficient businesses go under. It is fun to ride the curl of the tide, but just under the surface is the riptide just waiting for the unwary.

Progress in Schleswig was on the mind of many people. The Golden Jubilee had been a huge success; the United States was the leading nation in the world; the farm economy was strong and solid; and the businesses in Schleswig were strong and prosperous. A number of changes were taking place, however. Amos Sinn had bought the local funeral home; Al Stoneking bought the dry-cleaning business from John Gottberg; and Modern Appliance, run by Ray Schmidt, Julius and James Else, expanded its offering by buying out the hardware division of the Green Bay Lumber Company.

Along with growth and change in the business district, the residential district, too, was growing. A new housing project was planned for the east side of the railroad tracks along Maple Avenue. John Cassens was hired to level the ground with his Caterpillar. The first construction to start in that area was a café and motel built by Elizabeth Rock and Lillie Hollander, the nurses who had owned the Ida Grove Hospital. The Hilltop Motel was located at the apex of the triangle created by Highway 59 and Maple Ave. A number of new houses were built along Maple Ave in short order. The whole area was a major improvement to the town.

World and national events intruded on local concerns once more when the Communist forces in Korea attempted to take over that whole country and the United Nations sent military forces to repulse the attempt. With the United States being the dominant power in the world, the bulk of the armed forces came from America. Many of the veterans of the Second World War were recalled to active duty at a time when many of them had just started careers and families. It was not a pleasant experience. A number of new enlistees and draftees were coming of age as well–Bob Reimers and Dick Gottberg were the first ones to pass their military physicals. There was a lot of long, tough fighting before President Eisenhower arranged a cease-fire. Korea was divided, but the fighting was stopped by what turned out to be the longest standing cease-fire in history. On the home scene, this was the first war since the town was started that the residents could support without their neighbors looking at them suspiciously.

On the state level, a long-term move to emphasize soil conservation was underway. Farming practices up to this time involved plowing and planting in straight lines up and down the hills, but the Soil Conservation Service wanted to stop the tremendous loss of topsoil caused by this kind of tillage. One of their first efforts was to estimate the amount of topsoil being lost. This was accomplished by taking samples from the Boyer River after a rain storm. They estimated that from one storm alone 1,855,000 tons of soil washed under the highway bridge between 9:00 A.M. and 4:00 P.M. To prevent such occurrences, the Soil Conservation Service promoted contour plowing and planting, terraces on the hills, tiles for wet lands, grass turning strips instead of end rows, and grassed waterways. Demonstrations were used to prove their point. One of the more successful of such demonstrations on contour plowing was performed on the Waldo Winquist farm one mile south and one mile east of Kiron with almost a thousand people observing the demonstration. The county was divided into conservation districts, and one of the most successful districts was in southern Otter Creek Township where some of the farmers involved were Paul Baer, Henry Braase, Hans Jess, Stanley Baker, Harvey Mohr, Octavus Grill, Peter Pickel, Henry Miller, and Julius Braase.

A different and interesting event for our town in 1950-51 was the Coast and Geodetic Survey project. The object of the project was to make an extremely accurate topographical map of the Little Sioux watershed. They had to set up a series of reference points, one of which was located in the Schleswig Park near the shelter house. The exact latitude, longitude, and altitude were determined and inscribed on a brass plaque mounted on the spot, and a tower was established. Measurements were taken between it and other towers in the area. One such tower was located on the Eldo Hollander farm northeast of Schleswig. Schleswig was chosen because it is one of the highest points in the county, and it is on the very edge of the watershed.

Dr. John Hurd was elected mayor of Schleswig in 1950, and one of the first problems he encountered was the plan to sell the City Hall which was in the former Commercial Bank building. The new Fire Station next to the Community Building had a meeting room, and the Council thought it would suffice as a City Hall. The people of the town liked the distinguished looking former bank building as a city hall, and they presented a petition to the Mayor and Council stating they wanted to keep the city hall where it was and to improve it. The Council conceded to public pressure and kept the old city hall–but the improvements were quite a while in coming.

The railroad which had been planning to close down the Mondamin-to-Wall Lake end of the Punkin Vine Line, but up to now, had been persuaded to continue it. However, now the Missouri River bridge on the line was in bad shape, and the Chicago Northwestern decided not to repair it and to take out at least part of the line. Since Schleswig was still shipping a large number of cattle by train, they decided to leave the rails from Schleswig east, but all the rails west of Schleswig would be abandoned. Schleswig became the end of the line in October. Regular train service was down to one train a week, but part of the transportation problem was alleviated with the establishment of a passenger bus route through town.

Automotive events were making news in town. Everett Evers had built a prize winning stock car, and with Wilbert Namanny the driver for the vehicle, they won a number of races. Harris Grill had won the right to participate in a Safe Driving Clinic at the State Fair Grounds where the participants were treated royally in the capital city. In Schleswig, the streets were under the care of Street Commissioner, Oscar Moeller, who also took care of the water system and the sewers.

Sioux City was a regional shopping center and a major livestock market to where many Schleswig residents would make regular trips. The main intersection in the city was at Fourth and Pierce Streets which was the domain of a large burly policeman, known simply as Officer Baette. Once, while he was on his beat, a Schleswig resident, Carl Backhaus, attempted to make a U-turn in the middle of the busy intersection. Officer Baette called out, "You can't do that." Mr. Backhaus carefully surveyed the situation and replied in a very heavy accent, "I tink I can yust make it."

The medical care was about to undergo some drastic changes in Schleswig. Dr. Schultz had been practicing medicine here for fifty years, and, in 1951, the Business Club honored him for his contribution to the community. Also, in that year, a new hospital in Denison was completed, because the old wooden structure on the west end of town was no longer adequate. The new one was built on the old college campus grounds on the east edge of Denison, and it was constructed largely with federal, state and county grants. Because of this financing it was one of the few hospitals in the region that did not have to depend on its income to survive. Julius Rohwer represented Schleswig on the Board of Trustees. In Schleswig, two new doctors set up an office. Drs. Merlin Broers and H. J. Billerbeck were welcomed to the community. In 1952, Dr. Walter Schultz died. In 1953, Dr. Jones also celebrated his fiftieth year in practice, and he sold his office and practice to Dr. Broers. Dr. Billerbeck moved to Randolph, Nebraska. Later that year, Dr. Henry Jones also died. In a very brief time, the medical traditions that went back to the beginnings of the town were completely overturned.

The Business Club had long been active in promoting Schleswig businesses by sponsoring special promotions, sometimes as many as five and six times a year–including Santa Claus Day, Children's Day, Rooster Day, Trade Day and many more. They continued this effort with Dollar Day, Watermelon Day, Christmas Turkey drawings and a new Pancake Day that attracted 1500 people. The Business Club was, indeed, active and accomplished much for the community. Some businesses did individual promotions as well. Stern and Son sponsored a John Deere Day that attracted 500 people; Schultz Hardware brought in an announcer, Len Howe, from WHO Radio Station to do his show from the local store; Bill's Market brought in the WOW Radio Martha's Kitchen Show. The Farmers State Bank had become the largest bank in Crawford County. Tenhulzen and Sons opened a new feed store. The business district was quite active and strong.

Business was hampered slightly, however, by the price and wage controls brought on by the Korean War, but it did not last long. The war also brought a new activity to town. A Civil Defense sky watch program centered on the Geodetic Society towers and a Spotter's League could count on sixty volunteers to man their operation. The community gave its full support to the war effort and to the boys who were engaged in it.

The churches in town had developed substantial and stable congregations by this time. In 1950, the Friedens Evangelical and

Reformed Church installed a fine new organ. In 1951, the Immanuel Lutheran Church dedicated their new Church building, and, in 1952, they moved the old frame church building to Ricketts to be used as a Lutheran Church there. The Catholics formed the Neighboring Parishes organization to unite the members of the three parishes that met in the Schleswig area–the St. Boniface in Charter Oak, St. Rose of Lima in Denison, and the Sacred Heart in Ida Grove. Congregational identity had become a matter of growing importance in Schleswig.

In the Spring of 1952, the Missouri River went on a rampage resulting in the worst flood in memory. Much of the lower part of Sioux City had been destroyed, and there also was a great deal of destruction in Omaha, while in the area between, the river was up to twenty miles wide. A group of people from Schleswig, including Jute Bumann and Hugo Dahms, traveled as far as Yankton, South Dakota, so they could get around the flood to get to Omaha. The trip was made to attend the wedding of a young stock broker in whom they had a lot of confidence and with whom they had made friends–Warren Buffet.

Farming had always been a diversified operation, justifying a wide range of livestock on every farm. Poultry was a large part of every operation; hogs were the mainstay of most operations, and feeding cattle was the prestige end of the business. The Schleswig Cattle Train had become known as the Blue Ribbon Special and had grown to 97 carloads and was formed into two trains. Everyone possible tried to get in on the good times on the trip–even Hugo Kroeger, the mail carrier, fed out some cattle to be on the trains. Every farm also had something of a dairy operation. Crops, too, were diversified. Corn was the main crop, but oats was grown in quantities; barley and flax would be planted occasionally; alfalfa, red clover, and sweet clover were grown for hay, and the livestock needed a significant amount of pasture. All of the crops were used in the farm operation, and usually more had to be purchased. The diversity provided a certain amount of economic security, since all farm commodities were subject to economic cycles; and, when one commodity was low in prices, usually another commodity was up.

The average size farm was approximately 160 acres comprised of 50 acres of corn, 40 acres of oats, and the remainder in hay and pasture. One hundred head of feeder cattle, 200 head of hogs, 12 milk cows, 50 broilers, 50 laying hens, and a dozen geese or ducks provided the livestock for the farm. A third of each day was spent on chores caring for the livestock. All operations on the farm were labor intensive, and it was a balancing act to get everything done.

This arrangement was about to change though. The field of agriculture was about to experiment with specialization which would increase profitability when the prices in the specialized area were high, but it would introduce a strong undercurrent, a riptide of risk. It was a change that ultimately strongly affected the entire community. The first example of such a move occurred in 1952 when Werthus Grill, in conjunction with the Priebe Nursery Co in Manning, built a large specialized broiler chicken operation. The building was 40 feet by 80 feet with an 8 foot by 20 foot annex for feed and would hold 4000 chickens at time. All of the feeding was done by automatic conveyors, and the water was delivered through a pressure system. The entire operation was controlled through a system of pushbuttons making it the most advanced system of its type in operation.

A number of civic improvements were taking place around the county. In Schleswig, a new fire siren was mounted on a steel tower by the fire station, and Kiron paved its streets. The county had been attempting to control erosion with the use of Jackstones—cross-shaped concrete structures which were placed on stream banks to stabilize them. Many people in the county were agitating for more of the county roads to be graveled, but the Supervisors could not find the money for gravel even though smaller counties such as Ida County had most of their roads already graveled. The one shining spot under the control of the county control was the County Home which was self-sustaining and provided a quality service.

The role of Supervisor in Crawford County tended to be a controversial one. It was a position with enough power and control over a large enough budget, that it frequently went to the head of the holder of the position, and many supervisors became presumptuous and condescending, acting as though they were a level or two above the common resident. Of course, not everyone in the office fell into this trap, but few people have been able to use this office to start a political career, while more were to find themselves in legal trouble or even in jail. During the 1930's, the *Spotlight* magazine satirized the supervisors frequently and helped to keep them in line, but as soon as the *Spotlight* was gone, questionable things began happening in the courthouse again.

The Jackstone scandal broke in 1954. Jackstones had been used in the county for six or eight years, but as it turned out, a lot more jackstones were bought than were used, and the county was paying about three times what they were worth and not using them. Scores of them were found in a ditch near Ricketts, and the county had rented a lot behind the Farmers Lumber and Grain in Schleswig where many more jackstones were dumped and forgotten. A group of taxpayers requested an investigation, and the Attorney General's office looked into the matter. It was found that not only had there been questionable financial transactions with the jackstones, but also sales of county equipment such as caterpillars at below cost prices to contractors were discovered. There were a number of law suits which took place in a variety places in western Iowa, one result being that Supervisor Chris Olson from Manila was sentenced to prison for three years. Over the next few years, the supervisors found enough money to gravel most of the roads in the county.

A trial of another sort was taking place at this time. Jurgen Christensen was a supervisor from the Schleswig area. He was not directly tainted by the jackstone scandal and looked like he would win an additional term on the board. His opposition then tried a different tact. Realizing he would indulge in a drink or two more than he should, they arranged for the Highway Patrol to lie in wait and arrest him. He was brought to trial, and the opposition thought they had him dead to rights. When the jury went into deliberations, Jens Edsen, one of the jurors, made an impassioned speech.

"Government agents, hiding under the cover of darkness to entrap unsuspecting citizens was the way of the old country. Our people came to this country to be free of such practices. We should not allow such tactics to succeed here if we want to remain free." When he was finished, the jury voted to set Mr. Christiansen free.

A number of people were doing interesting things. Barney Boysen was about to throw a chunk of coal into his stove when he noticed a hole drilled into it and there was something in the hole, so he tried to extract it to see what it was. It was an unexploded stick of dynamite left by the miners! Donna Lou and Delores Kastner had the top pen of calves in 1951. At the Crawford County Centennial beauty contest, Ruby Pickel (Kastner) came in fourth. Walter Ernst won a prize in a bowling tournament on TV in 1954. Larry Worley showed the Grand Champion Steer at the County Fair in 1955. Elaine Marth was picked for the Girls All State Second Basketball Team. Dr. Hugo Moeller accepted a position as Professor of Medicine at the University of California. John Dodge and Roger Reinking became the first Eagle Scouts in the town's history in 1956. Doug Lyon was named to All State Team for Six-Man Football. Indeed our people were busy and involved.

Throughout much of its history, a large part of the business conducted in Schleswig was done on the basis of credit. Customers would charge many of their purchases and pay them when the income came in. The farm economy lent itself to this tradition, since large portions of income would come in only when the sales of livestock or of grain would be made. As a result, farm income would come in waves—not in a steady stream. Many of the merchants had "carried" a lot of people on the books during the depression when they did not have the money to pay their bills. Since then some large farming operations would run up huge amounts of debt during the year, and merchants would try to see that such bills were paid by the end of each year. Interest was usually not charged if the bill were paid; but, some large operators even demanded that, if they were going to make such large payments, they should receive a discount—and in a number of cases it was granted. As time went on, fewer discounts have been granted, but the tradition of encouraging the payment of accounts by the end of the year has continued, and as an incentive, many businesses hold appreciation parties with food and beverages for their customers.

A number of State Officials were becoming dissatisfied with the school system in the state. The country school system had been in operation for eighty years, and it was thought it to be time for a change. The average size sustainable farm had risen from 40 acres to 160 acres, and there was not the number of students in country school districts as there had been and as a consequence consolidation of the districts was being considered. Consolidating the school districts would also allow educational theorists to put some of the newest theories into practice. This was the case even though no educational theory to date had been able to statistically prove itself superior to the one-room school. The consolidated school could offer more resources, but it would lose ground in the all-important student/teacher ratio, although there would, of course, be more opportunities for additional levels of highly paid administrators. The final selling point was that in some areas of the state up to 70% of the farmland was not in a high school district. With property tax being the main support for schools and student cost going up to $280 per student, the state could no longer support the current system. The State Legislature initiated a system of cash incentives and restrictive rules that assured all the school districts in the state would be consolidated.

School consolidation was going to happen but just where the district lines were going to be set was a very controversial question. The Schleswig people thought a northern Crawford County district including Ricketts, Schleswig, and Kiron would be a practical solution. There was competition, however, with Charter Oak wanting the Ricketts area to enlarge its district; but, Schleswig won the area by promising to build and maintain an elementary school there for as long as possible. Charter Oak was unwilling to match the offer but still convinced a number of individual land

246246

owners to go their direction. Kiron, on the other hand, was being sought by Denison. Kiron had the added benefit of having a significant cash surplus on hand as well as having a strong tax base. They thought Schleswig would close their school if they were in the same district, but they might have a chance to have their own school with Denison. The distances would be too great to rely on buses they thought, so they voted to go with Denison. That was a major miscalculation as Denison applied the surplus to their building plan and closed the Kiron school almost immediately. A number of farmers west of Kiron had signed up with Schleswig, however.

When all the negotiations were concluded, and the district was approved in 1956, Schleswig had a school district of approximately 120 sections of land. The country schools were continued in operation until a new school building could be constructed which happened as soon as a bond issue was approved in 1957. It involved a new elementary school two blocks to east of the existing high school with ample ground was purchased to allow for a set of athletic fields. The facility was ready to be used for the school opening in the Fall of 1958 at which time all of the country schools were closed. The old country school buildings which had been so familiar and the land was auctioned off. Some of the schoolhouses were converted to residences and others were used for storage on local farms. Sadly, a tradition had ended.

Another tradition was ending in Schleswig as well. The Chicago Northwestern Railroad had petitioned the Commerce Commission for permission to abandon all that was left of the Punkin Vine Line, and permission had been granted. The railroad was going to pull out of Schleswig entirely. Julius Struck was on hand to see the first train arrive in Schleswig on July 24, 1899, and to see the last train leave on Saturday, February 23, 1957. The Blue Ribbon Cattle Trains were a thing of the past, and the huge engines with the seven foot high wheels, massive drive shafts, hissing power cylinders, high puffing smokestacks and shrill steam whistles would no longer be adding a bit of color and sound to the town.

The movement of freight had to go on, however, and the trucking industry was ready to try to take up the responsibility. Our town was certainly not without trucking facilities. Schleswig Transfer had been operating for some time earning a good reputation as a freighter and had recently earned some publicity for transporting a herd of burros from New Mexico to a farm near Dow City. Lucas Kusch expanded the family's long-time dray service to a full service trucking line. Some of the firms had semi-tractor and trailer rigs, but many of them had straight trucks. John Jors was one of the single truck operators. Harvey Linke would discount rates. Cecil Phillips ran several rigs. There were always a lot of interesting things going on at his place.

When the railroad left, there was even more trucking activity. Jack Suhr and Elmer Namanny put together a sizable operation. Chubby Schoenfeld, Zip Seimer, Albert von Gronau, Johnny Gosch, and Palmer Moeller were all in the business. Bob Baeth had a specialized operation in trucking milk. The Teut brothers, Roger and Ron, set up a coast-to-coast operation. Keith Worley established a large operation. Schleswig became one of the major trucking centers in western Iowa. The town was full of stories about the exploits of the truckers–stories about the close calls and unusual experiences they had on the road. One trucker would consistently charge his gas purchases and at the same time ask if he could cash a check for some money go on the town. When he would not pay his account, the gas station manager took him to Justice of the Peace Court where the trucker produced canceled checks on each of the days when gas was purchased for approximately the amount of the purchase. The case was dismissed, but check cashing policies were soon changed all over town.

When the railroad pulled out, a crew to pull up the tracks was sent in. The space of the right-of-way was put up for sale. It would have been a perfect time for the city to purchase sufficient land to straighten out the street pattern that had been disrupted by cross angle of the railroad tracks. Unfortunately, the proposal was not even considered, since the city government was in disarray. In the last election no candidates for Mayor were nominated, and the write-in vote was a tie—the office was awarded by the flip of a coin. There was no one watching out for the best interests of the city, and Schleswig lost the opportunity to make a major civic improvement.

The railroad land was sold mainly to adjacent land owners and promoters. Ben Bielenberg bought a large portion of the remainder. Part of it was subdivided for housing, and a portion of it was used to build a new church. The Friedens Church had decided to build, selecting a very modernistic design and a prominent place in the community on which to build it. The project was started in 1959 and completed in May of 1961, adding a beautiful highlight to the community.

One of the interesting characters around town was Andy Paulsen. Andy was a tall, slim, older gentleman who was often seen in a western hat with a cigarette dangling from his lips. He would have fit well in a western cartoon. In fact, back in the thirties he had gone to Hollywood to try to get a job as a drugstore cowboy. He was very good at rope tricks, a pretty fair pistol shot, and an excellent rider, but the competition was too stiff and the breaks didn't fall his way. For a while he ran one of the wildest bars in the county in Boyer, IA, but he generally made a living doing odd jobs—house painting and portrait photography. He was always good for a story or a magic trick. When some local boys had taken some naughty pictures of their girl friends out on 'Lover's Lane,' a half mile south of town, and were afraid to take the film to be developed in Hap Peter's Drug Store, because he would send the film away to be processed and someone along the way may report them to the authorities, they took it to Andy. He was glad to develop the pictures for the guys, and he made lots of copies and some of them got out around town. There were some mothers who were very down on Andy for a while. One of the mysteries of Schleswig is that when Andy died some years later, the fancy six-shooters from the old days that he was so proud of were missing. No one knows what happened to them.

In the business district, Roy Moeller from Kiron purchased Henry Brockmann's Produce Station in 1956. Earl and Ella

Schelldorf bought the Hilltop Motel and Café. Harris Grill set up a TV and Electronics sales and repair shop in the basement of the theater building and in 1957 moved to 206 Cedar Street where he demonstrated the first microwave oven in town. Leonhardt Schultz built a new apartment building. Harris Grill, Everett Evers, Dale Reese, and DeWayne Schultz built a go-cart track on the north end of the railroad right-of-way where the roar of the engines on the oval track attracted a lot of attention.

The Calf and Conservation Show in September was the major event of every year bringing all factions of the community together. In 1959, it was a larger celebration reflecting the sixtieth anniversary of the town, and it evoked more excitement than expected. Some local men had gotten into a gambling game run by the carnival, but they lost consistently and suspected they were being cheated. They demanded their money back. Shortly before midnight the "Hey, Rube," call went out to summon the carnival workers to the defense of their members. There was an altercation, and people were running all over the place. A large farmer was seen running across rows of bleacher seats with a carnival operator running after him swinging a hammer. A local man with some boxing experience quickly laid out a couple carnival workers. Fortunately, cooler heads soon prevailed, and the violence stopped, but the gamblers and the money were no where to be found. The festivities closed down early, but the stories lasted for a long time.

Andy Klotz had purchased and had been operating the Stoltenberg Grocery Store. When he had the opportunity to buy a larger operation in Mapleton, he took it and sold the Schleswig store to Kourt Smith. After Smith operated it for several years, it was struck with several fires in close succession. The Fire Marshals determined it was arson, and Mr. Smith was charged and convicted. The building at 121 Cedar Street was then converted to an electric appliance outlet operated by Harris Grill. The community was reduced to two operating grocery stores–Bill's Market and Behrmann and Company.

Schleswig had always been a close-knit community. The German language was spoken by many residents, and if one wanted to exclude a stranger, all one needed to do was to start speaking German. There had always been forces that prevented it from going too far, however. The anti-German pressure during the World Wars, the presence of Negro workers on the street crews, and the almost constant arrival of new German immigrants who knew the German language better than the natives. There was also a large group of seasonal workers to help with the farm work, particularly the harvest which was done mainly by hand. One of these was Stanley Baker from Missouri who stayed and prospered. Seemingly improbable, but true, Schleswig had a tradition of Jewish merchants, some of the names included Rubeck, Meisen, and the Merkin Brothers. The last of these, Jake Merkin, sold his grocery store and opened a bar on Fourth Street in Sioux City although his family stayed in the grocery business in Vermillion, South Dakota. Jake had a lot of interesting sayings. For example, during the holidays he would say "It was certainly a smart Jew that invented Christmas," as he rang up his cash register. By the 1960's, all of these influences had disappeared. Uno Laubert and Claus Jans were the last of the German immigrants who came to Schleswig to seek their fortunes. They stayed only a few months and moved on. Without these influences Schleswig became more closely-knit than usual. This lasted until enough new people moved into the area to open the society again some years later.

The most significant feature of these trends was not the social implications which eventually worked themselves out. The more important trend was economic in nature. It was entirely unnoticed at the time, but it was one of the undercurrents that could be seen mainly through hindsight years later. Starting in the late 1950's, Schleswig no longer had an appeal to outside groups. Individuals might start a business, but in general, workers no longer looked at Schleswig as a place of opportunity. Immigrants no longer looked at Schleswig as a place of promise for a new life. On the surface, Schleswig looked like a growing and prosperous community, but the economic underpinnings were eroding.

Some of the problems were not subtle, and, in some areas, diversification was openly discouraged. When Bohlmann Concrete Products decided to expand beyond their initial operation in Ricketts, they looked to Schleswig as a possible site for their new plant. A number of community leaders, especially those associated with the bank, discouraged them by saying Schleswig was an agriculture and retail center, and we should stay that way. Manufacturing would not fit well in our community. The Bohlmanns built a prosperous business in Denison. When the Godberson Brothers were looking for a new site for their manufacturing concern, Schleswig showed no interest so the Godbersons did not consider it, and their plant was set up in Ida Grove. Schleswig had placed some very heavy limits on its future growth.

Another area where business restrictions were promoted with widespread support was in the area of cooperative marketing. The Double Circle Coop had been active in the Kiron area for some time and had taken over the grain elevator, the lumber yard, a gas station, a hardware operation and more than sixty percent of the commercial activity in Kiron. The Schleswig people did not want that to happen in their town. The Coop made an offer to buy the Farmers Lumber and Grain, but it was strongly resisted and failed. All parts of the community pulled together to resist any additional inroads by the Coop, which was looked upon as a monopoly that exercised unfair competitive practices. The farmers had a good working relationship with the merchants and wanted to maintain it.

Competition was promoted, but the residents wanted it to be private competition. Competition was started in the feed and grain businesses when Feeders Supply Corporation was organized by Ben Bielenberg, Mr. and Mrs. Theodore Aldag, Mr. and Mrs. Howard Lenz, and Mr. and Mrs. Melvin Schlultz in 1960. The Stern and Son John Deere implement building was bought and converted to be used by the corporation which became an extremely successful operation.

Another successful feature of our society was the development of television. It had first appeared in the early 1950's, but few people had receivers. By the late 1950's it was receiving wider acceptance, and the number of homes with a television set was growing rapidly. The purchase of a television set was a social event in which friends and relatives would come to visit just to see the new set. The whole evening's entertainment would be centered around the set and the programs that could be pulled in on it. The screens were small and the picture was fuzzy, but the concept of television was captivating. TV was having a strong social impact as well. The whole nation was watching Milton Berle, world-class sports, and the Donna Reed Show. National network television, like no other force before it, functioned to homogenize the American society. The United States had always been a collection of ethnic, racial, and regional divisions each with its own clearly recognized identity. Newspapers and radio brought in an awareness of what other parts of the country were like but did not affect the barriers that divided them. Television, however, provided a clearly defined image to which people from all parts of the nation could aspire. It broke down the barriers and distinctions—which for some parts of the country was good. It marked the beginning of the end of many types of discrimination. It was not all good, however, in that it extinguished much of the diversity which gave this country its character. In Schleswig, it killed its German ethnic identity. Young people were impressed by new ideals, and they were no longer interested in the Platt Deutsche language and the German traditions and independent set of values. It took another generation for those who held to the traditional values to pass from the scene but the process was well on its way.

When the railroad pulled out of town, Schleswig became a
trucking mecca with a number of locally owned firms.

For some time the senior class in the high school had been
going to a major city in the region on a school-sponsored skip-day
trip. In 1961, Chicago was the selected city, and the trip and
tours of the museums, public places, the newly constructed
McCormick Place, and various scenic views went very smoothly.
However, near midnight, Principal John Burch called an unexpected class meeting at which approximately half the class showed
up in various states of inebriation. It appeared that Illinois law
prohibited the sale of alcohol to boys under the age of 21, but girls
could purchase it if over the age of 18. Some of the girls in the class
could legally buy liquor and did so, sharing it with a number of
their classmates, some of whom became rowdy enough to attract
the attention of the hotel management. They called the Principal
and thus the meeting. A number of the boys who were the worst
offenders were told that they could find their own way home the

next day—the school was no longer going to be responsible for them. Some of the boys went down to the stockyards and obtained rides with truckers from Schleswig who happened to be in the city, while others went down to the bus depot and purchased tickets home. Everyone made it back safely, but unfortunately, it was the last skip day trip the school sponsored.

That was not the end of the story, however. There was quite a furor that arose in the community directed at the school. How could the administrators take their children and transport them hundreds of miles to the midst of a major metropolitan area, and dump them there to find their own way home? That was not something they were going to allow without some kind of accounting. As a result, a special school board meeting was called to discuss the matter. The meeting was held in the multi-purpose room at the new school in which extra chairs had been set out which were filled by angry parents. At the appointed time the School Board filed in and took their seats behind a table facing the crowd. Superintendent Earl Christensen asked if anyone had a statement to be made, and after a moment of silence, a hand went up at the edge of the crowd. A short, solid man got up and slowly walked to the center of the room. He looked over the school board and then turned and looked over the crowd of parents. Then he quietly said, "What I see here is a bunch of damned fools . . . and I include myself in that group. These kids are our kids. What these kids did was wrong. It should be up to us to straighten them out. Let us do that and let the school board run the school." With that Herbie Miller went back and sat down. There was complete silence in the room. Everyone was not only surprised by what was said, but also by the quiet, unassuming, long-time resident who had said it. After a few moments, Superintendent Christensen asked if there were any more comments, and when there were none, the meeting was adjourned.

The school was doing a good job and was turning out some very good graduates. Among those going on for higher education were Karen Jess at the Des Moines Business School, Ken Jahde at

Missouri State, Regina Schultz at Drake University and Phil Rickert at Iowa State University. In 1961, three students tied for the highest number of academic credits earned in the history of the school. They were Marla Miller, John Cassens, and Larry Grill. People making collegiate honor rolls were Roger Petersen, Beth Krohnke, Swen Berger, Roger Reinking, Arlis Clausen, Gary Koch, Ron Kastner and Ron Clausen. Roger Reinking was nominated for a Woodrow Wilson Fellowship. As many as 25 to 30 percent of each graduating class was going on to higher education. Former teacher, Fran Allison was making a name for herself on television in her own show, "Kukla, Fran, and Ollie".

Athletics had always been strong along with academics. Schleswig's two mile relay team consisting of Bob Bartels, Phil Rickert, Wayne Miller, and Doug Lyon won the state track meet in 1957. Doug Lyon also set a school high jump record at six feet that lasted for 30 years. The Girls basketball team made the Sweet Sixteen at the State Tournament in 1961. They had to brave a blizzard to get to the Des Moines tournament, but they got there as did most of the residents of Schleswig and the surrounding territory. The baseball team won the conference championship in 1962. There was also a town softball team that was quite well known at the time. Roger Friedrichsen pitched a perfect game against a Danbury team in 1962.

Pulchritude also made a name for Schleswig. Diane Lenz (Rocker) became Miss Beef Empire in 1962. Marlene Henningsen (Lee) became Miss Crawford County in 1964.

One athletic activity for which the town did not have facilities was swimming. Those who were interested had to travel to Denison or Ida Grove to use their pools where swimming lessons were available. If there was enough interest, a school bus could be scheduled to transport the students. There had been talk for several years about building a swimming pool in Schleswig, but it would require voting in a bond issue to finance it, and there was a reluctance at assuming the amount of debt necessary to build the pool. The proponents continued to work on the project, however. Then a tragedy occurred which swung sentiment in favor of the pool. Harris Grill, a prominent young businessman, was drowned in the Missouri River where he had been helping his brother-in-law move a houseboat up the river. When the boat had snagged on a sand bar, Harris had apparently jumped into what he had thought was shallow water only to find it was much deeper, and had much stronger currents than expected. The shock of his unexpected death brought much attention to the pool issue. Swimming lessons and water safety became strong community concerns, and the bond issue was brought up and passed easily. The new pool was completed in 1963.

Always working to improve Schleswig's appearance, in 1963, Dr. Merlin Broers remodeled his office and had a new front put on the building. Byron Behrmann remodeled his grocery store and added a full line of fresh meats. Julius Rohwer had retired from the presidency of the bank and sold his shares in the corporation. That fall the Calf Show had a home talent show call the 'Schlesfest' which was a great hit. The following year Beep Sonksen and Melvin Miller built the B & M Drive-In on the highway north of town. In 1965, Werthus Grill opened a recreation center in the Krohnke building at Second and Cedar Streets. Always trying to improve—that was Schleswig.

One of the long-standing features of Schleswig life disappeared in 1963. Nellie Burmeister died in December of that year. Mrs. Burmeister's function was a rather interesting one, which in today's terminology, would have been called a Shaman or in the earlier days could have been referred to as faith healer, or simply as a healer, or by the derogatory reference—witch doctor. The practitioners of the ancient arts did not advertize this fact, but patients would seek them out for help. They had always operated as a counter point to the medical profession providing a service in offering a course of treatment in the gaps in medical science. They used incantations, spells, and unique concoctions to provide a patient a course of positive action in situations where medical science seemed lacking. One such procedure involved taking an object closely identified to the patient to the practitioner and have a ritual performed over it and have the patient or a family member bury the object in a prescribed manner in an area frequented by the patient by the light of the full moon while chanting a prescribed phrase. The patient and family members would then anticipate the relief of the symptoms–which occurred in a number of cases. There was a large variety of such procedures and a large vocabulary of special terms in their jargon. They had many terms, unknown to medical science, for diseases and conditions. These practices of the old ones date to antiquity and came down through the Black Forrest and across the oceans. They have been practiced in our community for as long as it was here. A practitioner would train his replacement, it would have to be a cross gender training–a man could train a woman or a woman could train a man but never one of the same sex. Some of the practitioners through the years were the Koch brothers southeast of town, Willie Bumann northeast of town, and in the very early days of Schleswig, Trina Rickert was the predominant proponent of these arts. These ancient traditions of Wicca came to an end in Schleswig with the death of Nellie Burmeister–as far as we know.

In the country, as a whole, the general theme was upbeat. John Kennedy was the President of the United States, and his youth and vigor was setting a positive tone for the country. Harold Hughes, a former truck driver from Ida Grove, was Governor of the State of Iowa. He, too, was creating a positive atmosphere for Iowa. He had been elected on a campaign of legalizing liquor by the drink by getting rid of the stodgy old laws that were not being observed anyway. His administration was a breath of fresh air in a state that had been stagnant for some time. While he was Governor, a small packing plant started in Denison called Iowa Beef Packers. It had a new idea of assembly-line processing for meat cutting, and once it got started, it did not stay small for long. It was soon followed by a Farmland Foods pork-processing plant and World Wide Meats, a frozen-food processing plant. In Ida Grove, the Godberson Brothers set up a plant to manufacture a hoist for farm wagons which soon developed other agriculture equipment. A line of marine equipment was added, and their GoMaCo Plant built a line of road construction equipment. In Holstein, Roger Claussen started a wood lamination plant calling it Van Top Industries. The number of good paying off-the-farm jobs increased significantly in the area.

The jobs were needed as the trends on the farm were for more and more specialization. The broiler chicken production only lasted a few years before the industry was concentrated in a few huge commercial operations in the southern states. Werthus Grill who had pioneered that type of operation in this area, converted his building to laying hens and went into egg production. A number of other large laying houses were established in the area which lasted a little longer because they were more labor intensive, and, as a result, it took a little longer for them to be concentrated–but that, too, eventually did happen. Poultry production disappeared almost entirely from this part of the state, and milk production soon followed the same pattern. First it was automated with milking machines, and then the move was to sell fresh milk rather than just the cream. The milk was picked up in ten gallon cans, and later, from bulk tanks on the farm. Requirements for sanitary milking parlors and for certified Grade A milk facilities increased investments, and the profit margins narrowed. When the business cycles turned down, the small and inefficient operators were squeezed out. Soon the whole industry would be concentrated in some other part of the country. Thus was the trend going through one commodity after another. Even in the area of crop production, specialization was occurring. More farmers were going to straight crop production and not bothering with livestock at all. The crops were being limited to corn and soybeans, and while Schleswig had for most of its history been a grain importing area, it now became a major grain exporting area.

The more specialized a production area becomes, the more efficient it becomes. More of the product can be produced with less resources and with less labor. The farm production was increasing and the number of farmers was decreasing as the size of the farms was growing. The Schleswig area was definitely feeling the change.

Lyndon Johnson won the Presidency with the biggest majority in years. He carried many Democrats into office on his coattails. His help was not necessary in Iowa, however. Harold Hughes was reelected with a larger margin than the President. War was declared on poverty, and the government was determined to raise the general standard of living of the whole country. The Democrats wanted to level the economic playing field, but this was not popular with those who wanted to concentrate wealth into their own hands. However, the common people loved it. There was a cloud on the horizon, however–Viet Nam. The French were having difficulty in controlling a Communistic insurgency under the leadership of Ho Chi Minh, and some American advisors were sent over to help organize the situation. Nothing they did seem to help, and, with each failure additional troops were sent over until the Americans were one of the main participants in the fight.

Harold Hughes spoke at the Calf Show in 1964. He had a large number of friends and acquaintances in Schleswig since he had been involved in the trucking industry in the area for years. For several years before becoming Governor, he had worked with the Commerce Commission to regulate and unify trucking rates. Schleswig being a center of the trucking industry made everyone here aware of his activities. Schleswig was written up in a feature article in *Business and Industry Magazine* at this time emphasizing the trucking industry located here. Harold Hughes repaid the friendship and loyalty of the people in Schleswig by supporting a request by the community to obtain a State-controlled retail liquor store. The Iowa Beer and Liquor Commission did establish a retail outlet at 31 Second Street with Herbert Miller being hired as the store manager.

Already in the early part of the 1960's it was becoming apparent that if Schleswig was to grow, it would need new areas in which to expand. At first there was interest in looking to the west and expanding into the Reinking farmland, but, by the time a formal organization was set up, the focus had changed to the Petersen farm on the south edge of town. The Schleswig Development Corporation with a Board of Directors including Harry Wellendorf, John Evers, Wm. Petersen, Edward Claussen, Milton Wasgren, and Ben Bielenberg purchased enough land to double the size of the town. Part of the land was used to develop a state-of-the-art sewage lagoon system for the town. Next to the town itself, a 51 lot residential development was laid out. Stanley Baker was the first person to build a house in the new Southern Heights Addition. The following year a 23-acre industrial park was laid out along Highway #59.

In 1966, a corporation was formed to layout a golf course on the remaining property. The officers and directors included John Evers, Dr. D.L. Schmidt, Richard Hansen, Edward Claussen, and Gerald Sonksen who contacted the Leo Johnson Company from Sioux City to plan and build a nine-hole golf course. Funds were raised to start this project and were supplemented with loans and government grants. A building committee consisting of Howard Lenz, Ted Hollander, Heinz Behnke, Dr. Merlin Broers, Wayne Schultz, and Burdell Jensen was then appointed to construct a club house for the golf course. They planned a 28' X 49' structure that was finished off in fine style using the German architectural motif.

At this time the Reverend Ralph Ratzlaff of the United Church of Christ was concerned about there being entirely too much frivolous activity occurring in town, so he stationed himself at the entrance of the V.F.W. Club and other such establishments on Saturday nights to get a close look at just who was indulging in unwholesome activities. He would then explain his observations during his sermons the next morning. He also wanted to make his parishioners more accountable for the financial support of the Church. He had some definite ideas to reform the community, but he did have some difficulty in getting them accomplished.

Calf auction during the annual Calf and Conservation Show.
Don Bielenberg calling, Swede Arnson and Ben Bielenberg
bid catching and Al Sedore clerking. A fifty year tradition.

The Grant Township Lutheran Church suffered a major catastrophe in the summer of 1969 when a tornado struck on July 28,
doing considerable damage to the Church building. The size of
the congregation had been dwindling for some time as the farm
population diminished, and, now, the burden of reconstruction
would have been prohibitive. Sadly, the decision was made to dis-
band the congregation in October of that year. The Church had
served its community for 89 years.

There was some excitement in Ricketts, too. Their bank had
been burglarized. The thieves had gained entrance by breaking
the hook on the screen door in back thus gaining entrance to the
basement. From here they dismantled a heating duct to gain access to the main floor where they then pounded a hole in the side

of the vault just above the safety deposit boxes. For all the careful planning, though, they discovered the bank did not store their cash in the vault, but kept it in a steel safe in the lobby. The sum total that the potential thieves were able to get for their efforts were the excess coins in the amount $2335.42 which was bulky and hard to handle. On the way out, one of the thieves ran into Mrs. Langholdt's clothesline and lost more than $700.00. There was virtually a trail of money leading out of town. Marshal Ben Carstensen, the county sheriff, state and federal investigators all investigated the event, but no arrests have ever been made.

Bill Wollenhaupt was involved in a very serious car accident in 1965, and as a result of the injuries he suffered in the accident, he was forced to sell his grocery store and his meat processing operation. Bert Redmond bought the grocery division, and Bob Bumann bought the meat and sausage division. Mr. Bumann expanded his business over the next several years, so much that he was in dire necessity of expanding his facilities. The State Meat Inspection Division, however, was making expansion difficult. They said the old slaughter house was no longer adequate, and any remodeling would require all new stainless steel fixtures. The whole project would require a considerable amount of new capital for which Mr. Bumann approached the bank to secure a loan. They, however, would only approve a full recourse loan, which required considerably more collateral than the amount of the loan—terms with which Mr. Bumann could not agree.

After the negotiations had broken off, the bank officers approached Bob Bumann with another offer. They would form a corporation to set up a new plant and buy his formula and trademarks and produce Schleswig Sausage. Bob Bumann would be hired to manage the production in the plant, and a sales staff would be hired to market the product. This plan was agreed to, and the first officers of the corporation were Amos Sinn, Erwin Voss, Robert Bumann, Robert Lyon, Dr. Broers, Bart Bielenberg, and Burdell Jensen. Corporate stock was sold, a Small Business Administration loan was secured, and additional local financing was worked out.

A site was selected in the new industrial park south of town, an architect drew up the plans, and a contractor was selected. It would be a million-dollar plant. However, undercurrents that could cause problems occurred almost from the beginning. In order for the plant construction to come in on budget, there had to be some cutbacks. The floor size of the plant was reduced, and some significant features such as a boiler room had to be delayed. The plant did open, and it began operations in which it custom butchered for local farmers, provided a local frozen food locker facility, produced a line of its own sausage products which it wholesaled to grocery stores, and it started a mail order gift package retail operation. The grand opening was held on July 6, 1972, with a ceremony including tours of the facilities, samples of the products, speeches, and celebrities including National Pork Queen Emma Schroeder.

It soon became clear that the shortcuts that were made in the construction were going to have to be corrected. Additional space had to be added to the plant, and additional equipment, such as a boiler, had to be added. It turned out to be more expensive to add it on later, but the construction financing had already been exhausted, and the money for the additions had to come out of the operating budget. The first marketing efforts did not work well either. Large amounts of product became outdated and had to be destroyed, and even labeling problems caused additional expenses. It was a sharp looking plant, and it produced some very good products, but it was getting off to a shaky business start.

Bowling had always been a popular sport in Schleswig. The bowling alley was located in the basement of the Odd Fellows building which was owned by Herbert Babbe and operated by Fritz Miller. By 1971, they both wanted to retire, but no one could be found to take over the operation. Bowling had been a part of the community since the days when they played nine-pin in the pasture at the old town of Morgan, and no one wanted to see the popular game disappear. The Community Club then stepped in and promoted building a new modern alley. An organization called the Schleswig Community Bowlers, Inc. was formed to accomplish this, and they bought the old Standard Oil Station at 201 Second Street and the lot just to the east. A new building was built with a café and bar on the west half and a bowling alley on the east half. Ironically, the bowling alley was built on the same location where there had been a previous bowling alley back in the 1920's. The completed structure was sold to Alvern Schoenfeld who made it a successful operation thus making it possible for him to pay off the note ahead of schedule.

Additional business activities were occurring in Schleswig, too. The Simonsen Company built a fertilizer distribution center on the old railroad right-of-way in the area behind the Community building—a site which had no street access, but right-of-way was open to traffic.

Three local insurance agencies merged into one—the Hugo Dahms Agency, the Claussen Agency of Schleswig, and the Claussen Agency of Ricketts—forming the new Shinco Insurance Agency for which Galen Ferry was hired as manager.

A number of local people were achieving notable individual accomplishments. Carol Lenz completed training to become an airline stewardess. Jean Weifenbach set a conference basketball scoring record and received All-State recognition. Cynthia Gosch was playing with the Midwestern College Packerettes in a National AAU Tournament. Jerry Struck became manager of the Computer Center at the Central Iowa Stockyards. Gayle Knief playing for the Morningside College football team attracted the attention of the Minnesota Vikings and began a professional football career. Betty Weifenbach was named Postmaster. Dick Streck received an outstanding customer service award. Mayor Ray Bumann hosted the Northwest Iowa League of Municipalities. He was able to give the visiting dignitaries an impressive tour of our town pointing out an impressive number of improvements and expansions. Mayor Bumann proved to be one of the more activitist mayors that the community had thus far.

A number of the executives from the Iowa Beef Packers, Inc. were living in Schleswig where they had made friends and were well accepted by the community. The workers at the IBP plant declared a strike at this time that went on for an extended period of time. Feelings were being inflamed, and there were some incidents of violence at the Dakota City headquarters plant. Then, word was received that a delegation from that area was going to intimidate the executives in this area. A special neighborhood watch was appointed by the citizens of Schleswig to be on guard against such activities in our town, and no incidents occurred locally.

A movement to investigate developing a nursing home in Schleswig was started. A committee was formed by the Community Club to see what would be required to build such an establishment. There was a great deal of interest in the community, since a number of senior citizens from Schleswig were in various nursing homes in other communities–enough to fill a nursing home if it were developed here. The committee found that a need's study would have to be approved by State agencies before such a facility could be opened or funding could be approved. While it did not appear that the need's survey would be a serious problem, it would take time and effort to obtain it. A sponsoring organization would also have to be designated, and the United Church of Christ agreed to be the sponsoring agency. The momentum behind the effort began to lag, however, since most of the energy was being used to develop the packing plant, the golf course, and the country club. There was just not the manpower or the focus to push through the nursing home effort, so it was put on hold for a while.

The war in Viet Nam was not going well either. More and more troops were being called up and sent to Southeast Asia, and more and more local boys were being included in the numbers. A former local boy, Roger Mohr, had taken over command of the National Guard Unit in Denison. The war was becoming less and less popular among the general population, and protests against it were larger and more widespread. President Johnson had refused renomination in hopes that it would help in achieving a settle-

ment. President Nixon was trying, with difficulty, to achieve a
peace with dignity, resulting in some prospects, but peace was not
achieved. Then the people of Schleswig were shocked to hear of
the death of a popular and promising young man—Dallas Nihsen.
He had been serving as a door gunner with a helicopter crew on a
number of missions when he had been wounded. He succumbed
to his wounds on April 15, 1972.

An international event of benefit to the community did occur.
A trade agreement had been reached with the Soviet Union, and
part of the agreement provided that the Soviet Union was required
to purchase a minium amount of feed grains from the United States
each year. This provided a baseline demand amount under the
grain markets and assured a stable farm income for a number of
years to come. The whole local farm community benefitted from
this arrangement.

The general prosperity that the community was experiencing,
and the prospects that it would be a continuing state of affairs,
caused a rather unusual phenomenon. The community saw a substantial influx of returning native sons. Usually there was an out-
flow of children to find their fortune and fate in other parts of the
country, usually in the cities. Now, however, they were coming
back. There were the prospects of making a good living on the
farm again, and the businesses that supported the farms were doing well. A large number of young people returned from California, Missouri, Minnesota, Nebraska and the Dakotas, wherever
they had gone for an education or a job, where they had been
teachers, corporate employees, professional people and a variety of
occupations. They came home and took over the family farms, the
family businesses, and opened up new activities. A new level of
vigor revitalized the community.

Vigor was something that would be needed as Schleswig was
planning to put on a celebration for its Diamond Anniversary on
the seventy-fifth year since its founding. Everyone agreed it should
be as large an effort as the one for its Golden Jubilee in 1949. The
various organizations around town each began forming plans for

their part in the festivities, and a number of fund-raisers were begun to finance the activities. One of the most successful was a street party with a barbequed pork dinner and a beer garden which was dubbed with the name 'Beerfest.'

The celebration was held on the September 5-6-7, 1974. A renewed interest in the history of our community developed, and the *Schleswig Leader* published a series of historical articles by Myra Hamann, and a book on the history of the town was published by Lillian Jakso and Emma Struck. A record number of families signed up to sponsor a pen of calves in the Calf Show that would take place during the celebration; a beard club was established and most of the men in the community began growing a beard. Contact was made with Schleswig's sister city and namesake—Schleswig, Germany—in which an invitation to attend our Celebration was extended.

On the Wednesday evening before the celebration, a reception was held in honor of the delegation from Schleswig, Germany, which was headed by the Burgermeister of Schleswig, Germany, Bodo Richter. The following day there was a large Children's Parade of which the Grand Marshal was Jim Henry, a television celebrity from Sioux City, where he had hosted the very popular Kid's Korner children's program. The entire town was decorated. Every storefront window had a display of historical artifacts, and there was a large carnival with rides all over the business district. In the evening, there was a Schlesfest style home talent show.

The next day a German Costume Style Show was held. A wide variety of very colorful and varied ethnic costumes were displayed. There were so many they were broken down into divisions—a Women's Division, a Teenage Girl's Division, a Family Division, a Couple's Division and a Mother and Daughter Division. The judging of the beard contest was also broken down into divisions—the Full Beard Division, Part Beard Division, and the Mustache and Goatee Division. Each of these divisions was broken down farther by age groups—the under 35, the 35 to 55, and the over 55. Sandy Evers was crowned Jubilee Queen. The church groups put on din-

ners at noon during the celebration. In addition, a school food
stand operated on the street outside the City Hall, and a Futjenhaus
sponsored by V.F.W. Auxiliary was set up in one of the buildings
to serve the German pastry. A water fight between fire departments was held with over twenty competing teams. The Schleswig
Fire Department was the victor.

A huge Grand Parade was held with floats from all of the busi-
nesses, civic organizations, surrounding communities and numer-
ous individuals participating. There were several bands, color
guards, fire departments, and military displays. The Shriner's White
Horse Patrol was here as well other groups from their organization.
Visiting dignitaries including Governor Robert Ray, Congressman
Wiley Mayne and the mayors of many cities and towns including
Mayor George Cole from Sioux City. Special guests, including Mrs.
Frank Forney, the first baby born in Schleswig and the oldest citi-
zens in the community, John D. Moeller, age 96, and Lena Reese,
age 93 were featured in the parade.

The evening of the final day was reserved for nationally known
entertainment. Seats were set up on the upper half of the 100
block of Cedar Street with a stage on the lower end of the area.
Archie Campbell, a member of the very popular network televison
show HeeHaw, was the headliner, and the musical group, the
Blackwood Singers, as well as other groups, preformed. The crowd
was so large and the area was so packed, that the performance was
interrupted on a number of occasions by medical and similar emergencies.

The Jubilee was a tremendous success. There were tens of thousands of people attending each day, and they were well entertained.
The town had celebrated well, and it had something to celebrate.
The community was generally prosperous, and it had achieved
significant growth and development. In fact, it had reached a pin-
nacle of physical development. New things would evolve in the
future, but, on balance, the town as a whole was near the top of its
development.

Progress comes in waves like the tides. It will wash well inland, and then recede. The tide will raise all ships, and when the tidal wave recedes, riptides are created just under the surface. The riptides carry the unwary deep under the surface and far out to sea. Somehow, analogies from the sea seem appropriate to an area whose ancestors lived not far from either the North Sea or the Baltic Sea. Many of the old adages even survived, for example one is about the sky, "Red sky in the evening, Sailor's delight, red sky in the morning, Sailor take warning." The tides of economic progress provide a profit for all businesses, but when the backwash comes, the weak and inefficient businesses go under. It is fun to ride the curl of the tide, but just under the surface is the riptide just waiting for the unwary.

X. REDUCTIONS

1975–1999

It is very easy to assume that when things appear to be going well that everything is good, and it will go on forever, but that is the time to examine carefully the footings on which they are based. Nothing, however, goes on forever. Not things, not people, not communities, not even whole economies. The time to be most observant is when things are going the best. Caution must prevail. Problems can come in a variety of forms. They can be short-sighted, self-inflicted problems, or they can be caused by outside influences; they can be repetitions of previous conditions; or there can be undercurrents of conflicts. Problems do occur and fully as often as do the good times. The bad times seem to have a sharper edge, however. Our Grandfathers and Great-grandfathers knew this when they first came to this part of the country. They worked at it, and they persevered, and they built this country. They enjoyed doing it. They nurtured the good times and did not let the bad times get them down. They had a sense of accomplishment. It would be too bad if the present generation had to close down the West that our forefathers had so much fun opening up.

Farming was going especially well. Foreign trade treaties had used up grain surpluses and farmers responded by going into a full-production mode. Prices were strong and incomes were good. Farmers had money which they were willing to spend on bigger equipment, more chemicals, and larger farms. The price of land finally met and exceeded the prices set during the land speculation right after the First World War. Before World War I, a living could be made on forty acres, after World War II, it grew to 160 acres, and by the 1970's the average size farm was going over 320 acres. As a result, larger farms meant fewer farmers.

The timeline for farms was growing, too. At least a half a dozen farms a year were becoming century farms meaning they had been in the same family for a hundred years–truly a remarkable feat.

All of this progress though was causing costs to go up faster than the grain prices. Machinery was becoming very expensive, and so was seed, fertilizer, and chemicals. Of course, an integral part of modern farming has always been farm credit. It took a lot of money to obtain land and to raise a crop. A good banker can help sustain a good operator through the economic cycles. The income history of a farm would provide a baseline for the amount of credit that would be extended for its operation, but this method of evaluation was in for a change. The Department of Agriculture farm credit agencies began using the value of the land rather than its income potential as a basis for credit. As land values spiraled up, the more credit became available. The problem was that if land values came down, there would not be enough collateral to cover the loan, and foreclosure procedure might be necessary. Commercial banks began using the same procedures, and they also began requiring a net-worth statement and a master note which would tie up all the assets a farmer had regardless of the size of the loan. Along with these conditions, the interest rates went on an upward spiral along with the inflation of general prices. Credit and interest became a much more predominant ingredient in the farming equation than it had ever been in the past.

The conditions began to put a squeeze on some farmers. As in numerous times before, the response was the emergence of a new farm organization–the American Agriculture Movement–which started among the wheat farmers on the high plains. By 1977, they were proposing a farm strike in which they wanted farmers to refuse to plant crops until they were guaranteed full parity– the profit level of the pre First World War expansive period. The farming community was still too independent to achieve that level of cooperation. The farmers around Schleswig watched the developments but continued operating in their usual way.

Returning natives and a number of young executives and workers from the IBP plant in Denison had chosen to live in Schleswig. This group of young people organized a chapter of the JayCees of America. Such interest was generated that they enjoyed a large membership from their beginning. In 1975, they asked the Community Club if they could take over and continue the Beerfest activity the Community Club started as a fund-raiser for the Diamond Jubilee. The Community Club gave its blessing, and the Beerfest became the primary fund raiser for the JayCees for the next dozen years. It brought in thousands of dollars each year and was nearly enough to provide the JayCees with their entire budget each year. The JayCees also had their jelly sales and other traditional fund-raisers, but the Beerfest was its forte. The JayCees contributed to many civic improvement projects in the community from flagpoles at one end of town to park improvements on the other end. Some of the early leaders were Dick Uhl, Roger Bumann, Leon Gosch, and Al Sedore.

The sister-city relationship with Schleswig, Germany, was getting stronger. A tour group went to Germany to visit the sites from where their ancestors had come and were royally received. Then in 1977, a group of 34 people from Germany visited here during the Calf Show. Among them were Wilhelm and Adried Jons from Schleswig, Germany, who stayed at the Alvena Lohse home. They were so impressed by the Calf Show that they offered a free trip to Germany to one of the Show participants. Patricia Ehlers, daughter of Mr. and Mrs. Howard Ehlers, won the trip. The Ehlers made the trip that fall, and in the following year they sponsored an exchange student from Germany in their home.

After a difficult beginning, the situation at the Schleswig Sausage plant had stabilized. Joe Neppl from Wall Lake was hired as General Manager and with him in charge of general operations and Bob Bumann in charge of production, the plant produced a steady output and sales record. It was still somewhat less than the organizers had hoped for, but at least it was operating smoothly. Employment was being provided for a number of families in Schleswig, and Schleswig Sausage was gaining a reputation for a quality product. The gift pack sales were growing strongly, although the wholesale market was not as strong as had been hoped.

At this time, a second attempt at sponsoring a nursing home was made. The State regulations had tightened up since the last attempt, but it was still possible to receive approval. However, it would take more work, and the enthusiasm just was not as strong this time. Consequently the effort was put on hold again.

The young women of the town were not going to let the men have all the glory with their JayCee organization, so a Chapter of the JayCee-ettes was formed, coming up with their own ideas, their own projects, and going their own independent way. They made some major civic improvements, such as a fence on the highway side of the park and sponsoring such events as the annual Easter Egg Hunt. They definitely made major contributions to the community.

On Main Street, Bill's Market had been purchased by Don and Sharon Thompson. Don had been teaching in the Schleswig school system where he had been a major influence in the musical presentations including the Swing and Supper Shows that had become extremely popular. Now, he was going to enter the business district in a big way. He changed the name of the business to Don's Market, and provided a full range of grocery and fresh meat products, and, in addition began a catering service.

In the 1976 Calf Show, a small, new event was started and was hardly noticed. Most people were preoccupied with the traditional events of the Calf Show to notice a change. In a small building at 109 Cedar Street, the first Schleswig Amateur Wine Contest was held–an idea of Joan and John Cassens. They, together with other local wine makers such as Douglas Lyon, Byron Behrmann and Larry Grill, put together a formal judging to evaluate their home-made products. Wine and beer had been made by a variety of people in the community for some time, and with a little publicity, it was surprising the number of entries that were submitted. A very distinguished panel of judges evaluated the wines including James Oberding from the Iowa Beer and Liquor Control Commission in Des Moines, Dr. Merlin Broers from Schleswig, and Dr. Earl Christensen from Harlan. The Best of Show Wine was entered by Glen Houpt from Sioux City, and second place over all was won by Walter Wellendorf of Sac City. It was such a success that the contest was tried again the next year. It has become an annual affair drawing contestants from long distances.

Other events were occurring, such as the Schleswig–Ricketts High School Band achieving the distinctive honor of winning the Governor's Cup competition. With the distinction, they were awarded the honor of leading the Iowa State Fair Parade the following year. The Boy Scouts inducted six boys to the rank of Eagle Scout. The Eagle Scout program in Schleswig was beginning to be noticed. The rank of Eagle Scout is a distinctive honor that requires a great deal of dedication and work that less than one out a hundred boy scouts achieves. It was unusual for a town as small as Schleswig to have a record of 24 eagle scouts as Schleswig did at this time.

The Krohnke Building on the corner of Second and Main Streets had been the hallmark of the business district for the last 75 years but now was becoming dilapidated and run down. There was little interest in rejuvenating the structure so the City purchased the building and decided to demolish it. This posed a problem, however. The building next door–the original Christiansen Grocery Store which was now being used as the Schleswig Library–had been built onto the Krohnke building without its own supporting wall. The Krohnke Building had to be demolished in such a way as to allow the back wall to remain and support the side of the Library. It made the operation much more tricky and expensive. The City Council's first suggestion was to take the library down, too. It proposed to build a fancy new city hall and, on the site of the two buildings. They proposed a $160,000.00 bond issue to finance it. At the same time the Fire Department proposed a

$150,000.00 bond issue to build a state-of-the-art fire station. Both bond issues failed by substantial margins. The City Council then proposed to save the library building and to look for a new use for the vacant lot in the center of town.

The firemen waited a year and proposed a much more modest fire station, and the bond issue went through without much opposition. The Krohnke Building lot became the focus for a new Post Office building. The Farmers State Bank was considering a major expansion and their plans included the building where the Post Office was currently located. The City agreed to sell their lot to a developer to build a Post Office building on the old Krohnke Building location.

A number of German visitors were coming through Schleswig following the immigrants that had come from their regions in Germany. Among these were Gustav Box, Yogi Reppmann, and William Pautsian. Some of them became acknowledged experts on this theme. Unlike the Germans who came to Schleswig throughout most of its history, these visitors came to see our community and then returned to the Old Country. They had no desire to stay.

The Jaycees were holding their Beerfests on Thursday evenings. It was an awkward time to have a celebration, but it was the only time when the taverns in the town would close to allow them to have a time without competition. Even with such restrictions, the event was growing each year. Jaycee Park Committee Chairman, Larry Grill, was able to obtain some property in the south part of town for the group. The organization developed the land into a playground for the children in that part of the community. It took several years and a lot of effort, but it has been a nice addition to the town.

Byron Behrmann had been visiting with his sister, Lois Ipsen in Des Moines when she told him about a new program the State of Iowa was starting. It was called the Community Betterment Program. The communities in Iowa would be called upon to organize a local Community Betterment group to encourage and report on civic improvements in its locale and, if necessary, initiate such improvements. Once a year there would be a Recognition Day in Ames where the reports would be evaluated and prizes would be awarded by the Governor. Byron checked to see if there would be any interest in Schleswig. Within a short time there was a local Community Betterment Organization in operation. There was no shortage of civic improvement to report on. The organization put together a report book and submitted it for the 1979 Recognition Day.

Remodeling was the major theme of the year in town. The Farmers State Bank was undergoing a major renovation which would include all the buildings in a half a block of the business district. A design that reflected German architecture would be used. It was also the next step on the shifting door of the bank. The original bank in 1899 had its main door on the corner of the building. The renovation in 1938 moved the door part way up Second Street. During the renovation in 1960's the door was returned to the corner, but now it was put back part way up Second Street. The Shinco insurance office would occupy part of the bank building. A new Post Office was being built as was a new Fire Station. Schleswig Motor Supply moved to Cedar Street. The Texaco station was being converted to self-service, and a convenience store called the Pump–N–Shop was being added. The swimming pool was also being remodeled and shower rooms were redone. All in all, remodeling certainly was a top priority.

At the same time some of the old landmarks of the town were disappearing. The old Shinco building was being torn down to make way for a parking lot for the Post Office. It had been constructed in 1900 as an ice house for the first saloon in the town. The demolition crew had some difficulty with the foot thick, sawdust packed walls. The old blacksmith shop was also being razed. It had been operated for years by Neil Koch, the blacksmith from Hohenzollern, and had been operated many more years by Johannas Gosch.

New faces were showing up around town, too. Dr. Gary Polking had started a dental practice and built an office near the Country

Club. Merle Bielenberg bought the Schleswig Lanes. Lee Hollander had returned to operate Hollander Motor Company. The bank had brought in a new officer, Norman Rossow, from a bank in Battle Creek. The bank here had grown to the extent that another officer was needed, but when Norm came in, he brought enough new customers with him that the work load changed very little.

Individuals were receiving recognition, too. Doug Lyon received a double award. He was awarded the Governor's Leadership Award at the Community Betterment Recognition Day, and he won the Grand Prize at the Schleswig Wine Contest. Kristy Miller was named Iowa Pork Queen in 1977. Ede Bubke received a nursing degree. May Lou Evers became the first woman elected to the City Council. Elvera Hollander was awarded the Friends Education Award. Long time teacher, Duane Goode, was named principal at the high school. Two boys, Corey Neuhaus and Jeff Thompson were not only named as Eagle Scouts, but they received the Bronze Palm for additional service, which is the highest award obtainable in Scouting.

A number of insurance companies can receive a tax break on their income if they donate a portion of their profit to good works. Such companies include Aid Association for Lutherans, Woodmen of the World and several others. Usually a local committee is formed to evaluate local requests. In Schleswig, Don Thompson has been very active in forming and operating a local committee for the Aid Association for Lutherans. They have provided funds to people with individual hardships, to match fund raisers of worthy organizations, and to provide money for many other worthwhile causes. Through Mr. Thompson's efforts and those of his committee the community has had the benefit of thousands of dollars of aid.

Efforts at the school won the Boyer Valley Conference basketball title, and the Schleswig–Ricketts High School Band raised money to sponsor a tour of Canada where they participated in an international competition.

Some excitement in town was caused when dangerous gasoline fumes were discovered at a number of places in the sewer system. The State Fire Marshal was called in, and an exhaustive investigation was made. The elusive leak turned out to be an old railroad fill pipe that had not been disconnected from a storage tank, and over the years had rusted through and leaked gasoline which had found its way into the sewer system. Fortunately, no spark had ignited it or a town-wide explosion could have resulted. Another problem was developing at the Sausage Plant at this time. The water it was receiving from the City was too high in bacteria for Federal Food Inspection standards. Somewhere along the extended mains there was a source of contamination, so additional chlorination and other similar measures had to be taken to cure the problem.

In the meantime a final effort was made to secure a nursing home for the community. This time it was thought there was a good chance of achieving their goal. Some of the members from the prior committee such as Edward Claussen, Larry Clausen and Erwin Voss were joined by new members—Rev. Fred Moore and Al Jorgensen. Much of their confidence was based on the addition of Al Jorgensen to the committee. He had been a local sales representative for feed companies for years, but recently he had taken an administrative position with a nursing home chain. His company would do much of the compliance and need surveying that was necessary for the State regulatory authorities in exchange for a management contract. This sounded promising, and the wheels were set in motion. In the years, since this project had been started, the state regulations had continually become more stringent. At the same time more and more surrounding communities had been building their own nursing homes, and despite the additional professional help, the State authorities rejected the needs study. They said there were sufficient residential and medium care facilities in the area. A possibility existed that a high-level nursing care facility could be approved, but it would cost more and would be more difficult to build and to manage. Neither the management company nor the local committee wanted to attempt that type of facility. Consequently, the effort was abandoned.

Although the Nursing Home idea failed, Larry Miller, a local contractor, had been seeing a number of Federally-financed retirement apartment complexes being developed in various communities around. He proposed that if Schleswig could not get a nursing home, it should try for a retirement apartment complex—but, business considerations prevented him from getting the project started. However, the concept was brought up at a JayCee meeting where it met with some interest. JayCee president, Larry Grill, checked into the requirements for the project which required a separate corporation and an independent board of directors. He adopted a set of Articles of Incorporation and had them accepted by the Iowa Secretary of State and completed the application processing through the Farm Home Administration. A public meeting was called and a board of directors was elected. The original board members were Larry Grill, Don Thompson, Ray Miller, Jeff Iversen, Judy Gierstorf, Sharon Thompson, Margaret Kohles, Eldo Hollander, and Evelyn Johnson.

Once the organization was structured and the Board of Directors elected, the next step was to find a location and to raise the money locally to buy it. Four or five possible sites were identified, but there was something wrong with each one. The area was either too small, or too far from the business district, or on the wrong side of a busy highway—always something. Finally, enough land could be pieced together on the old railroad right-of-way on the far side of the United Church of Christ. A fund-raising drive was successful, and the land was purchased. The FHA approved the plans, and an architect was hired and bids were let for the construction.

The following year a new board of directors was elected. They included Larry Grill, Don Thompson, Ray Miller, Al Sedore, Merle Ernst, Burdell Jensen, Arlene Miller, Leroy Hight, and Joyce Petersen. Petersen Construction was awarded the contract, and the project was underway.

International affairs began once again to intrude the local corn-fields. The Soviet Union invaded one of its smaller neighbors, Afghanistan. The whole free world protested. President Carter demanded they withdraw. His protest was ignored, and the action he took was to declare an embargo on all trade with the Soviet Union. This move effectively canceled the agricultural trade treaty we had with Russia. As a result, there was no longer an outlet for our crop surplus, and any future surplus would drive down the market prices. At the time it looked like the embargo was the direct cause of major change in the direction of American agriculture. However, in the light of historical perspective, we now know that the Soviet Union was already on the verge of bankruptcy. It could not afford to continue the treaty under any circumstances, let alone at the same time it conducted a war. The war in Afghanistan turned out to be the same type of long drawn-out affair the Viet Nam War had been for the United States. The difference was that while the United States was strong economically, the Soviet Union was not. Our Central Intelligence Agency had misinterpreted the strength of the Soviet economy and was caught off guard by its collapse. The records now show how weak their economy actually was even then. But whatever the cause, the treaty was over, and the markets had to find their own price level.

For years farm production levels had been high and were increasing. A number of farmers in our area discontinued all livestock production and specialized in grain cropping. The amount of grain produced and shipped out of town was prodigious. Even visitors from Germany who knew little about our system commented that it seemed like we were overdoing crop production. The two grain elevators in town were extremely busy during the harvest season. Tractors, wagons, and trucks came in from all directions. Lines several blocks in length waited to unload grain so they could go out to the farms to get more. The grain company employees had to be especially vigilant. At least one young farmer was caught trying to take the same load of grain across the scales of both elevators and be paid twice. On the whole, however, things remained remarkably orderly.

The Community Betterment group decided it would be a good idea to find out just what the community valued and the directions in which it wanted to go. To do this they organized an opinion survey. They contacted the Agricultural Extension Service to help set up the survey correctly and to help with the evaluations. The results showed that the residents of Schleswig were strong supporters of their community. The breakdown of results indicated that they would prefer to buy products they needed locally. This was especially true of Veterinary services, insurance, hardware, and farm supplies. Groceries, appliances, and cars were close to the break-even area. Services were given very strong ratings with the possible exception of the quality of the water. Organizations and activities were given very good ratings. Suggested new activities, such as increased senior citizen activities, were more popular with the people not involved in the groups than they were supported by the people who would have qualified for the service. The school was very strongly supported. The survey indicated a desire to see more emphasis on academics and less on extracurricular activities, but solid support to maintain the local school was strongly expressed.

RAGBRAI, the Register's Annual Great Bike Ride Across Iowa, is an annual bike ride completely across the State of Iowa from the Missouri River to the Mississippi River. The ride is sponsored by the Des Moines Register newspaper, and at least ten thousand riders ranging in age from seven months to 83 years participate in some part of the ride. The stream of riders seems endless as they form a procession down the roads. RAGBRAI came through Schleswig on July 27, 1981, and many organizations had prepared for their arrival. A dozen stands providing all kinds of food and beverages had been set up in the City Park, but alas, when the day arrived, the weather would not cooperate. The temperature dropped into the fifties, and a strong head wind came from the east, bringing in the rain. It was a thoroughly miserable day. Many of the bikers, after the long trek from Mapleton, could not find the energy to go on. Instead of a brief pause on the ride, the park, and then the whole town, began to fill with discouraged bikers. The business places filled up, and many residents took the riders into their homes and let them dry off and warm up. Roger Wonder in the clothing store nearly sold out the entire store including a lot of outdated styles from the basement. Warmth, not style, was the order of the day. The grocery store sold out of plastic garbage bags in which a neck holes were cut, and then were slipped over the shoulders to serve as temporary rain coats. By mid-afternoon it became clear that many of the riders would not be able to make it to their next campsite at Lake City, so a rescue effort was organized to transport them to the camp. Anyone with a truck, pickup, or a vehicle with a trailer was recruited for the effort. At least three semi rigs, 12 straight trucks, and numerous pickups and cars responded to the call. Many of the rides were free and some charged enough to cover expense. The riders were just glad to reach their destination even though they were packed in the vehicles as tightly as they could be. It was a day that went down in infamy among the riders and is still referred to as "Soggy Monday."

Always open to suggestion, the Betterment Council initiated an idea for a project suggested by Larry Grill. It was to establish a community endowment fund for which contributions were to be solicited, and the funds were to be invested. The income from the investments would be used to support civic improvement projects. An advisory group of a wide range of interest groups from the community would determine which projects would be funded and to what extent. The organization was named the BASIC Fund. BASIC is an acronym for Betterment According to Schleswig Interorganizational Consensus. Mr. Grill wrote up the Articles of Incorporation and had the organization recognized as a non-profit organization and then took an additional step and had the Internal Revenue Service designate it as an organization to which contributions could be used as charitable contributions on an income tax return.

An extensive effort has been made to explain to the public about the purpose and structure of the BASIC Fund. Gradually, it caught on and contributions have come in. It was promoted as a repository for memorials to residents who had died. Rather than to send flowers or such temporary reflections of sentiment, a permanent beneficial gift could be made for the benefit of the community. To encourage this, a Memorial Book was established in the library. A page in it is reserved for each person for whom a memorial contribution was made. Family or friends can enter anything they wish on that page from obituaries to photographs. Over the years, the BASIC Fund has grown slowly but surely and has provided tens of thousands of dollars for improvements in the community. It has been very successful and has been copied by a number of cities and groups.

Schleswig would occasionally lose a business, but one of the things that the Betterment Council noted in its record book in 1980 was that seven new businesses had started in town during this year. Schleswig Foods was begun by John Cassens and sold to Donna Meeves and Bernadine Kragel. Creatively Yours hobby and gift shop was set up by Larry Grill, Renewit Shop was opened by May Lou Evers, Modern Appliance was purchased by Mike and Jackie Goodin, Uncle Lee's Pizza and Subs was opened by Lee Hollander, and Dr. Allen Meisner remodeled the motel into a veterinarian clinic. These new ventures made some fine additions to our business district.

Hollander Motors received some national attention for a rather innovative sales promotion. They began selling vehicles by the pound instead of by the vehicle. The prices ranged from a nickel a pound for some pickups to $1.82 for some cars. This truly created some interest in a commodity-sensitive community. Word of it spread far and wide. In fact, it was the object of a feature on the Today Show on network television.

The Business Club held a special banquet to honor Emma Behrmann who, with her late husband Hans, had been involved in a major business in the community for sixty years. It was held in the Sirloin Steak House and was very well attended.

At the school, the music department was making news again. The vocal group–Southwind–was preforming at the Iowa State Fair. The High School Band won the Governor's Cup and was awarded the honor of leading the Iowa State Fair parade the following year. In the whole history of the Governor's Cup, it had only been won by a small school (Class C) twice. Both times it was won by Schleswig–first in 1976, and then in 1980. Under the direction of Victor Wood, the band was doing great things. The school lost one very good teacher that year–Arlene Miller retired after 32 years of teaching.

Farming had long been known as a hazardous enterprise. The Department of Labor declared it at the top of the list, farming having proved itself more hazardous than coal mining. The work was done with large and powerful machines working under stress on uneven ground and usually under time constraints determined by the weather. Problems could crop up in the least expected places. For example, Wayne Lafranz was quite careful in his operation and still had a large poultry barn burn down. Fortunately, no one was injured, but whenever there was an injury or incapacity, the neighbors were quick to pitch in and help. This tradition was as old as the community, and there was a need for it usually once or twice every year. One of the largest outpourings of help occurred when Bruce Grill caught his arm in a hay baler and as a result had to have his hand and part of his arm amputated. More than three dozen farmers turned out to help harvest his crops. They brought so much machinery and equipment that there was virtually a traffic problem in the fields. The crops were harvested quickly and efficiently. On such occasions the farm wives usually came along to help provide food and refreshments for the workers.

In the early 1980's, the weather was not cooperating with the farmers. Since it had been dry for some time; the crops suffered and at the same time prices had been dropping. Economic problems that had started with the wheat farmers on the high plains were spreading to this area. Farmers who owned their land were able to shift some of their operating loans to the farmland which was a risky maneuver, especially if the value of land should decline. The farmers who rented their land were in immediate trouble. The bank made every effort to shift these farmers to the Production Credit Association which was the federally run credit source of last resort.

The Department of Agriculture Feed Grains Program provided payments to farmers who would agree to certain program restraints which required a certain amount of land being taken out of production. Also provided for payment was storage of grain if the farmers kept it off the market. As a result, a large number of grain bins were constructed on farms for this purpose. The Federal government thought it was in the national interest to keep the agricultural infrastructure in place and was willing to put tax dollars to work to do it. Interestingly enough the farmers decried as waste funds spent on welfare to the poor or for corporate bailouts which were coming from the same source as their own agriculture payments. The real problem with the program was that it used prior production as the basis for the payments. This meant the farmers who worked their land the hardest with the least regard for conservation received the largest payments. The farmers who had tried to be responsible and had used good conservation practices were penalized with lower payments.

Competition for good people always creates problems for small companies. Joe Neppl left the Schleswig Sausage plant for a better job. A succession of new managers came and left in short order. The wholesale market was crucial to the plant's success, and none of the new managers could develop the market. The Board of Directors was becoming more and more involved in the actual operation of the plant as their concern grew, and the bank was becoming more concerned that the debt was not being paid down as planned. Desperate now, the Board devised a plan to market a new product consisting of individual slices of sausage that could be vacuum sealed and would not need refrigeration. The hope was for a new product that could be marketed as a ready-to-eat snack food. The first samples looked good. A good-sized order was placed and distributed to various convenience outlets where it was discovered that the packaging had not sealed properly. Most of the product spoiled and had to be destroyed causing a large financial loss. At about this time Eddie Claussen announced that the bank had found a buyer for the plant. The name of the buyer nor the details of the terms could be disclosed. The Board of Directors, discouraged by the outcome of their efforts to make the plant profitable, were ready to talk. The stockholders also disappointed by the plant's lack of performance agreed to let the Board negotiate a sale. When an agreement had been reached in December of 1981, it was announced that Richard Beatty, an executive with Farmland Foods in Denison, was the buyer. He agreed to take over the indebtedness of the plant, and to pay a small stipend for the remaining equity. The bank was glad to see the loan covered, and the stockholders hoped to see the Schleswig Sausage tradition continued and some employment maintained for the community.

Johannes Gosch retired and turned the Gosch Farm Store over entirely to Charles Evers giving up the Minneapolis Moline dealership in the process. This left Schleswig without a major implement dealership. At one time there had been four of them: the Gosch Minneapolis Moline dealership, the Petersen and Marth Massey Harris dealer ship, the Stern and Son John Deere Dealership and the Don Dodge and Son International Dealership, but, one by one they each quit operation, and now there were no more implement dealerships.

President Reagan established several policies at this time that were devastating to this part of the country. First, he initiated a fiscal policy that brought interest rates up to 16 to 20 percent and held it there for five years. In an industry like farming in which the profit rate in an average year had been squeezed to 10 to 15 percent, even the most efficient operators were in trouble. Secondly, he reformed the income tax system. The top rates were lowered from 40% to 28%, but on the lower end of the range the 9%,

11% and 14% tax rates were all raised to 15%. At the same time, a wide range of deductions and tax breaks were eliminated. While the wealthy enjoyed a substantial tax saving, the moderate-income person realized a sharp increase in taxes. Finally, he engaged in a public-spending campaign the likes of which this country had never seen. There were no limits on the raids on the national treasury. Much of the money went to the defense department to engage the Soviet Union in an arms race with the object of draining their economy dry. The plan failed because the Soviet Union did not respond. Their economy was already virtually dry. The national debt ballooned out of all proportions. Interest expenses on this debt unbalanced the national budget for years after he left office. The effect on small business and family farms was devastating. The effect on small towns such as Schleswig was so crippling that it has not recovered from its effects and may never recuperate.

As the economic pressures on the rural economy grew, the banks and the Production Credit Association were trying to help their clients get past the current crisis. When the debt grew to the extent that the interest payments alone were more than the expected profit even in an average year, there was virtually no hope of recovery. The banks began refusing to continue to provide credit, and the desolate alternative was a farm sale. The renters were the first to go, but the farmers who owned their lands were soon seeing debts as high as $2000 to $2500 per acre build up, and the price of land began to decline. Financial institutions were demanding payment, or they would initiate foreclosure proceedings, and, in many situations, there were not enough assets left to cover the debt.

While the economic outlook was bleak, the human spirit was much more buoyant. It will not be held down for long periods of time. In Schleswig the Country Club was the center of Summer activities. Tuesday was ladies' night, Wednesday was the men's steak fry, Thursday was for couples. The weekends were being filled by a variety of tournaments. In the Winter, league bowling was well established. A group of Denison businessmen bought the bowling alley and hired Glenn and Jerrie Wigg to manage it. The Schleswig Enterprise Corporation was in charge of operations at the Community Building. Directors were selected for a three-year term, and they were responsible for managing the activities and to serve as hosts and bartenders—serving without pay but receiving a share of stock in the corporation. Along with dancing, the main social activity in town, as it has been since town began, was card games. Whenever several people had a few free moments, it was not unusual for a deck of cards to appear.

There were some tragedies that occurred at this time, too. Dr. Al Meisner, who had become a very popular member of the community, was killed in an automobile accident. He was hurrying from one client to another when he collided with another vehicle on a rural hilltop. Another horrible tragedy happened when Al Janssen, a popular farmer, was suffocated when he was sucked into a bin of grain by the agitating action in the grain caused by an unloading auger. The community mourned both unexpected deaths.

Date (Amanda) Bumann was a gentle lady who grew up and lived all her life in Schleswig marrying Jute Bumann, a successful and prosperous farmer. She was involved in many of the activities that occurred in town and was especially active in her church, serving as a Sunday School teacher for decades. Her husband had been an astute investor, having been one of the original investors in Warren Buffet's Berkshire Hathaway Company. Upon her death, she willed the stock and other securities to the United Church of Christ to form an endowment fund for the benefit of both church and community improvements. When the value of the stock rose from $600 dollars a share to nearly a $1000.00, the Church committee on finance thought it was too risky and sold the stock and invested the money in Certificates of Deposit at the local bank. The move proved short-sighted as the share value of the stock rose to over $70,000.00 per share. The difference was in the multimillion dollar range. But with the remaining money, the Church has financed a number of good works and has provided scholarships for a number of deserving students. Date's contribution continues to be a strong beneficial influence in the community.

When times are tough, some ideas that would not receive much consideration are given a second look. One such idea that came up at this time was for the exploration of oil. One of the principal areas for such activity was along the old rift valley to our east. A number of wells were drilled, some with questionable techniques, others with very sophisticated equipment. Oil was found, and, while it was of good quality, it was not in commercial quantities. Some of the wells were within five miles of Schleswig. Several major oil companies increased the interest by leasing mineral rights in a wide area. It created a lot of interest, but it did not turn into a viable business opportunity.

For more than sixty years, the Farmers Lumber and Grain Company had been the cornerstone of the commercial activity in the community, but, it, too, was beginning to show its age. The smaller number of farmers raising livestock meant feed sales were down; the low prices for grain meant there was less profit in handling it, and the fewer dollars in farmer's hands meant that fewer farm supplies would be sold. A succession of managers serving the old business was starting to run it into debt. The bank advocated letting individuals take over the part of the operation rather than let the corporation run into too much debt. The Board of Directors was all farmers, who relied on the bank for credit to operate their farming operations, decided it might be time to dissolve the corporation. They agreed to sell the grain operation to Les Schultz, the former manager of that part of the corporation. Although his bid was not the highest, the consensus was that he represented the best chance for the business to continue and to maintain some competition in the industry. The Board hoped to find a buyer for the lumber and hardware portion of the business and advertized for sealed bids. It was an unorthodox situation, for they required the bids be submitted before an inventory of the property was taken. Thus a bidder had no idea what he was bidding on, and the Board rejected a proposal to sell the stock on a commission basis.

The only thing left open to them after having gone this far was to hold an auction. The business was pieced out at bargain basement prices. The real property was bought by John Schultz, who ran a lumber yard in Kiron. It was hoped he would maintain a lumber yard in Schleswig, but he was soon offered a good price for the property by Terra Chemical Company, and he sold it. The property was combined with the former Simonsen Fertilizer operation, and Terra Chemical became distributor of farm fertilizers and chemicals. Schleswig no longer had an outlet for lumber nor for general farm supplies, although some other businesses did put in short lines of such merchandise.

Other businesses were running into trouble, too. The Sirloin Steak house had bought out Walt's tavern next door and expanded their floor space. Business, however, began to decline, and in 1984 they were forced to close. They were not alone. Hollander Motor Company, a 67-year-old business, went out of business as did Dick's Skelly Service. In 1986, Don's Market closed, and so did the Iowa Liquor Store. The economic problems may have started on the farm, but their effects were definitely felt in town.

The farm crisis of the 1980's resulted in 60% of the small farms going out of existence. As a result, the effect in town was to have 70% of the business also go out of business. The interesting thing about the farm industry is that when a farmer goes out of business, the farm does not go out of production. The land is incorporated into a larger farm. Larger farms mean fewer farmers. With fewer customers, there is less likelihood that the business district of the town will recover.

Not everything was disappearing from town, however. The Crawford County Development Corporation was established to encourage business to locate and expand in Crawford County. Norman Rossow had become a member of this group, and when he saw a company that might work in Schleswig, he would approach them. One of the contacts paid off. Charles Bryson was looking for a place to set up a new business–CB Electronics. He had developed a new product–the Pulpit Phone–that he wanted to produce. It would be used in Churches to broadcast their sermons through regular phone lines to shut-in parishioners. He organized his company and sold stock in it locally. He purchased the former Hollander Motor Building and remodeled it to his company's specifications.

At the time he moved to Schleswig, Mr. Bryson contacted Northwestern Bell Telephone Company. He approached them about the possibility of doing warranty repair work on their telephones. After demonstrating his capabilities, the company offered him more work than he expected. The Pulpit Phone was put on hold for a while, and the telephone repair took first priority. The business grew rapidly, and the Hollander Motor building was soon being used to capacity. Expansions included the purchase of the former liquor store for a sales and repair outlet and the Gosch Farm Store for a product return inspection operation. Various other buildings around town were rented for storage. Employment grew to 85 employees which was contributing a significant payroll to the community.

When there is an economic upheaval such as the community was experiencing, the local grapevine becomes rife with rumors and accusations. There were stories of unfair advantage being taken, of secret deals, of wealth being accumulated at the expense of others. Very little of the talk could be verified, but it was all stated with certainty. There may well have been illegal insider dealing to get below market positions or deceptions to get a better deal. A lot of people were under a lot of stress and susceptible to being taken advantage of by an unscrupulous operator. Some of the stories were true, but some were the grossest type of misrepresentation. There was no way to determine the difference. It did appear that moral fiber behind business deals was declining, or at least, that was the general appearance.

All of the farmers who survived in business in this era were dependent on the Federal Feed Grains Program. In 1985, the government revamped the program and put in place a variety of conservation measures. Erodible land had to be terraced. Wet lands had to be preserved. If their guidelines were not followed, program payments were denied. More restrictions were placed on crop production and on the amount and nature of set-aside acreage to be taken out of production. Farmers had less and less control of what they could plant, and where they could plant it. This, of course, was disruptive to the morale in the farm community where independence has always been supreme.

The largest diversion from these problems involved school programs. The varsity athletic programs were extremely popular, and the pageantry of a high school football game was very captivating. The colorful action under the lights on a crisp fall evening was exhilarating. The crowds were large and enthusiastic, and the games were usually followed by a variety of house parties. The teams responded by providing good performances. In 1984 and in 1988 the football teams won the State Championships in their division. The band was also doing very well. It was invited to perform in San Antonio, Texas, and the money was raised to send the entire band to participate. Additional bus loads of music boosters also made the trip. School spirit was at its peak.

The Community Betterment Group was also enjoying a great deal of success. They had been regularly receiving awards in their division at the Fall Achievement Day held in Ames, and a number of local people had received the Governor's Leadership Award. They had taken the German Band to perform at the Recognition Day in Des Moines and had set up a Fudjen House to distribute the pastry from their booth. All in all, their efforts garnered a great deal of good publicity for the town. The crowning achievement came when the Governor's council decided to establish an overall Best-in-the-State award. The first year it was awarded, 1984, Schleswig received the honor. In the words of Master of Ceremonies, Don Stone from Sioux City, there are some communities that are just so far above their contemporaries they should not be judged in the same categories—and Schleswig, Iowa, is certainly one of these. Locally, the community was certainly enhanced by the large number of projects the organization initiated or encouraged.

Above: School activities were very popular and well attended.
Below: Truck convoy to the aid of bikers on "Soggy
Monday."

Because some unfortunate things had happened in previous years, a prom party was organized in the Community Building with activities that were to continue all night. If participants would stay all night, they would be served breakfast in the morning. Halloween was another activity that was the focus of change. It was proposed that a Harvest Festival replace the traditional Halloween activities because it was thought there was too much latent Satanism in contemporary Halloween. Indeed, there appeared to be an obsession with underworld influences in Schleswig. Ever since the release of the movie "The Exorcist," there appeared to be a growing concern with devil worship and satanic possession. Strange stories of hauntings in and around Schleswig were causing much concern. Lutheran ministers were even conducting exorcisms. The Harvest Festivals were short lived, however, and the obsession with Satan and his minions faded equally as quickly. Trick or treaters returned to the streets of Schleswig, but mischief and vandalism on Halloween seemed to be abating. While costumes were still devilish, the activities had become more gentile.

An interesting story about a past Halloween surfaced about this time. Back in the 1920's, a group of young men from the community which included John Jakso, Jr., Bart and Ben Bielenberg and some others were out on Halloween. This was in a day when there were still many outhouses in use in town. The boys had a car and a trailer and decided it would be funny if they were to move some of the outhouses out of sight. They loaded a number of outhouses on their trailer. To hide them, they loaded the outhouses into a boxcar on a railroad siding. There was a lot of fuss the next morning about the missing outhouses. When the boys thought they had enough fun out of the joke, they went to return the outhouses only to discover the train had hooked up the boxcar during the night. It was nowhere to be found! The culprits thought maybe it would be best not to let on that they knew anything about the whole situation. That could have been the end of the story, except—after more than fifty years had passed—a small story appeared in "Cappers Weekly" magazine. Under the title of "Strange

Stories" a man from central Kansas had written that outside of his town there was an old railroad siding and on it had been an old abandoned boxcar that had been sitting there for decades. One day he and a friend had decided to see just what was in that boxcar. It was so rusted they had a hard time getting the door open. When they did, to their amazement, it was filled with old used outhouses. There is no way of knowing for sure if those were the Schleswig outhouses, but the coincidence is strong.

Don Thompson had been directing the choir at the Lutheran Church for a number of years when he proposed that the choirs from both churches in town combine and form the basis for a community choir. He was instrumental in putting the group together inviting people from surrounding communities to join. An excellent musical program in the form of a holiday cantata has been put on for a number of years. They perform in both churches and in surrounding towns, all of which look forward to enjoying the talents of their people.

As successful as the Calf Show had been through the years, it was having difficulty now. The cattle prices were so low, the children were losing a significant amount of money on their calf projects. The Calf Show had provided entertainment for young and old through the means of a carnival, but it was becoming more and more difficult to get good rides. For these reasons, some people in the community advocated discontinuing the show. The bulk of the population demonstrated support for the tradition, however, and it was continued, although it limped for a few years. Although the JayCees were continuing the Beerfest, their number was getting smaller, and it was getting difficult for them to manage the affair. The Jaycee-ettes had decided to drop their national affiliation and began operating under the name Chapter II. They continued to be active though and put on a number of activities including a Spring Style Show in the Community Building.

Farming still held a great deal of appeal for those involved. The farmer could basically run his own business, work at his own schedule, enjoy the great outdoors every day, and gain a feeling of independence unavailable in almost any other line of work. The vast majority of the farmers worked hard, cooperated with their neighbors, and strived to live the good life. They would like nothing better than to do their own thing in their own way. However, that was not always possible. There have always been a few farmers willing to take advantage of others, and a number of others who were willing to do things under stress that they would not do under normal circumstances. They paid close attention to each other and were quite aware of what was going on in the countryside. As it was once stated, farming is really a spectator sport.

Conditions on the farm in the later part of the 1980's were slowly improving. One of the features of the Federal Farm Program was that it required farmers to maintain crop insurance, which added expense, but they complied. There were stories circulating about how it could be worked for the best benefit. It was said that shell corn could be used to fill a silo and covered with silage. When crop yields were estimated, they would come in low to increase a claim. If insurance adjusters were too busy to get to a farm before harvest, a small strip of the crop could be left for them and the rest harvested. Tales circulated of gross mutilation of these strips using everything from bull whips to dragging barbed wire across them to make the loss look worse. There were even stories about strips being planted in a field using old seed without the benefit of fertilizer or herbicides. The only purpose for such a strip would be to leave it as an insurance strip if necessary.

The prices of grain were finally going up, but the best profits could be made on hogs. The traditional mortgage payers were coming through again. This phenomenon was not ignored by a number of major interests in the agriculture economy. Efforts were made to consolidate and mass produce pork. Some confinement buildings were built, and mass farrowing operations were attempted, but the technology was not at the level where it could be accomplished at this time. It was the focus of considerable interest, however. Schleswig Specialty Meats became involved with the pork speculation by working on a contract to produce specially processed pork for the Japanese market. In the process, they discontinued producing the entire line of Schleswig Sausage products and remodeled the plant. The contract to produce meat for the Japanese fell through, but unfortunately, the smokehouse and slaughter facilities had been dismantled. The plant continued, but it now processed short line products for other packing plants.

Dr. Broers retired in 1989. He sold his practice and his office to the Crawford County Memorial Hospital which decided they would like to retain the practice, but they did not want the real estate. A proposal was made to the people of Schleswig in which they would sell the Office building to a Schleswig organization and would rent it back and to operate a medical practice on a part-time basis with doctors from Denison. The BASIC Fund was selected as the most likely organization to hold title to the building. The BASIC Fund agreed in effect to buy the building, collect the rents, and use the money to pay off the building. The medical service did not last long. Within a short time one after another doctor withdrew his services from Schleswig. The BASIC Fund had to hold fund-raising drives to pay off the building and then apply for grants to maintain it. Medical service in town was left in the hands of Dr. Doris Nahnsen who had opened the Schleswig Chiropractic Clinic a few years before.

The Jaycees were not able to find enough workers to put on the annual Beerfest in 1989, so the Community Club took on the responsibility for the event. They called upon a group of former Jaycee officers (who had long since passed the age level of the Jaycees) to use their prior experience to put on the festival. The new drunk driving laws were having an effect on the size of the crowd, and the population in the Schleswig community had become smaller. The name of the event was changed to Summerfest, and the emphasis was to direct it toward more family appeal. Sadly, the activity became a little smaller each year.

In 1992, however, a new group proposed a new direction for the Summerfest. The group adopted the name Schlesfest. They proposed capitalizing on the German name that our forefathers had fought to maintain, and the German traditions of the community. They envisioned an event which would feature German theme entertainment, much of which would be imported directly from Germany, and paid for by a moderate cover charge. There would be a variety of food and activities sponsored by community organizations which would be used as fund-raisers for those organizations. It was hoped that the German theme would revive community spirit and attract people to the community, while at the same time strengthen the groups that participated in the activity.

The effort ran into trouble from the start. The timing of the first Schlesfest was set to coincide with the very popular model plane air show in Ida Grove. It was hoped that a significant number of the huge crowds attracted to that event would come to this event which was scheduled at a time when little was to be going on there. The first year, the Department of Transportation closed the highway to Ida Grove for repairs making it difficult for people to get to Schleswig. Within weeks after the first event, the Air Show was reported to be up for sale, and it was moved to Ankeny. There would be no piggybacking on that activity for the Schlesfest. Then a group in town wanted to change the emphasis from German style entertainment to Country Western. They said the German traditions were dead and should be forgotten. They did not succeed, but it caused a rift in the support for the organization. Another source of resistance was the cover charge for the entertainment. Although moderate when compared to charges for similar entertainment in other locations, a cover charge was new to Schleswig. In the past the same organization that put on the entertainment sold food, beverages or ran some activity to recoup expenses. This time the entertainment was much more expensive, and the only income was from the cover charge. Resistance was strong and much of the audience was becoming nonresidents who came into town for the event. Finally, the tradition of volunteer support for any activity that was put on for the community benefit dwindled to a skeleton crew. The last Schlesfest was held in 1994.

The school was also becoming an object of controversy. As the population of the area declined, so did the class sizes in the school. The Iowa Department of Education initiated a number of policies to eliminate small schools and to consolidate activities on the theory that large class sizes were more cost efficient and offered more educational alternatives. Open enrollment offered students the opportunity to pick their schools even if not in their community. Financial restrictions were imposed if designated planning objectives were not given consideration. Whole grade sharing between schools was initiated, and, once established, was made irreversible. The pressure was strong. School Superintendent, Warren Andrews, presented the proposals for consideration to the school board. The reaction in the community was strong. The school had long been the center of pride and the focus of activity. The athletic teams and the music department were very strong and received near universal support of the town. Many of the children had received a strong academic start here and had gone on to significant accomplishments. At the time the school was receiving good publicity on TV by the showing of the Quiz Bowl team under the direction of math teacher, John Cassens. It didn't seem possible, but there were a number of groups had lost faith in Schleswig's ability to survive the many problems that had beset the community. They thought it would be best to align ourselves with other communities. Superintendent Andrews resigned and then withdrew his resignation. The controversy grew and the community developed deep and sharp splits.

Various alternatives were proposed. It was suggested that Schleswig combine schools with Denison or Charter Oak or Mapleton or Ida Grove or remain independent and rely on technology such as the Iowa Fiberoptic Network to provide diversity of opportunity. Superintendent Andrews was replaced with Bill Wright. Mr. Wright was working part-time for the Schleswig School System and also holding a position as an administrator in the Denison School System. This set a clear direction as to the outcome to the school controversy. Save Our Schools committees were established and were quite vocal–but to no avail. Whole grade sharing on the high school level was initiated with Denison Schools. In 1994, the high school was closed, and the following year the building was sold. The divisions and resentments in the community would take years to heal.

The banking business was experiencing some interesting changes, too. The Ricketts bank was robbed for a second time in 1991, but this time the thieves were quickly captured and convicted. The Schleswig bank was building a state-of-the-art Automatic Teller Machine at a location on the north side of town near the highway. The Ricketts Farmers Savings Bank was merged with the Schleswig bank, and a number of personnel changes were also taking place. Edward Claussen retired from the presidency of the bank in 1990, being replaced by Larry Clausen. He, in turn, was replaced by Jon Sailer in 1992. Norman Rossow accepted a position as Executive Vice-President of a bank in Merrill, Iowa, in 1993 and a number of his clients left the bank when he did. Jim Anderson joined the bank as an officer. Alan Wiess became part of the staff in 1994, and Todd Schultz in 1996. That was the same year that Edward Clausen retired as Chairman of the Board of Directors. The Board reflected the bank's heavy emphasis on agricultural lending–the majority of the directors having an interest in farming. The bank celebrated its 75th anniversary in 1994. The bank policy seemed to be changing, too. The farm crisis had been moderating since the late 1980's, but there were still a number of farmers who were in shaky financial circumstances. The bank policy seemed to involve moving these accounts out of the bank or close them out before they became a liability to the bank. Speculating on bank policy was becoming a community past-time.

Boy Scouting had been a strong feature in Schleswig since 1910, during which time, countless numbers of boys participated in the programs. In the last forty years, the Eagle Scout program was particularly strong. It takes a lot of time and effort to complete the requirements to become an Eagle Scout. Since John Dodge and Roger Reinking became the first Eagle Scouts in 1956, nearly fifty boys had achieved the rank in Schleswig. This an outstanding achievement for a town of less than a thousand population. A number of these boys also earned Bronze Palms, which is a designation above Eagle Scout. Incredible as it seemed after 86 years, the Boy Scout program in Schleswig had to give up its charter in 1996 and cease to exist. The difficulty of getting leaders and with all the school activities now located in Denison made it almost impossible to maintain a chapter in Schleswig. The boys that were interested had to join the Denison Boy Scouts.

On the farm, the Federal Feed Grain program had carried the surviving farmers through the 1980's farm crisis. The situation was improving; surpluses were held in line by reducing production because of required set-aside acres. It was not a quick nor uniform recovery, but there was an occasional windfall. 1993 was a very wet year causing flooding all over the Midwest. Des Moines lost its water system to severe flooding. The entire State was included in a presidentially-declared disaster area. There were so many crop damage claims that appraisers were not able to adequately investigate them all. When this became known, the number of claims grew substantially. One young farmer, who did not think he had serious damage, was so pressured by his fellow farmers he felt obligated to at least submit a claim and let the appraisers determine his condition. With very little evaluation, he was awarded a claim large enough to buy a new pickup. After that year, there were a lot of new pickups around town. Soon thereafter another technique was developed. Some of the larger farmers in the area would go in after corn harvest in late November and plant a crop of winter wheat. At that late date, there was very little chance for a crop to develop. The next Spring, if the crop did not materialize, it would be turned in for Federal crop insurance. The claims were seldom disputed.

Not all of the breaks went in favor of the farmers, however. A marketing technique known as hedge-to-arrive was becoming popular. It involved a farmer delivering his grain to an elevator in the fall, but the price would not be determined until the farmer requested it some time in the next six to nine months. The idea was to allow the farmer to gain the advantage of the basis change. The basis is the difference between the cash price at the moment and the commodity futures price. This difference was greatest in the Fall after harvest and smallest in the next Summer. The farmer could pick the most advantageous time to price his crop and gain a moderate increase in income. The elevator would hedge the crop against any price fluctuation until the farmer decided. The elevators would not charge for this service but used it to attract business. In the 1996–1997 marketing season, a price inversion took place which caused the futures contracts that the elevators held to suffer large losses. The hedge-to-arrive contracts were mainly oral contracts, and the elevators began to send out letters that the farmers interpreted as changed to the terms of the contract. The elevators began to try to shift some of the futures losses to the farmers, and they began trying to cancel the contracts and settle the sale at the current disadvantageous prices. Some farmers who did not think they had any liability were receiving bills for tens of thousands, and sometimes for hundreds, of thousands of dollars. Some speculators who did not understand how the procedure worked even tried to enter contracts in the Summer and thought they could make money by claiming a sales price in the Fall. That was the wildest type of shear speculation. Most Schleswig farmers avoided the most serious features of this problem. It was most troublesome in north central Iowa, but there was enough around here to sting in some cases.

C B Electronics, the largest source of non-farm jobs in the community, was also getting into trouble. Low cost new telephones were cutting sharply into the need for warranty repair work. Charles Bryson, president of the company, tried desperately to find alternative business activities. He established a telephone parts wholesaling outlet and attempted to create an international marketing setup. Nothing he did resulted in a long term business operation. He attempted to rekindle interest in his original invention—the Pulpit Phone. He attempted to build a new plant to develop it south of town in the new industrial park under an innovative tax increment improvement plan. It involved the cooperation of then Mayor Norm Rossow and State and County authorities. Continual construction delays doomed this approach, however. He then attempted to start production in an existing plant in Spencer. By this time, the short obsolescence cycle of electronic products had taken effect. A great idea in 1986 was behind the times in the mid 1990's. C. B. Electronics closed its doors in 1997.

The people of Schleswig had gone through tremendous amounts of stress and pain in the previous number of years. Changes had occurred in all phases of the community. It was difficult to recognize the Schleswig now, based on the features that had existed in the community. The riptides and undercurrents that threatened various features of the community had all come to the surface, and the effects were devastating. They had ripped apart almost everything that had come to be familiar in the community.

Long-standing traditions were destroyed. Many features of the community remained in form only; they had been changed drastically from their former function. For example, the Cemetery Board proposed a fund drive to improve the entryway to Morgan Cemetery. Normally it would have been an automatic accomplishment, but in these times it failed. The Schleswig Enterprise Board had so much trouble recruiting help to operate the Community Building, they contemplated reorganizing or closing down operations. Many people had lost everything they had hoped for and had worked years to achieve. Farms were lost and businesses had been closed. Many people became bitter because of what happened to them and because of the unfair advantages others seemed to be achieving. It was not always a pleasant time just to be around town. It was also a time when there were no leaders in the community. There was no one in the community who could influence more than a few colleagues or friends. Throughout our history there had always been influential leaders—men like Julius Rohwer, Bart Bielenberg, John Evers or Ennis Stoltenberg. There were not only no leaders, there was little chance leaders could be developed.

Several people tried to organize some positive action. They became the object of ridicule, derogation, and ostracization. It soon became clear that anyone who reared his head would find it the target of verbal blasts from every direction. The back biting was quite vicious. This was the type of situation that could only be cured by the passage of time. Gradually, the situation did improve. It was a slow process, but no one can remain despondent forever.

When the psychological situation did improve, it did so in a very different town. The business district was in shambles. More than a third of the commercial buildings in town were vacant, and a number of those remaining businesses were smaller activities than they had once been. Many of the institutions usually associated with a viable community were missing. The family farm was no more. There were families living on farms, but the synchronized family effort was not there. It would have involved a man working a home farm operation with a wife helping with the operation or running a portion of it, such as a poultry operation, and the children working with the parents and having regular farm chores. Instead, now the farmer may be working land 10 to 20 miles distant, the farm wife would likely be working at a job not related to farming, and the children would likely be involved in activities that had nothing to do with farming and would also be miles away. By this time most farmers were farming from 1000 to 1500 acres. It was a new world.

While this may not have been a shining hour in the history of Schleswig, it was not all totally black either. There were some good things happening. They were just fewer and farther between. In 1993, the town passed a bond issue by a slim margin to replace the swimming pool. The old one was showing its age and had developed a number of problems. In 1994, the Farmers Coop of Arcadia bought Feeders Supply, Inc. Melvin Schultz had wanted to sell the business for some time and some thought he may just shut it down. The Coop purchase has been somewhat controversial, but it is a viable and active ongoing business in town. Carlton

Petersen became Mayor. He started quietly but has been a positive force for the community. Teuts remodeled the Standard Station and included a convenience store in 1995. Chubby Schoenfeld, who had been running the bowling alley, sold the pin setting machines when league bowling could no longer be maintained. And in 1996, he sold the building to Arlo and Darlene Jensen. Under the name "Shorty's" they changed the emphasis to a café with a large meeting room where the lanes had been. Shirley VanSickler bought Fat's Place and under the name "Friends" expanded the kitchen and food service. The Schleswig Library undertook an extensive remodeling project that made significant improvements to both the interior and the area behind the library. It was a distinctive improvement to the town. In 1997, Bert Schauer bought the Pump–N–Shop and expanded the food service and sold it to Jim and Jamie Summers.

Stock car racing has been growing as a national sport, and the Crawford County Speedway in Denison is the regional center for this activity. Over the years there have been a variety of entries from Schleswig, participating with a varying degree of success. Our current standard bearer is Tim Clausen in car number 23.

Off-the-farm jobs in the area had not been growing at an encouraging rate. Iowa had a thirty year run of Republican governors who ran for office on the claim of being pro-business. Every year the business climate of Iowa as reported in financial magazines seemed to slip lower. The only permanent jobs in any numbers in the area were at the packing plants in Denison and the manufacturing plants in Ida Grove and Holstein which dated back to the Hughes era. If anyone needed to look for a different line of work, he would have to leave the community.

The medical service in the community went through a rather tumultuous time during this period. When Dr. Broers retired in 1989, the availability of doctors went to a part-time basis with the doctors coming up from Denison. That lasted only a brief time and the Doctors Office was vacant for years. The BASIC Fund maintained it as best they could without funds. In 1995, they sold it to the Horn Memorial Hospital in Ida Grove. Horn Memorial remodeled the office and put a doctor in on a part-time basis. This stirred the Board of Directors of the Crawford County Memorial Hospital to take action. They had been pressed from the East by the Carroll County Hospital and they were losing patients in south to Council Bluffs and Omaha. Mapleton was setting up a large clinic to the west. Obviously, they did not want to lose any more market area such as Schleswig, so the Crawford County Medical Clinic opened at 116 Cedar Street. Several doctors were rotated through on a weekly schedule. This was good since the doctor provided by Horn Memorial Hospital ran into problems with the Board of Examiners and had to withdraw. The Doctors Building sat empty until 1999 when it was again put up for sale. Through it all, doctors were again practicing in Schleswig.

One of the major problems that had been plaguing Schleswig since it was founded a hundred years ago was an adequate water supply. The quantity of water was usually adequate, but the quality was lacking, and an occasional problem would arise with the nitrate level in the water. In a dry year the quantity of water was borderline. The shallow wells depended entirely on surface water and could be subject to pollution. The deep well had extremely hard, mineral-saturated water. Fritz Berger, a long time plumber in the area, had said that in the 1950's most wells in the area were clean and pristine, and the water was good, but by the 1980's, and later most of the wells had developed coatings that could probably be attributed to new agricultural practices. The quality of the water had become questionable. All through the 1990's the Rural Water Association had been working on developing a plan for northern Crawford County. Mayor Petersen and the City Council came to an agreement with the Association to include Schleswig in their water network. The source of the water was to be the Denison Municipal Water Department. Denison had access to the glacial aquifers with huge volumes of water, and they had plants to treat the water. A plan was devised to build a water main from Denison to Schleswig for which a bond issue to finance it was passed. The water line was completed and put into operation in 1996. The plan was then extended to include local rural residents and to extend the mains to Ricketts and Charter Oak. There was also the future prospect to extend the lines to Kiron and possibly to Arthur. To accommodate this expansion a new water tower had to be built. The site for the tower was to be on the south edge of Schleswig near the Schleswig Specialty Meats plant. A 400,000 gallon tank was constructed in 1998 and put into operation in 1999.

The farm economy was as volatile as ever and may have become more so. At least, it was not all negative. President Clinton had gotten the budget deficit under control and had set in place a set of policies that encouraged economic development. The general economy of the country, including the farm economy, responded positively. The Republican Congress passed the Freedom to Farm bill which removed most of the restrictions on farm operations. Farmers were no longer required to take part of their land out of production when supplies of commodities were high, and they were no longer required to conform to conservation practices. They would still receive, as a transition measure, government payments for a number of years without restrictions on their operations. After seven years of declining payments, they would cease and there would no longer be a safety net in the farming industry. Farmers would be on their own to swim or sink. The farmers like it all. They were again in control of their operations. The supply of commodities was tight, and foreign sales were strong in 1996 and 1997. Farm prices were higher than they had ever been. Corn reached a price of over $5.00 a bushel and hogs were over $50.00 per hundredweight. Hogs were selling at a higher price than beef, which was very unusual, but this was not a point of large local concern. During the farm crisis of the 1980's, the cattle feeding industry had largely shifted to huge corporate feedlots in the western states. It had only partially come back when times improved. More than fifty percent of cattle production remained in the hands of less than three percent of producers in the nation. There were some cattle-feeders in the area, and they were surviving, but the emphasis was on the hogs. Confinement hog operations had been attempting to consolidate the hog industry for years. They were now getting many of the production problems solved.

A new set of players appeared on the scene at this time. Packing plants and huge corporate operations began offering to build confinement hog facilities for a farmer and hire him to operate a hog feeding operation in the building and after ten years, the building would be the farmer's. Quite a few farmers accepted the offer. The next step was to offer the farmer what generally became known as a ledger contract. Under this arrangement a farmer would be guaranteed a certain price for his pork–$40.00 per hundredweight was a common figure. If the price went lower, the farmer would still get $40.00 but the deficit would be banked and when the prices went more than $40.00 he would not get the higher price until the deficit was eliminated. That was also a very popular concept. A construction boom was occurring in the countryside. It was difficult to drive across Iowa without there being a new hog confinement within one's field of vision. It appeared that a vertical integration of the industry was in progress. Farmers without a contract with a packing plant had a hard time finding a buyer for their product. The big outfits were going to control the industry.

In 1998, farm production responded to the high prices with a large increase in production. At the same time the economic collapse in Asian rim countries and in Russia caused foreign exports to be curtailed sharply. Throughout the year farm prices trended downward. Not just one commodity but nearly all areas of production were going down sharply. Corn was down below $2.00 per bushel; soybeans were below the $5.00 per bushel area; hogs were down to $10.00 per hundredweight. These were prices that had not been seen for many years. Some prices were approaching those of the depression years of the 1930's. Congress has been reluctant to revise the Freedom to Farm Act, but some Federal support seems necessary.

This wood carving of our community's symbols—
a Bavarian Man and our City Crest was made by artist-in-
residence Don Thompson and is located at the entrance to
town.

Schleswig's Centennial occurs in 1999. It has had a rollicking and turbulent hundred years of history. Plans for the celebration have been under the guidance of Mayor Carlton Petersen for the three years leading up to the event. The prospect of the Centennial has been one of the unifying features in the community. Schleswig is a community that no longer entertains many illusions or presumptions concerning its future. It has recently gone through throes of self derogation and has been forced to reevaluate its identity. The process is not complete, but it is well on its way. Nearly everyone in the community is looking forward to a new century—to a new beginning. They want to build our community in new directions to fit new circumstances. Old attitudes and prejudices of the residents have been ripped apart. They are ready to embrace new ideas and to evaluate new situations on their merits. They are ready for a new time. Schleswig will be going into its new century ready to handle whatever comes its way. It knows not everything will be positive. That point was driven home by a recent tragedy. The home of Larry Beeck, a prominent local farmer, was totally demolished by a gas explosion. Mrs. Jolene Beeck was in the house at the time and, after several weeks of intensive treatment, succumbed to her injuries. It brought forth the empathy and sympathy of the entire community but emphasized the vulnerability with which each one in the community has in approaching the future. This point was reinforced by a series of tornados which hit the community on May 16, 1999, destroying three farmsteads and damaging several more.

Schleswig had achieved a good attitude to face its future. It will not be a future that will look anything like its past. It may not be a future that is being visualized at the present time. It will be a successful future none-the-less. The people will make it so. They have the ability to solve its problems and the desire to do so. A lot of good people have left, but there is good stock still here and some good new stock has come to live here, too. The soil on which our forefathers built is still fertile. Our future generations will respect it and enjoy it. The fields and streams will be there to renew our spirits and remind us of our upbringing.

Small boys and dogs love to explore creeks and streams. There is something intriguing about these irregularities in the rolling curves of our landscape. There is always the prospect of discovering something new and different. Fields and cropland offer broad ranges of uniformity and consistency. All of the diversity of nature seems to be crowded into the creeks and streams. Flowing streams glisten in the sunlight. Wet rocks shine in multicolors. Fish flick through the waters. There is a multitude of sounds. The water tinkles over the streambed, birds sing in the trees, the wind rustles the leaves, a squirrel chatters and rabbits rustle in the grasses and weeds. Side ditches and gullies offer a sense of mystery. Time just seems to disappear in these environs.

APPENDIX I

Schleswig Centennial

Thursday July 22, 1999

4:00–7:00 Health & Safety Fair.

7:00 P.M. Flag Raising and
Opening Ceremonies.
@ Flag Pole by the
City Maintenance Bldg.

Time Capsule
St. Rep. Hoffmann
St. Senator King
Supervisors and
County Officials
City Council

Friday July 23, 1999

9:00 A.M. Viet Nam Wall @ Park

All Day Food tents & Beer Garden Uptown

10:00 A.M.–4:30 P.M. Craft Show @ School

11:00 A.M.–1:00 P.M. Lunch @ Comm. Building

12:00 Noon Carnival Opens.

1:00 P.M. Pedal Pull and Petting Zoo.

2:00–9:00 P.M.
Antiques & Classic Cars
Antique Tractors
Toy Show.

5:00–Closing. Tent Show.

6:00 Announce King and Queen and
Grand Marshall of the Parade

8:00 P.M. Polka Dance

Saturday July 24, 1999

9:00 Calf Judging.

10:00 F-16 Fly-over
Grand Parade
White Horse Patrol
20 Shriner Units
Viet Nam Wall at the Park
Craft Show at the School

All Day: Food tents & Beer Garden

11:00 AM-1:30 PM Lunch at the

Community Building

12:00 Noon Carnival Opens
Pedal Pull
Petting Zoo

1:00 White Horse Patrol at
Football Field

2:00-Closing Tent Show
Antique Tractors & Cars
Toy Show

3:00 PM Firemen Water Fight

5:00 PM All-School Reunion

8:00 PM Announce Pickup Winner
Teen Dance

Sunday July 25, 1999

8:00 AM Joint Church Program

9:00 AM Breakfast
Vietnam Wall
Craft Show

11:00 Kiddie Parade

12:00 Noon Carnival Opens

12:00 Noon Carnival Opens
Tractor Pull

2:00-Closing Tent Show
Antique Tractors & Cars
Toy Show

9:30 PM Cash Drawings

Top of the Hill Tent Show

Friday July 23, 1999

5:00 P.M. Schleswig German Band, Dancers and Singers.

5:30 P.M. Barbershop Quartet.

6:00 P.M. Sisters Act, Danbury, Iowa .

6:30 P.M. Hergert-Formation, Schliusingen, Germany.

7:00 P.M. State Fair Singers and Jazz Band.

Saturday July 24, 1999

2:00 P M. Schleswig German Band, Dancers and Singers.

2:30 Hergert-Formation, Schliusingen, Germany

3:15 Peter Petrashek, magician.

3:30 Heimat–Taenzer German–American Society of Omaha.

3:50 Peter Petrashek, magician.

4:10 Heimat– Taenzer, folk dancers.

4:30 Peter Petrashek, magician.

4:45 Nishna Valley BlueGrass Assn

5:30 P.M. Hergert-Formation, Schleusingen, Germany

6:15 Bobby Allen Band

Sunday July 25, 1999

2:00 P.M. Schleswig German Band, Dancers and Singers.

2:30 Duane Pichelman.

3:00 Manning LiederKranz Singers.

3:30 Peter Petrashek, magician.

3:50 Duane Pichelman, musician.

4:15 Holstein German Band.

4:45 Peter Petrashek, magician.

5:00 Holstein German Band.

5:20 Peter Petrashek, magician.

5:30 Hergert-Formation, Schleusingen, Germany.

6:15 P.M. Bobby Allen Band.

SUNDAY JULY 25, 1999

2:00 P.M. Schleswig German Band, Dancers and Singers.

2:30 Duane Pichelman.

3:00 Manning LiederKranz Singers.

3:30 Peter Petrashek, magician.

3:50 Duane Pichelman, musician.

4:15 Holstein German Band.

4:45 Peter Petrashek, magician.

5:00 Holstein German Band.

5:20 Peter Petrashek, magician.

5:30 Hergert-Formation, Schleusingen, Germany.

6:15 P.M. Bobby Allen Band.

APPENDIX II

The Legend of the Schleswig Saddle

For the first forty years of the history of Schleswig there was a leather and harness shop on the corner of Second and Birch streets. For most of these years it was operated by Adolph Hansen. He was a craftsman at his trade, and, in the very early days of the town, he built a special saddle in his shop designed in a style that had been popular with the cowboys of the old West in the 1870's and 1880's. It had a straight fork and a pancake saddle horn incorporated in its very distinctive design.

Unfortunately, by the turn of the century that style had become obsolete. The saddle sat in his harness shop for years. Mr. Hansen had marked the price down to ten dollars but there were no takers. It looked as if he had wasted his time in making that type of saddle.

Many of the German immigrants who came to Schleswig immigrated first to the Clinton, Iowa, area and later came west. One young man who immigrated to Clinton with his parents at the age of two in 1880 did not follow the pattern. William Henry Dethlef Koerner had other ideas and he had a special talent. He like to draw and he honed his skills until he became an accomplished artist. His works appeared in a number of magazines and publications. A number of them, especially the *Saturday Evening Post,* used many of his works on their covers.

He became a member of the Brandywine school of artists and his work became quite well known. His favorite theme was to paint scenes of the old West and in his day he was as well known as some of his contemporary artists such as Charles Russell and Frederick Remington.

One of the reasons for his success was his penchant for authenticity. He wanted every detail to be just right. This is where the Schleswig Saddle comes in. Through mutual acquaintances, Mr. Koerner learned about the old style saddle in the Hansen Harness Shop and he made a special effort to buy that particular saddle.

Once in his possession, the saddle became the model for the western saddles that appeared in his paintings. W.H.D. Koerner was a very prolific artist. In his lifetime he produced more than 2000 works of art. At the time of his death in 1938, he was known as one of America's premier artists.

Today, Koerner's works are on display in art galleries and museums throughout the nation, especially in the West. The Whitney Gallery of Western Art in Cody, Wyoming, in addition to his art, has on display a reproduction of his studio where he created many of his works. The gallery has reproduced the studios not only of Koerner but also those of Frederic Remington and Joseph Henry Sharp.

In this way, William Henry Detlef Koerner immortalized the lowly, unwanted saddle from the old harness shop in Schleswig, Iowa, in his works of western art. When in an art gallery, take notice of Koerner's work and take pride in our community's contribution to it.

APPENDIX III

Schleswig, Germany

Dr. Holger Rüdel, Schleswig:
The City of Schleswig in the State of Schleswig-Holstein, Germany

"The traveler, who comes from the south, is usually amazed by the attractive location of Schleswig, which is mostly surrounded by the Schlei and rising horseshoe-shaped heights," wrote Theodor Fontane, when he visited the city in 1864. "The quiet stillness here is serene. The romantic and historical feelings that old cities tend to have are everywhere around here."

The heart of the city is the Schlei, and like Fontane thought, it's less a river than a 40-kilometers-wide inland arm of the Baltic Sea. At one time this passage was Schleswig's gate to the world. This place was already known in 804 AD in France. During the 9th and 10th Century the location for the most important Port worker and craftsman workstation of Northern Europe was built. At the time, however, the city was known by a Scandinavian name, Haithabu. The wealth of the settlement attracted plunderers and conquerers. After many terrible battles, Haithabu was destroyed, in the middle of the 11th century. Most inhabitants left that location and created a new city 3 km away on the north bank of the Schlei, Schleswig. It took over the role of Haithabu for many decades as the international port and commercial metropolis. In the 13th century it lost its rank to the queen of the Hanse, Luebeck, and sank into provinciality. The turn came in the middle of the

16th Century, when the city developed an important principality. But this glamourous time also came to an end, when the Danish crown took over the duchy 1713.

In the 19th Century the city was swept up in the growing tide of Nationalism. In 1848 large sections of the Schleswig-Holstein population rose against the Danes in order to create their own state with their neighbor Idstedt, which was defeated 2 years later. In 1864 Schleswig readied itself for the Schleswig-Holstein conflict again: Together with Austrian troops Prussia defeated the Danish army. The new gentlemen let Schleswig develop as capital of the Prussian province Schleswig-Holstein.

This status remained up until the end of the Second World War, but with its museums, the palace, the tremendous cathedral, the national file and other points of attraction Schleswig could attain an important new position as the cultural center of the country. And so those 30,000 inhabitants (counting the city) welcome their guests today to a town without a hectic pace, yet with many cultural attractions—just as Schleswig's new slogan reads, "friendly cultural city."

Translated by:
Yogi Reppmann
3 Lincoln Lane
Northfield, MN, 55057
Tel: (507) 645-9161
http://moin-moin.com